IFIP Advances in Information and Communication Technology

472

Editor-in-Chief

Kai Rannenberg, Goethe University Frankfurt, Germany

IFIP – The International Federation for Information Processing

IFIP was founded in 1960 under the auspices of UNESCO, following the first World Computer Congress held in Paris the previous year. A federation for societies working in information processing, IFIP's aim is two-fold: to support information processing in the countries of its members and to encourage technology transfer to developing nations. As its mission statement clearly states:

> IFIP is the global non-profit federation of societies of ICT professionals that aims at achieving a worldwide professional and socially responsible development and application of information and communication technologies.

IFIP is a non-profit-making organization, run almost solely by 2500 volunteers. It operates through a number of technical committees and working groups, which organize events and publications. IFIP's events range from large international open conferences to working conferences and local seminars.

The flagship event is the IFIP World Computer Congress, at which both invited and contributed papers are presented. Contributed papers are rigorously refereed and the rejection rate is high.

As with the Congress, participation in the open conferences is open to all and papers may be invited or submitted. Again, submitted papers are stringently refereed.

The working conferences are structured differently. They are usually run by a working group and attendance is generally smaller and occasionally by invitation only. Their purpose is to create an atmosphere conducive to innovation and development. Refereeing is also rigorous and papers are subjected to extensive group discussion.

Publications arising from IFIP events vary. The papers presented at the IFIP World Computer Congress and at open conferences are published as conference proceedings, while the results of the working conferences are often published as collections of selected and edited papers.

IFIP distinguishes three types of institutional membership: Country Representative Members, Members at Large, and Associate Members. The type of organization that can apply for membership is a wide variety and includes national or international societies of individual computer scientists/ICT professionals, associations or federations of such societies, government institutions/government related organizations, national or international research institutes or consortia, universities, academies of sciences, companies, national or international associations or federations of companies.

More information about this series at http://www.springer.com/series/6102

Kevin Crowston · Imed Hammouda
Björn Lundell · Gregorio Robles
Jonas Gamalielsson · Juho Lindman (Eds.)

Open Source Systems: Integrating Communities

12th IFIP WG 2.13 International Conference, OSS 2016
Gothenburg, Sweden, May 30 – June 2, 2016
Proceedings

 Springer

Editors
Kevin Crowston
Syracuse University
Syracuse, NY
USA

Imed Hammouda
Chalmers and University of Gothenburg
Gothenburg
Sweden

Björn Lundell
University of Skövde
Skövde
Sweden

Gregorio Robles
Universidad Rey Juan Carlos
Madrid
Spain

Jonas Gamalielsson
University of Skövde
Skövde
Sweden

Juho Lindman
Chalmers and University of Gothenburg
Gothenburg
Sweden

ISSN 1868-4238   ISSN 1868-422X (electronic)
IFIP Advances in Information and Communication Technology
ISBN 978-3-319-39224-0   ISBN 978-3-319-39225-7 (eBook)
DOI 10.1007/978-3-319-39225-7

Library of Congress Control Number: 2016939373

Printed on acid-free paper

This Springer imprint is published by Springer Nature
The registered company is Springer International Publishing AG Switzerland

General Chairs' Foreword

Free/libre open source software (FLOSS) has had a disruptive effect on the software industry and the ways that organizations and individuals create, distribute, acquire, and use software and software-based services. The FLOSS movement has created new kinds of opportunities for software developers, such as the emergence of new business models, knowledge exchange mechanisms, and collective development approaches. Many organizations that have been known for developing proprietary software are now actively involved with FLOSS. FLOSS adoption continues to grow among businesses, governments, and other organizations. FLOSS remains important for educators and researchers, as well as an important aspect of e-government and information society initiatives, providing access to high-quality software and the code used to create it. On the other hand, the movement has introduced new kinds of challenges, especially as different problem domains embrace openness as a pervasive problem-solving strategy. FLOSS development projects can be complex yet widespread and often cross-cultural. Consequently, they require an interdisciplinary understanding of their technical, economic, legal, and sociocultural dynamics.

The goal of the 12th International Conference on Open Source Systems, OSS 2016, was to provide an international forum where a diverse community of professionals from academia, industry, and the public sector, as well as diverse FLOSS initiatives, could come together to share research findings and practical experiences. The conference also provided a forum for sharing information and education with practitioners, for identifying directions for further research, and for being an ongoing platform for technology transfer, no matter which form of FLOSS is being pursued. The major conference theme was "integrating communities", with related themes addressing FLOSS as innovation, FLOSS practices and methods, FLOSS technologies and applications, and economic organizational and social issues of FLOSS.

Many people contributed greatly to putting together the conference this year and we owe them all a great deal of thanks. The conference program benefited from the considerable effort and contribution of time from the program chairs, Björn Lundell and Gregorio Robles, and the organization of the conference from the local conference organizer, Juho Lindman. Without their work, the event would not have happened. Sincere thanks also go to Jonas Gamalielsson for his work as proceedings chair and to Jesús M. González-Barahona, Daniel German, and Barbara Russo for their roles as industry, tutorials, and panels chairs, respectively. We also thank the members of the Program Committee and the many reviewers for their input in shaping the program.

The team of publicity chairs, led by Andrea Capiluppi, our publicity and social media chairs, comprising Jaco Geldenhuys (Africa), Tetsuo Noda (East Asia), Jamshaid Iqbal Janjua (Central Asia), Megan Squire (North America), Daniel Weingaertner (Central and South America), Ioannis Stamelos (East Europe), and Terhi Kilamo (Western Europe and Nordic), did a tremendous job by promoting the conference, thus ensuring that there was wide interest in the event in the form of submissions as well as participation. Sincere thanks also go to Dimitris Platis, our web master who has been maintaining the website of the conference.

We also wish to thank the two universities that were involved in the organization, Chalmers University of Technology and University of Gothenburg for their support regarding the event: These universities have been of great help and financial assistance. We also wish to thank the sponsors of the event, the IFIP Working Group 2.13, and the past conference organizers, who provided a great deal of assistance during the preparation of the program as well as the actual event.

Finally, we humbly wish to thank the authors and conference attendees without whom there would be no technical program. We hope you enjoy what you have created!

Imed Hammouda
Kevin Crowston

Program Chairs' Foreword

It is a great pleasure to welcome you to the proceedings of the 12th International Conference on Open Source Systems (OSS 2016). The range of papers published in this book, "Open Source Systems: Integrating Communities", provides a valuable contributions to the existing body of knowledge in the field. Contributions cover a range of topics related to FLOSS, including: organizational aspects of communities; organizational adoption; participation of women; software maintenance and evolution; open standards and open data; collaboration; hybrid communities; code reviews; and certification.

The OSS 2016 conference represents a long-standing international forum for researchers and practitioners, involved in a range of organizations and projects, to present and discuss insights, experiences, and results in the field of FLOSS. The maturity of research in our field is also reflected in the range and number of excellent contributions received.

We were very pleased to have received 38 contributions (31 full and seven short paper submissions) for the technical program, from which we included 13 full papers and three short papers (representing an acceptance rate of 41.9 % for full papers). Every paper received at least three reviews by members of the Program Committee, and was carefully discussed by Program Committee members until a consensus was reached. Based on the reviews for each paper, one of the two program chairs initiated an online discussion among the reviewers in order to reach consensus. The two program chairs facilitated this process for the different papers. All decisions were based on the quality of the papers, which considered the reviews and the outcome of the discussions. No minimum or maximum number of papers to be accepted was targeted.

The program also included two keynotes (by Leslie Hawthorn and Robin Teigland) and one panel discussion on the future of open source research. In addition to the main OSS 2016 conference, we also included a doctoral consortium, two invited talks (by Jesús M. González-Barahona and Jens Weber), and two associated workshops.

We want to give special thanks to all the people who allowed us to present such an outstanding program, and we would especially like to mention the following: the Program Committee members and additional reviewers; the session chairs; all the authors who submitted their papers to OSS 2016; and the general chairs (Kevin Crowston and Imed Hammouda). We are also grateful to a number of other people without whom this conference would not have happened, and with respect to preparing the proceedings we would like to specifically mention Jonas Gamalielsson for his support.

April 2016

Björn Lundell
Gregorio Robles

Organization

Organizing Committee

General Chairs

Imed Hammouda — Chalmers and University of Gothenburg, Sweden
Kevin Crowston — Syracuse University, USA

Program Chairs

Björn Lundell — University of Skövde, Sweden
Gregorio Robles — Universidad Rey Juan Carlos, Spain

Local Organizing Chair

Juho Lindman — Chalmers and University of Gothenburg, Sweden

Proceedings Chair

Jonas Gamalielsson — University of Skövde, Sweden

Industry Chair

Jesús M.
González-Barahona — Universidad Rey Juan Carlos/Bitergia, Spain

Tutorials Chair

Daniel German — University of Victoria, Canada

Panels Chair

Barbara Russo — Free University of Bozen-Bolzano, Italy

Publicity and
Social Media Chair

Andrea Capiluppi — Brunel University London, UK

Publicity Co-chairs

Africa

Jaco Geldenhuys — University of Stellenbosch, South Africa

East Asia

Tetsuo Noda — Shimane University, Japan

Central Asia

Jamshaid Iqbal Janjua   Al-Khawarizmi Institute of Computer Science,
University of Engineering and Technology, Pakistan

North America

Megan Squire   Elon University, USA

Central and South America

Daniel Weingaertner   Universidade Federal do Paraná, Brazil

E. Europe

Ioannis Stamelos   Aristotle University of Thessaloniki, Greece

W. Europe, Nordic

Terhi Kilamo   Tampere University of Technology, Finland

Webmaster

Dimitris Platis   University of Gothenburg, Sweden

Program Committee

Alberto Sillitti	Center for Applied Software Engineering, Italy
Andreas Meiszner	SPI - Sociedade Portuguesa de Inovação, Portugal
Anthony I. (Tony) Wasserman	Carnegie Mellon University - Silicon Valley, USA
Björn Lundell	University of Skövde, Sweden
Carlos D. Santos Jr.	University of Brasilia, Brazil
Chintan Amrit	University of Twente, The Netherlands
Cornelia Boldyreff	University of East London, UK
Davide Tosi	Università degli Studi dell'Insubria, Italy
Diomidis Spinellis	Athens University of Economics and Business, Greece
Dirk Riehle	Friedrich Alexander University Erlangen-Nürnberg, Germany
Fabio Kon	University of São Paulo, Brazil
Giancarlo Succi	Innopolis University, Russian Federation
Gregorio Robles	Universidad Rey Juan Carlos, Spain
Gregory Madey	University of Notre Dame, USA
Ioannis Stamelos	Aristotle University of Thessaloniki, Greece
Imed Hammouda	Chalmers and University of Gothenburg, Sweden
James Howison	University of Texas at Austin, USA
John Noll	LERO-University of Limerick, Ireland
Jonas Gamalielsson	University of Skövde, Sweden
Joseph Feller	University of Cork, Ireland

Juho Lindman	Chalmers and University of Gothenburg, Sweden
Kangning Wei	Shandong University, China
Kevin Crowston	Syracuse University, USA
Klaas-Jan Stol	Lero, University of Limerick, Ireland
Maha Shaikh	London School of Economics, UK
Netta Iivari	University of Oulu, Finland
Richard Torkar	Chalmers and University of Gothenburg, Sweden
Roberto Di Cosmo	Université Paris Diderot, France
Sandro Morasca	Università degli Studi dell'Insubria, Italy
Stefan Koch	Bogazici University, Turkey
Stefano Zacchiroli	Université Paris Diderot, France
Tommi Mikkonen	Tampere University of Technology, Finland
U. Yeliz Eseryel	University of Groningen, The Netherlands
Walt Scacchi	University of California, Irvine, USA

Advisory Committee

Alberto Sillitti	Center for Applied Software Engineering, Italy
Tommi Mikkonen	Tampere University of Technology, Finland
Anthony I. (Tony) Wasserman	Carnegie Mellon University – Silicon Valley, USA

Sponsored by

Software Center

INFORMATION AND COMMUNICATION TECHNOLOGY   A CHALMERS AREA OF ADVANCE

BUSINESS REGION GÖTEBORG

Supported by

UNIVERSITY OF
GOTHENBURG

CHALMERS

Doctoral Consortium Supported by

US National Science Foundation

Contents

Short Papers and Tool Demonstration

Panel and Workshops

Full Papers

The Role of Local Open Source Communities in the Development of Open Source Projects

Sinan Abdulwahhab, Yazen Alabady, Yacoub Sattar$^{(\boxtimes)}$, and Imed Hammouda

Department of Computer Science and Engineering,
Chalmers and University of Gothenburg, Gothenburg, Sweden
sattaryacoub@gmail.com, imed.hammouda@cse.gu.se

Abstract. This paper investigates the position of local open source communities (LOSCs) in the development of open source projects (OSPs). We have conducted an empirical study to examine the role of LOSCs, their way of working, and the benefits/challenges they experience compared to the overall global community. The qualitative investigation consisted of ten semi-structured interviews with members within different LOSCs. The results confirm the importance of LOSCs and the pivotal role they play in the development of OSPs. In many cases, they act as the middleman between individual members and the project's global community. However, LOSCs have their own kinds of challenges.

1 Introduction

Open source software projects in general offer their code in an open and accessible form to the public. By being open and accessible any person with the right skills may join the community for the purpose of improving the software [1]. Developers benefit from contributing to open source projects (OSPs) in different ways including recognition from their peers, the fame they get from contributing, the advantages of the tool they create, or simply for the money [2]. In addition to developers, open source communities involve a wider set of stakeholders such as users, sponsors, and eventually business professionals [1].

The development of Open Source Projects (OSPs) is typically driven by the contributions of a geographically distributed community of people under the steering of a small core of project leaders. Yet many projects highly depend on the efforts of smaller local communities that meet face to face to work on the projects. Local communities have different purposes, some of them are educational, some promotional, some social and some are driven by financial interest. We argue that this trend has become significant and is gaining momentum through the important rise of meetups where people meet in local restricted settings to share common interests. Examples of open source communities which operate locally include Linux User Groups (LUG) and Ubuntu's LoCo teams [25,26]. We refer to those as Local Open Source Communities (LOSCs).

The purpose of this study is to understand through an empirical investigation the way of working of LOSCs, their role and the different factors influencing their operations. In particular, the paper investigates three research questions:

© IFIP International Federation for Information Processing 2016
Published by Springer International Publishing Switzerland 2016. All Rights Reserved
K. Crowston et al. (Eds.): OSS 2016, IFIP AICT 472, pp. 3–15, 2016.
DOI: 10.1007/978-3-319-39225-7_1

- What interaction patterns are established between LOSCs and other stake-holders in open source projects?
- What is the role of LOSCs in the development of open source projects?
- What are the challenges/benefits that those communities face/bring when developing open source projects?

The study is based upon several interviews conducted with different LOSCs operating locally in different parts of the world. This paper proceeds as follows. In Sect. 2 we present a characterization of LOSCs. In Sect. 3 we discuss our research methodology. We then present our findings in Sect. 4 and discuss them in Sect. 5 in relation to existing literature. Finally, we conclude in Sect. 6.

2   Local Open Source Community (LOSC)

According to social science, a local community is a group of interacting people sharing an environment. In human communities, intent, belief, resources, preferences, needs, risks, and a number of other conditions may be present and common, affecting the identity of the participants and their degree of cohesiveness [23]. A local community is where a group of people living in a common location interact, share the same interests and contribute to each other's social or material values within a shared geographical location [23].

In open source, there are many communities that are acting locally city wise, region wise or country wise. These communities have objectives and characteristics which their members follow while working on OSPs. Examples of these communities along with their main objectives, characteristics and distribution are discussed below.

A Linux user group (LUG) is a group of developers who gather within a location and provide support, advocacy, education and a social environment for Linux users whether they are experienced or novice [15]. Furthermore, they meet face to face or via IRC to exchange information and work on various OSS projects by developing, making configurations and fixing bugs [15]. There are different characteristics a LUG can have such as a need for a website, a meeting location and a meeting time [15]. Also, LUGs are commonly known to be distributed city wise [26].

Another example is Ubuntu's LoCo teams which stand for Ubuntu's Local Community teams. They are to some extent similar to LUGs, there is a LoCo team in almost every country and sometimes more than one, like in the United States where they have it state wise [16]. The users' expertise in LoCos range from Linux experts to entirely new users [22]. LoCo teams get together to achieve objectives that include advocating Ubuntu, providing support, organizing release parties and more [22]. In order to join a LoCo team and socialize with other Ubuntu users, one has to look for a LoCo in their area, if not existent, they are allowed to start a new one with other users in the area if they are available [25].

Another example is Mozilla's Community Sites (MCS). Within MCS there are some which are locally distributed; these are commonly known as local

MCS [24]. Commonly, MCS are distributed country wise [27]. Local MCS work in a hierarchical manner and engage in various tasks such as: localization, promotion, quality assurance, documentation and extension development [24,28]. The number of members varies among different communities, and communication mechanism varies from IRC chat to mailing lists. However, it is mandatory for local Mozilla communities to have their own specific website for information and communication mechanism [24,28].

We refer to such initiatives as Local Open Source Communities (LOSCs). The goal of this paper is to investigate LOSCs by looking into their role in open source development, what challenges and benefits they bring or face and what interaction patterns they have with OSPs stakeholders.

3 Methodology

In this work, we decided to use a case study as our research strategy. A case study is an empirical inquiry that investigates a contemporary phenomenon within its real-life context, especially when the boundaries between the phenomenon and context are not clearly evident [19]. This fitted well our case given that the boundary of LOSCs in relation to individuals and global communities has not been widely studied and is not yet fully understood. With a case study, we can collect qualitative data from different developers within the local communities.

3.1 Data Collection Procedures

Since we adopted the approach of collecting qualitative data, our aim was to conduct a number of interviews of five local communities. We have interviewed people with different roles in those communities: organizers, leaders of specialized groups, and developers. This variation helped provide different perspectives regarding the purpose of the local communities. Since the size of the sample is very small and there is no population information available, we have adopted the maximum variation sampling for both the developers and the local communities [21]. The method of data collection which we chose was the "direct method" which involves conducting interviews and the direct involvement of people [21]. We have conducted a pilot test to estimate how much time it would take to answer our questions and whether our questions were clear enough to the interviewees to provide good answers. During the interviews, different open questions were used followed by specific ones, which follows the "funnel model" [21]. With that design of data collection procedure we could achieve more solid results.

3.2 The Interview Questions

In order not to miss any details of our research agenda, the interview questions were derived from the list of our research questions. The interviewee's understanding of LOSC have been ensured before starting the interviews in order to prevent any misinterpretations. The list of interview questions is as follows:

1. From your experience, how do local community branches contribute to OSPs?
2. What is the difference between local branch projects and the global community projects for OSPs?
3. Why do people join LOSCs? What motivates them?
4. What are the relationships between local community members? Is it different from that between the members of a widely distributed global community?
5. How do the local communities impact the open source ecosystem?
6. How do the local communities impact the local industries?
7. What kind of challenges could a local community introduce to OSPs?
8. How can a local community benefit open source organizations and projects?
9. What benefits does the local community obtain from OSPs?
10. What challenges does the local community face when working on OSPs?

3.3   Method for Analyzing the Data

In our study, we have interviewed two developers from each of the five different LOSCs. The data we got from the interviews are mostly qualitative data. When relying primarily on qualitative data, triangulation is the best technique to use [21]. Triangulation is a data analysis technique that means studying an object from different angles and thus it provides a broader result [21]. Triangulation is also important in order to increase the precision of our research [21]. Data source triangulation is a type of triangulation where the data is collected by using more than one data source or by collecting the same data at different occasions [21].

We started with summarizing the interview data. We then sorted, organized and categorized the answers depending on which research question it is related to and who answered what. This made it easier to later analyze the data. With the sorted data, we used triangulation by analyzing what each developer answered comparing the answers in order to come up with a general result.

3.4   Validity Threats

Although we have lots of data, there could be some threats to its validity [21]. As construct validity, the interviewed person may have interpreted our interview questions in a different way than we did. This is something which we came across in some of the interviews, specifically when we mentioned the word "local" in association with open source communities. Some of the respondents considered that all open source communities whether global or local to be the same. We addressed this concern by explaining the topic, titles and interview questions clearly and with examples for the subjects. In order to reduce this as much as possible, we had many discussions about the interview questions and we also pilot-tested them to make sure they are interpreted the same way by both the interviewer and the interviewees.

There is also the threat to the external validity. In order to minimize this, we tried to interview as many different open source communities as possible.

With data from two developers each from five different well-established LOSCs, we should be able to get a generalized result.

One more validity threat is the threat to the reliability of the study. Should another researcher conduct the same study, they should, hypothetically, get the same result. In order to reduce the reliability threat, all researchers discussed the details of the research agenda to avoid possible misunderstanding among researchers and researcher bias. We also included two interviewees per case to remove possible interviewee's bias. Finally, we have our interviews recorded and transcribed not to miss any important details.

4   Results

We have identified three dominant organizational roles within a LOSC. First, each LOSC has an organizer, which can be seen as a local project leader. It is the organizers' work to build and grow the local community. The steps they follow to attract the developers include finding a friendly meet up place where they gather and socialize with other developers sharing the same interest. Also an organizer usually forms a mailing list or some mean of communication in order to get hold of developers for the purpose of recruiting them into the local community. The second dominant role is a developer role with tasks including development and contribution to the open source project. The third organizational element is the specialized groups within a LOSC itself. Those are smaller groups in charge of specific tasks in the local community. For instance some groups focus on very specific localization or functional features.

The discussion below is structured along four subsections each related to one of the research questions. Subsection three and four will cover the third research question. We have conducted ten interviews, three interviews with organizers of LOSCs, four interviews with local developers within a LOSC and three interviews with special groups within a LOSC. The interviewees were part of different LOSCs that are part of several open source organizations. The organizations are Linux, Meteor, Mozilla, Ubuntu and Google (buzz project).

4.1   First RQ: LOSC and OSP Stakeholders' Relationship

There were different points of view regarding different interactions between a LOSC and other OSP stakeholders. We will present the LOSCs organizers', the LOSCs developers' and the LOSC special groups' points of view.

On the Interaction Between LOSC and the Global Community. Organizers of LOSCs engage with the global community via participation in discussion boards, mailing lists and other events where members of the global community are present. LOSC developers typically contribute with what they develop within a LOSC to the project using the LOSC as medium for getting support and feedback. As reported earlier, we observed the presence of special groups within a LOSC itself. These groups support the global community with contribution around their very specific agendas.

On the Interaction Between Different LOSC Members. In the LOSC organizers' perspective it was emphasized that the organizers try to keep the LOSC members working on the project at hand. The members should not mix their work with their daily life's work. On another note, it was mentioned that socializing with people who use similar language/thinking is an important aspect and it makes the development more efficient.

The LOSC developers' point of view showed that the relationship between LOSC members is based on socializing factors and collaborating with others to be more effective in working.

The LOSC groups' point of view was a bit different than the others. While socializing may have been a factor, making profit was reported as an important factor. Joining to meet interesting people to work locally on profitable things is an important aspect. A group mentioned that their group was assembled at the start to work on a commercial idea, along with their contribution to the open source project.

On the Interaction Between LOSC Members and Local Industries. The organizers' point of view was described as moral. It was said that the focus of the community should be more on issues like freedom of the software and public good when working with projects in contrary to the industry goal of making profit. Furthermore, the idea of seperating LOSC and profession was enforced by the organizer and the community to remove any severe collision.

The LOSC developers' point of view seemed different from that of organizers. They mentioned that the industries could hire people from these communities. Working with open source helps being noticed by the industries. Working in LOSC increase the chance of being noticed since this activity involves a lot of interaction with the local stakeholders including the industry.

The LOSC groups' point of view was similar to that of developers. It was said that "a group of three developers I know have worked on a project and they have managed to contribute to some extend towards that project. The meteor organization has noticed their contribution and offered them a job in San Francisco".

4.2   Second RQ: LOSC Role in Development of OSPs

From the LOSC organizers' perspective, a LOSC promotes and inspires local people to use free open source technologies, as the LOSC localizes the content of open source and promotes material on a more practical level. These LOSCs work on collaborative projects and the resulting product gives benefits to both the LOSC itself and the society as a whole. Furthermore, their roles in OSP development are not limited to promoting. Various members have different roles and tasks in the LOSC as some of them provide significant code contributions to OSP.

Different LOSCs differ in their work process, however, these LOSCs share the same ethical guidelines of separating daily profession from their work on OSP, even if some of their work is in the open source field. As they contribute to these OSPs, LOSCs use the materials and know-how of the associated open source communities.

LOSC stakeholders usually partake in discussions online and they organize and take part in international gatherings to work with other associated LOSCs from time to time on large OSPs. This grants a larger chance of solving issues in OSP development in terms of manpower. Also, this provides a larger motivational force when a large group of individuals work together, as it increases the chance of success.

According to a LOSC organizer, in order to maintain an OSP un-abandoned, it is his job to motivate developers to engage in meetups to work together and increase motivation. So in this sense, it is his job to keep the project alive locally, and possibly get more developers to contribute. The developers mostly contribute to such projects for fun and to feel part of something great. This does not disclose the fact that some projects end up being marketed for profits as the LOSC members sometimes choose to go commercial with their project by changing its license. This is because OSP can be highly beneficial and could bring large income if promoted properly. Another aspect is that some companies pay developers to join LOSCs in order to contribute to OSS platforms or tools, which the company wants to keep alive.

According to one interviewee form the Google buzz project, the role of a LOSC is to advertise and to promote the OSPs which they are contributing to. From his experience, the roles that LOSC members play in the development of OSP are not limited to coding, as promotion and marketing are big beneficial roles for OSP. For instance, members of LOSC present the project they are working on at meetups or promote it online on forums, with the purpose of attracting interest and new members. Another interview with a LOSC member from a LUG suggested the same thing, where he said that the development and success of the LOSC help the OSS movement to grow. Also, LOSC members -primarily organizers- help in structuring the OSP which the LOSC is working on in order to avoid issues in the future and to increase the chances of project success.

One of the interviewed developers made a point, as a group from his LOSC played a role in the development of an OSP and after it was released, they were still contributing by adding new packages, fixing bugs and constantly coming up with new ideas and features to the OSP. Some of his fellow LOSC members were seeking jobs, which is why they took part in the development of the OSP. This plays a big role in the expansion and spreading of OSP, as many start to contribute to them and see it as an opportunity to gain reputation which attracts job offers.

We could see the differences in the perspectives of the roles a LOSC could have in the development of an OSP. According to advertisers, promoting and marketing the project making it beneficial and profitable is what a LOSC does when taking part in an OSP. On the other hand, the developers' point of view was that LOSC helps in keeping projects alive by constantly contributing to them and adding new additions to them. From organizers perspective, LOSC helps attract developers and keeping projects alive, and if the LOSC stopped having meetups, then the developers would start to lose motivation to work on the project and might lead them to abandoning the project they are working with, which would result in project's end.

4.3   Third RQ: Benefits the LOSC Bring and Obtain When Working in an Open Source Project

There are many benefits for joining LOSCs. This ranges from being a part of something greater to humanitarian reasons and enjoyment. We gathered ten data points regarding this topic, one of the biggest reason is altruism. Helping others by working with OSPs is a factor which leads many enthusiastic developers to join this cause, in a sense this practice would be a way to satisfy our nature to help.

Social factor and it's benefits encourage many to join. It helps developers to grow and work in an environment which one can get an indication on how the industry operates. Other benefits include sharing ideas within the LOSC, being able to discover new ideas and create them. This leads to improving one's business relationships and goal orientation.

The last and probably the biggest motivation was experience and creating opportunities for future work. Many work with open source to get some recognition. It could be through the open source product itself or popularity from code repositories. Several interviewees clearly stated they received many job offers due to their contribution and local recognition from OSPs which they have worked on. This has been reported to be the biggest beneficial factor of joining LOSCs and OSPs.

4.4   Fourth RQ: Challenges Which the LOSC Bring/Face When Working in an Open Source Project

From the organizer point of view, the main challenges were limited funding and tool changes. Due to organizers focus on promotion and the nature of open source, economical cost was a challenge often faced. Another challenge was the fact that the results may not meet the goals set for a code distribution. Another challenge that a LoCo organizer mentioned was that the LOSC scene is dying since many developers are working directly within the global communities instead of joining LOSC as he sees it. Lastly tool changes are a challenge faced. The challenge revolves around how to introduce new tools to a LOSC. This could lead to structural challenges and efficiency problems with project development.

From a LOSC group point of view, the challenges faced by groups are more general. The biggest challenges usually include meeting up with the group since time and place could be an issue as most of the members work in their spare time and individuals have different schedules based on their separate life styles.

From one LOSC member point of view, the challenge which LOSC members face is adaption, whenever there is a new tool introduced or when faced with structural changes. The majority of members in a LOSC are developers, and whenever there is a new tool introduced many try to reject the idea at first. This is because when they are required to use the tool, the adaption process slows down the development process and some at the start might be too conservative to learn it. This leads to slowing down not only the process but also the workforce. Another issue is related to structural changes. According to some of our interviewees when a structural change occurs the members of the community tend to get the shorter stick. They have to adapt, learn and understand the changes which sometimes lower the morale of the members.

5   Discussion

In this section we use our findings to discuss the importance of LOSCs, the main motivations to join them and the challenges faced.

5.1   On the Importance of LOSCs

We have found out a number of important aspects when it comes to the importance of the LOSCs.

Collaborative Work. The collaborative work which LOSCs provide is quite important. While working on an OSS project there are tools which allow the developers to work collaboratively. These tools are for example the discussion boards which help developers get more support or tools like GitHub which helps them organize their contributions. Those tools are accessible to the LOSC members. However, talking face to face, socializing and working in a team together in the same place is more collaborative and more efficient. Furthermore, joining a LOSC gives developers coding experience and social industrial experience by working in an office like environment and collaborating with developers of various skill sets.

Meeting People with the Same Views. Within a LOSC you could meet people who share the same views and goals as you. Maybe those people you meet could be your future teammates who work with you on something you both are interested in. We found out such relationships within the groups in the LOSCs. Such relations are hard to run into in the open source communities since global interactions are mainly in the cyber world.

Interaction with Industry. Many global community developers try to earn respect and good reputation in the OSS community by contributing with code [10]. This is a common way for a global community developer to be noticed by the industry. LOSC introduces a new way for developers to be noticed by the industry. By meeting people from the industry at a LOSC, members within that LOSC will have a higher chance of being hired at industries since their work, skills and contributions might get noticed by those people.This indicates that a LOSC member has a higher chance of being noticed by industries compared to a global community developer.

Promoting Open Source. On a different point of view, the LOSC could be considered as a mean to inspire people to use free open source technologies. The meetings and socializing aspects along with the support provided by the experts within the LOSC could assist in inspiring people to use and contribute to the open source. The LOSC can also be used as a way to promote different OSPs and different open source tools.

5.2   Why People Join LOSCs

Open source community's work force is to a large extent based upon volunteers. The majority of these volunteers work for free and on their spare time but what is the golden factor which makes them join?

There were several factors in the literature findings such as motivation to learn and create, social motivators, flow motivators and altruism motivators. Those motivators helped open source community developers to contribute to OSPs [9]. Other motivations include intrinsic factors and extrinsic factors [4,6,13]. From our interviewees we had factors such as social reasons, future work criterion, enjoyment, self-improvement and humanitarian. If we would compare these factors form both sides we can clearly see all of them match each other, even though the wording is different.

5.3   Common Challenges Associated with LOSCs

While working with open source or any kind of work in general anomalies might emerge in forms of challenges; the nature of the challenge differs when comparing literature and our gathered data points. According to the gathered challenges from the literature the three biggest challenges are; low level activity and performance, lack of documentation and support roles, and the forking of projects and high-end users' product development [11]. Another very common challenge that many would face is the lack of focus on documentation and support, the need of a decent user interface and backward compatibility which is found in different OSPs [11]. From our interviews we gathered three different challenges from different views. First view was organizers' point of view where the concern revolved around promotion of LOSC and tool introduction to the LOSC. Second, local groups' view is the issue of time and date. Third, LOSC members' view, organizational and structure changes.

5.4   A Conceptual Model

Figure 1 depicts an overall conceptual model for LOSCs as described in the previous discussion. There are both internal and external stakeholders that regulate

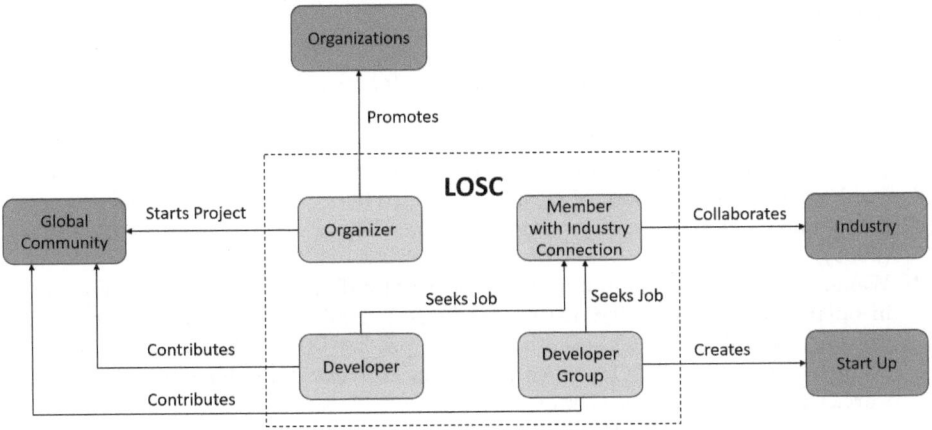

Fig. 1. Conceptual model for LOSCs.

or influence the working of LOSCs. In addition, the figure highlights the different interactions and relationships between those stakeholders. In order for LOSCs to operate sustainably, it is important to understand the expectations of each stakeholder in terms of what it receives and what it provides. However, because the proposed conceptual model explains the phenomenon of LOSCs applied to a limited number of cases, the conceptual model needs to be tested further and linked to theoretical studies in related fields such as social sciences.

6   Conclusions

We conducted this work with the aim to understand the role of LOSCs in the development of open source projects. In order to achieve this we have chosen a case study strategy as our research methodology. To investigate our topic in-depth, we conducted ten interviews with members of several LOSCs, who had different roles within those local groups. From our results we concluded that both LOSCs and OSPs do impact each other. Some impacts are beneficial such as code contributions, project localization and promoting within the local region. Others represented challenges such as financial challenges and project abandons.

We have also discussed motivations as to why people join LOSCs rather than being in contact solely with the global community. Motivations included the need of being part of something big while working locally, helping humanity by offering free software and socializing with people who share the same interests.

A total of ten interviews have been conducted in order to investigate LOSCs. The study should therefore be classified as a preliminary inquiry, as opposed to a substantial research which examines the OSS community dynamics over time across the various local OSS projects. Our future work consists of studying factors of success and failure of LOSCs and how to build and grow sustainable LOSCs. We also plan to widen our study to other open source projects and compare between different LOSCs within the same project.

References

1. Bonaccorsi, A., Rossi, C.: Why open source software can succeed. Res. Policy **32**(7), 1243–1258 (2003)
2. Godfrey, M.W., Qiang, T.: Evolution in open source software: a case study. In: Proceedings IEEE, International Conference on Software Maintenance (2000)
3. Dahlander, L., Magnusson, M.G.: Relationships between open source software companies and communities: observations from nordic firms. Res. Policy **34**(4), 481–493 (2005)
4. Wang, F.R., He, D., Chen, J.: . Motivations of individuals and firms participating in open source community. In: Proceedings of 2005 International Conference on Machine Learning and Cybernetics, Vol. 1, pp. 309–314. IEEE, August 2005
5. Wang, Y., Guo, D.: EMOS/1: An Evolution Metrics Model for Open Source Software. Unpublished Paper (2007)
6. Deci, E.L., Koestner, R., Ryan, R.M.: A meta-analytic review ofexperiments examining the effects of extrinsic rewards on intrinsic motivation. Psychol. Bull. **125**(6), 627 (1999)
7. den Besten, M., Dalle, J.M., Galia, F.: The allocation of collaborative efforts in open-source software. Inf. Econ. Policy **20**(4), 316–322 (2008)
8. Ghapanchi, A.H., Aurum, A.: The impact of project capabilities on project performance: case of open source software projects. Int. J. Project Manage. **30**(4), 407–417 (2012)
9. Baytiyeh, H., Pfaffman, J.: Open source software: a community of altruists. Comput. Hum. Behav. **26**(6), 1345–1354 (2010)
10. Feller, J.: Perspectives on Free and Open Source Software. MIT Press, Cambridge (2005)
11. Lerner, J., Triole, J.: The simple economics of open source (No. w7600). National Bureau of Economic Research (2000)
12. DeKoenigsberg, G.: . How successful open source projects work, and how and why to introduce students to the open source world. In: IEEE 21st Conference on Software Engineering Education and Training, CSEET 2008, pp. 274–276. IEEE, April 2008
13. Lakhani, K., Wolf, R.G.: Why hackers do what they do: understanding motivation and effort in free/open source software projects. In: Feller, J., Fitzgerald, B., Hissam, S., Lakhani, K. (eds.) Prespectives on Free and Open Source Software. MIT Press, Cambridge (2003)
14. Dick, S., Sadia, A.: Fuzzy clustering of open-source software quality data: a case study of Mozilla. In: International Joint Conference on Neural Networks, IJCNN 2006, pp. 4089–4096. IEEE, July 2006
15. Moen, R.: Linux user group HOWTO (2004)
16. Ubuntu LoCo Teams List — Ubuntu LoCo Team Portal (n.d.). http://loco.ubuntu.com/teams/. Accessed 13 Dec 2015
17. Raymond, E.: The cathedral and the bazaar. Knowl. Technol. Policy **12**(3), 23–49 (1999)
18. Mockus, A., Fielding, R.T., Herbsleb, J.D.: Two case studies of open source software development: Apache and Mozilla. ACM Trans. Softw. Eng. Methodol. (TOSEM) **11**(3), 309–346 (2002)
19. Yin, R.K.: Case Study Research: Design and Methods. Sage publications, Thousand Oaks (2013)

20. Creswell, J.W.: Research Design: Qualitative, Quantitative, and Mixed Methods Approaches. Sage publications, Thousand Oaks (2013)
21. Runeson, P., Hst, M.: Guidelines for conducting and reporting case study research in software engineering. Empirical Softw. Eng. **14**, 131–164 (2009)
22. Bacon, J.: The Art of Community: Building the New Age of Participation. O'Reilly Media Inc., Sebastopol (2012)
23. Beck, U.: Risk Society: Towards a New Modernity, vol. 17. Sage Publications, Thousand Oaks (1992)
24. Mozilla Community Sites (n.d.). https://wiki.mozilla.org/MCS. Accessed 13 Dec 2015
25. Ubuntu Wiki (n.d.). https://wiki.ubuntu.com/LoCoFAQ. Accessed 13 Dec 2015
26. UK Linux User Groups (n.d.). https://lug.org.uk/uklugs. Accessed 13 Dec 2015
27. Contacts, Spaces and Communities - Communities (n.d.). https://www.mozilla.org/en-US/contact/communities/. Accessed 13 Dec 2015
28. MCS/Planning (n.d.). https://wiki.mozilla.org/MCS/Planning. Accessed 13 Dec 2015

A Study of Concurrency Bugs
in an Open Source Software

Sara Abbaspour Asadollah[1]([✉]), Daniel Sundmark[1], Sigrid Eldh[2],
Hans Hansson[1], and Eduard Paul Enoiu[1]

[1] Mälardalen University, Västerås, Sweden
{sara.abbaspour,daniel.sundmark,hans.hansson,
eduard.paul.enoiu}@mdh.se
[2] Ericsson AB, Kista, Sweden
sigrid.eldh@ericsson.com

Abstract. Concurrent programming puts demands on software debugging and testing, as concurrent software may exhibit problems not present in sequential software, e.g., deadlocks and race conditions. In aiming to increase efficiency and effectiveness of debugging and bugfixing for concurrent software, a deep understanding of concurrency bugs, their frequency and fixing-times would be helpful. Similarly, to design effective tools and techniques for testing and debugging concurrent software understanding the differences between non-concurrency and concurrency bugs in real-word software would be useful. This paper presents an empirical study focusing on understanding the differences and similarities between concurrency bugs and other bugs, as well as the differences among various concurrency bug types in terms of their severity and their fixing time. Our basis is a comprehensive analysis of bug reports covering several generations of an open source software system. The analysis involves a total of 4872 bug reports from the last decade, including 221 reports related to concurrency bugs. We found that concurrency bugs are different from other bugs in terms of their fixing time and their severity. Our findings shed light on concurrency bugs and could thereby influence future design and development of concurrent software, their debugging and testing, as well as related tools.

Keywords: Concurrency bugs · Bug severity · Fixing time · Open source software

1 Introduction

With the introduction of multicore and other parallel architectures, there is an increased need for efficient and effective handling of software executing on such architectures. An important aspect in this context is to understand the bugs that occur due to parallel and concurrent execution of software. In this paper we look into how the increase of such executions have impacted a number of issues, including the occurrence of related bugs and the difficulty to fix these bugs compared to fixing non-concurrent ones.

K. Crowston et al. (Eds.): OSS 2016, IFIP AICT 472, pp. 16–31, 2016.
DOI: 10.1007/978-3-319-39225-7_2

Testing and debugging concurrent software are faced with a variety of challenges [1]. These challenges concern different aspects of software testing and debugging, such as parallel programming [2], performance testing, error detection [3] and more. Since concurrent software exhibit more non-deterministic behavior and non-deterministic bugs are generally viewed to be more challenging than other types of bugs [4–6], testing and debugging concurrent software are also considered to be more challenging compared to testing and debugging of sequential software.

Developing concurrent software requires developers to keep track of all the possible communication patterns that evolve from the large number of possible interleavings or concurrently overlapping executions that can occur between different execution threads through utilizing the shared memory.

Handling the many execution scenarios that this results in is a notoriously difficult task in debugging and makes it equally hard to create test cases [7].

In the study presented in this paper we are particularly interested in isolating concurrency bugs from other types of bugs (non-concurrency bugs) and analyzing the distinguishing features in their respective fixing processes. Hence, the main emphasis of this research is on concurrency bugs, and to explore the nature and extent of concurrency bugs in real-world software. This exploration of bugs can be helpful to understand how we should address concurrency bugs, estimate the most time-consuming ones, and prioritize them to speed up the debugging and bug-fixing processes. Also it could be helpful for designers to avoid the errors that are more likely to occur during the early phases of the software lifecycle.

In our study we address the following research questions:

- **RQ1:** How common are different types of concurrency bugs, compared to non-concurrency bugs?
- **RQ2:** How much time is required to fix concurrency bugs, compared to fixing non-concurrency bugs?
- **RQ3:** Are concurrency bugs more severe than non-concurrency bugs?

In this study we investigate the bug reports from an open source software project. We classify bugs into two distinct groups, i.e., concurrency bugs and non-concurrency bugs. We classify the concurrency bugs based on bug type, severity and fixing time. We compare the non-concurrency and concurrency bug in terms of their reporting frequency, severity and fixing time. Our results indicate that a relatively small share of bugs is related to concurrency issues, while the vast majority are non-concurrency bugs. Fixing time for concurrency and non-concurrency bugs is different but this difference is not big. In addition, concurrency bugs are considered to be slightly more severe than non-concurrency bugs.

2   Methodology

In this study first we start with *Bug-source software selection* in order to select a proper open source software for our study. Second, we identify the set of concurrency bug reports in the issue tracking database of the selected project through a keyword search in *Bug report selection*. Then we manually analyze the full set of identified bug reports in order to exclude those that are not concurrency-related. Finally, in *bug reports classification* process, we collect data for the concurrency bugs, and classify the bug reports based using the classification scheme described in Sect. 3. The following subsections describe the steps of this research process in further detail.

2.1 Bug-Source Software Selection

We were interested in an open source application that coordinates distributed processes with significant number of releases and an issue management platform for managing, configuring and testing. We selected the Apache Hadoop project[1] as the open source project for our study. The full justification for selecting Hadoop as our study object is provided in the list below.

(1) Hadoop has changed constantly and considerably in 59 releases over six years of development. (2) Due to Hadoop's key concept of parallel and distributed abstraction it is recently adopted by several big companies (i.e., Facebook, Ebay, Yahoo, Amazon and more). (3) Detailed information on bugs and bug fixes are openly available. (4) The Hadoop framework has been widely adopted by both the industry and research communities [8]. (5) It has a web interface for managing, configuring and testing its services and components.

Hadoop tracks both enhancement requests and bugs using JIRA[2]. JIRA is an issue management platform, which allows users to manage their issues throughout their entire lifecycle. It is mainly used in software development and allows users to track any kind of unit of work, such as project task, issue, story and bug to manage and track development efforts.

2.2 Bug Reports Selection

In this stage we selected the concurrency bugs from the bug report database including bugs from different versions of Apache Hadoop, including bug reports from the period 2006–2015, i.e., the last decade. In total, the Hadoop bug report database contains 4872 issues in this period that are tagged as "Bug"[3].

We automatically filtered reports that are not likely to be relevant by performing a search query on the bug report database. Our search query filtered bugs based on (1) "Bug" as report type, (2) the status of the report, and (3) keywords relevant to concurrency. Figure 1 summarizes the bug report selection process.

In filtering based on *"Bug" as report type* step, we practically searched in the Apache Hadoop report database for the reports with issue type "Bug" according to our main objective and bug definition.

---

[1] https://issues.apache.org/jira/browse/hadoop.
[2] https://www.atlassian.com/software/jira.
[3] Bug is "a problem which impairs or prevents the functions of the product" [9].

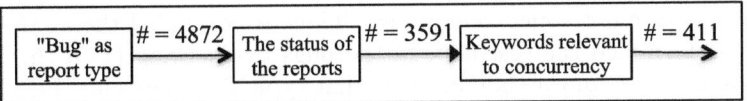

Fig. 1. Bug report selection workflow

In filtering based on *the status of the report* step, we searched for bugs with "Closed" (i.e., this report considered finished, the resolution is correct) and "Fixed" resolution status (i.e., fix for this issue has been implemented). We only selected "Fixed" and "Closed" reports since unfixed and open bug reports might be invalid and root causes described in the reports could be incorrect. It would then be impossible for us to completely understand the details on these bugs and determine their types.

In filtering based on *the keywords relevant to concurrency* step, we decided to use the keywords that could help us to include the bug reports were compatible with the scope of this study. In identifying such keywords, we reviewed the keywords utilized in similar previous studies [1,10]. The keywords included in the search, i.e. the terms, are as follows. After filtering we obtained a final set with 411 reports.

thread, blocked, locked, race, dead-lock, deadlock, concurrent, concurrency, atomic, synchronize, synchronous, synchronization, starvation, suspension, "order violation", "atomicity violation", "single variable atomicity violation", "multi variable atomicity violation", livelock, live-lock, multi-threaded, multithreading, and multi-thread.

Table 1 shows the bug count across the different stages of the bug report selection process. Note that this selection process may have some limitations, discussed in more detail in Subsect. 5.1.

Table 1. Report counts from different stage of bug report selection process

Filter	Selected reports	# of reports
2006–2015 & Bug & Fixed & Closed	Total Hadoop bug reports	3591
	Keywords match related bug reports	411
	Concurrency bug reports analyzed	221
2006–2015 & Bug & Fixed & Closed	Sample of **non-concurrency** bug reports	221

2.3 Manual Exclusion of Bug Reports and Sampling of Non-concurrency Bugs

In this stage we manually analyzed the 411 bug reports obtained in the previous step[4]. The manual inspection revealed that some of the bugs that matched the

---

[4] We provide the raw data of this study at https://goo.gl/sr6iDQ.

search query were not concurrency bugs. Thus, we excluded them. More specifically, we determined the relevance of the bugs by checking (1) if they describe a concurrency bug, and if they do, (2) what type of concurrency bug is it. The latter is done, by comparing their descriptions (or explanations) with our concurrency bug classification (Sect. 3.1). If we could not map a report with any class we excluded that report from our set. We also excluded reports with very little information, since we could not analyze them properly. After filtering we obtained a final set with 221 concurrency bugs.

As explained in Sect. 1, our main objective is understanding the differences between non-concurrency and concurrency bugs. For comparison purposes, we randomly sampled an equally sized subset of non-concurrency bugs that were reported during 2006–2015 and were "Fixed" and "Closed". These bugs were used for comparative analysis between the concurrency and non-concurrency bug sets. In this study, we use the term *non-concurrency bugs* instead of *sample of non-concurrency bugs* for all comparative analysis.

2.4 Bug Reports Classification

We analyzed the issues and information contained in the reports using them to map to the concurrency bug classification manually. Each bug report contains several types of information, which were valuable in recognizing and filtering the concurrency bugs with other types of bugs to aids us understand the characteristics of bugs. The bug reports contained for example the description of the bug with some discussions among the developers on how to detect, where to detect (bug localization) and how to fix the bugs. Typically most of the reports include a description of the correction of the bug, and a link to the the version of the software where the bug has been corrected, and even the scenario of reproducing the reported bug. The reports also contain additional fields such as perceived priority, created date, resolved date, version affected and more.

We used different types of fields in order to explore the concurrency bug issues in the Hadoop project. We used the *priority* field to estimate the severity of the bug. The interval between the *Created date* and *Resolved date* fields was used to calculate the amount of (calendar) time required to fix the bug (fixing time).

3 Study Classification Schemes

In order to perform the bug classification process we defined three main classifiers and grouped the reports based on these classifiers. The classifiers were **Type of concurrency bug**, **fixing time** and **severity**. These three classification schemes are described in detail below.

3.1 Concurrency Bug Classification

In [10], our main contribution is a better understanding of the different types of concurrency bugs. We classified and mapped the relevant bug reports related to the types of concurrency bugs using a classification of concurrency bug types. It categorizes concurrency bugs into seven disjoint classes (i.e., **Deadlock**, **Livelock**, **Starvation**, **Suspension**, **Data race**, **Order violation** and **Atomicity violation**).

3.2 Fixing Time Calculation

This class shows the time duration (days) which developer (or debugger) spend to fix a reported bug. **Fixing time**, calculated by subtracting the *Created date* and *Resolved date* fields of the bug.

3.3 Bug Report Severity Classification

In order to define priority for each issue based on developers' perspective we used a classification scheme similar to the classification defined in [9]. **Blocker** shows the highest priority. It indicates that this issue takes precedence over all others. **Critical** indicates that this issue is causing a problem and requires urgent attention. **Major** shows that this issue has a significant impact. **Minor** indicates that this issue has a relatively minor impact. **Trivial** is the lowest priority.

4 Results and Quantitative Analysis

This section provides the analysis of the data collected for bugs obtained from the Hadoop project bug database. We used 442 bugs (i.e., 221 are concurrency bugs while the rest are non-concurrency bugs sampled for our analysis) reported between 2006 and 2015. The bug selection process is described in Sect. 2.

RQ1: How common are different types of concurrency bugs, compared to non-concurrency bugs?

As seen in Fig. 2(a), out of the 3591 bugs reported in the Hadoop database, 221 (i.e., 6.15 %) bugs are related to concurrency issues and are causing a certain type of concurrency bugs, while the rest (i.e., 93.85 %) are identified as non-concurrency bugs.

The 221 concurrency bugs were further categorized according to the concurrency bug classification in [10]. As mentioned already in Sect. 3.1, this taxonomy defines seven types of concurrency bugs. For the sake of this study, we have added *Not clear* category to the taxonomy. The *Not clear* category includes reports that cover bugs related to concurrency and parallelism, but are not classified according to the concurrency bugs taxonomy. For these bugs, the summary and description of the report shows it is a concurrency bug, but further classification of bug type is prohibited by a very project implementation-specific explanation of the bug details and solution.

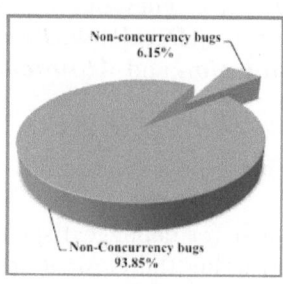
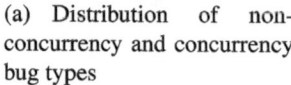

(a) Distribution of non-concurrency and concurrency bug types

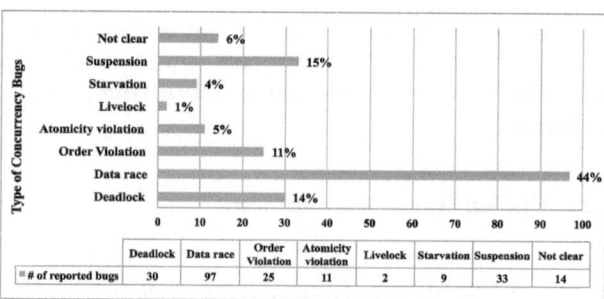

(b) Distribution of concurrency bugs

Fig. 2. Distribution of bugs

In addition, we investigated the frequency with which each type of concurrency bug appears, with the aim of getting insights into bug prioritization. In Fig. 2(b) we show the number of concurrency bugs according to their category and how often they are reported in the data we collected. From a total of 221 bug reports, almost half of them (i.e., 44 %) concern data races (or race conditions), a well-known and common concurrent bug [11]. In addition, about 15 % of the reports reported the *Suspension* bug type and only two bug reports were categorized as *Livelock* bugs.

Answer RQ1: Only 6.15 % of the total set of bugs are related to concurrency issues, while the majority of bugs (i.e., 93.85 %) are of non-concurrency type.

RQ2: How much time is required to fix concurrency bugs, compared to fixing non-concurrency bugs?

In order to gain better understanding on how difficult is to fix concurrency bugs in comparison with non-concurrency bugs, we conducted a quantitative analysis of the effort required to fix both concurrency and non-concurrency bugs. This effort was measured as explained in Sect. 3.2. We used this time as an indicator for the complexity involved in fixing these bugs.

Table 2(a) lists the detailed statistics on the obtained results for fixing time of concurrency and non-concurrency bugs. These results are also summarized in Fig. 3(a) in the form of box-plots (the vertical axis scale of the plot is logarithmic). Interestingly, the fixing time for concurrency and non-concurrency bugs is very similar, with an average of 58 days and 54 days for fixing concurrency and non-concurrency bugs, respectively.

Table 2. Descriptive statistics results for concurrency and non-concurrency bug sets in terms of fixing time.

(a) Fixing time comparison

Fixing time \\ Bug	Average	Minimum	Maximum	Median	Standard Deviation
Concurrency	58.3	0.1	1221.0	13.1	143.4
Non-concurrency	54.2	0.1	998.1	7.9	133.3

(b) Fixing time comparison for concurrency bugs

Fixing time \\ Concurrency bug	Average	Minimum	Maximum	Median	Standard Deviation
Deadlock	43.1	0.1	943.2	4.3	171.5
Data race	80.0	0.1	1221.0	17.0	181.4
Order violation	54.9	0.1	471.3	20.4	100.6
Atomicity violation	39.1	0.2	253.7	19.7	72.3
Livelock	16.9	15.0	18.9	16.9	2.7
Starvation	24.4	1.0	89.2	12.8	29.6
Suspension	38.5	0.5	197.2	17.9	46.9

To evaluate if there is any statistical difference between concurrency and non-concurrency bugs fixing time we use a *Wilcoxon Signed Rank* test, a non-parametric hypothesis test for determining if there is any statistical difference among two data sets, with the assumption that the data is drawn from an unknown distribution. We use 0.05 as the significance level.

In addition, we calculate the *Vargha-Delaney A-statistic* as a measure of effect size [12] for analyzing significance. This statistic is independent of the sample size and has a range between 0 and 1. The choice of what constitutes a significant effect size can depend on context. Vargha and Delaney [12] suggest that A-statistic of greater than 0.64 (or less than 0.36) is indicative of "medium" effect size, and of greater than 0.71 (or less than 0.29) can be indicative of a "large" effect size.

We are interested in determining if the fixing time for concurrency bugs is similar to the one for non-concurrency bugs. We begin by formulating the statistical hypotheses as follows: the null hypothesis is that fixing time of the concurrency and non-concurrency bugs sets have identical distributions (H_0) and the alternative hypothesis is that the distributions are different (H_1). Based on the p-value of *0.027*, which is less than 0.05, we reject the null hypothesis. That is, the fixing time of concurrency bugs and non-concurrency bugs are statistically different. When calculating the Vargha-Delaney A-statistic we obtained a value of *0.560* which indicates a "small" standardized effect size [12]. From our results, we can see that the fixing time for concurrency bugs is different from the fixing time for non-concurrency bugs, but that this difference corresponds to a "small" standardized effect size.

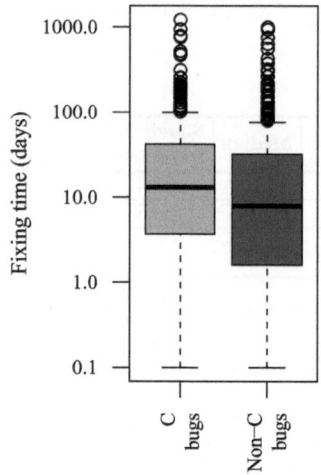

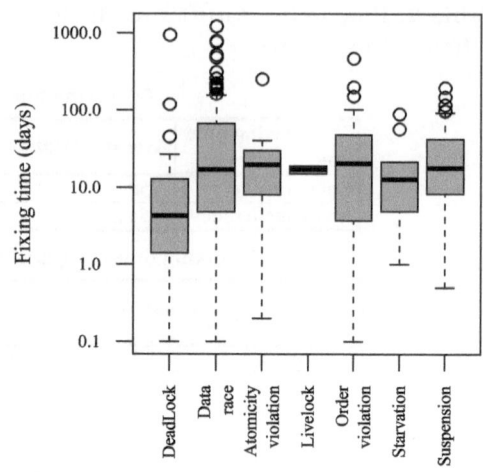

(a) Fixing time comparison for concurrency (C bug) and non-concurrency bugs (Non-C bugs).

(b) Effort required to fix each type of concurrency bugs.

Fig. 3. Fixing time analysis; boxes span from 1st to 3rd quartile, black middle lines are marking the median and the whiskers extend up to 1.5x the inter-quartile range while the circles represent the outliers.

We were also interested in understanding the differences between fixing time for each type of concurrency bugs. Figure 3(b) summarize our results in the form of box plots. It is obvious that *Data races* took the longest time to fix (i.e., 80 days on average). *Order violation* and *Deadlock* type of bugs took less time (55 and 43 on average, respectively) while *Livelock* and *Starvation* type of bugs took shorter fixing time (17 and 24 days on average, respectively). Table 2(b) lists the detailed statistics on the obtained results for each type of concurrency bugs. To evaluate if there is any significant statistical difference between the different types of concurrency bugs, we use a *Wilcoxon Signed Rank test* and calculate the A-statistic effect size. To this end, we report in Table 3 the p-values and the effect size for each type of concurrency bugs. The tested hypotheses are formulated as follows: the null hypothesis is that fixing time results between two different bug types are drawn from the same distribution and the alternative hypothesis is that the fixing time results are drawn from different distributions. We use a traditional statistical significance limit of 0.05 and Vargha and Delaney's suggestion [12] for statistical significance. Examining Table 3, we can conclude that the null hypothesis is accepted with p-values above the traditional statistical significance limit of 0.05 for the majority of bug types except for *"Deadlock-Data race"* and *"Deadlock-Suspension"* pairs where the null hypothesis is rejected. This shows that the bug fixing time is not different except between "Deadlock-Data race"

Table 3. Wilcoxon test for concurrency bugs fixing time comparison

H_0 H_A	Hypothesis test result	Deadlock	Data race	Order violation	Atomicity violation	Livelock	Starvation	Suspension
Deadlock	P-value	-	0.007389	0.03635	0.06946	0.1476	0.128	0.001921
	A-statistic	-	0.7951961	0.2046976	0.0892762	0.0154108	0.0735466	0.2636306
Data race	P-value	0.007389	-	0.9368	0.9595	0.9702	0.646	0.5778
	A-statistic	0.2048039	-	0.1302476	0.0572856	0.0100967	0.0507493	0.1589967
Order violation	P-value	0.03635	0.9368	-	0.9452	0.8894	0.6391	0.6888
	A-statistic	0.2826018	0.8697524	-	0.0990541	0.0181741	0.0821554	0.2936019
Atomicity violation	P-value	0.06946	0.9595	0.9452	-	0.9231	0.7902	0.6644
	A-statistic	0.2983314	0.9427144	0.2428526	-	0.0195557	0.0879477	0.3191625
Livelock	P-value	0.1476	0.9702	0.8894	0.9231	-	0.8128	0.8869
	A-statistic	0.3081093	0.9899033	0.2548624	0.1121267	-	0.0919864	0.3364332
Starvation	P-value	0.128	0.646	0.6391	0.7902	0.8128	-	0.4343
	A-statistic	0.2998193	0.9492507	0.2444468	0.107716	0.0195026	-	0.3216601
Suspension	P-value	0.001921	0.5778	0.6888	0.6644	0.8869	0.4343	-
	A-statistic	0.2806356	0.8410033	0.2166543	0.0958657	0.017377	0.0797641	-

and "deadlock-Suspension". For example, in Table 3 we show the obtained p-value of *0.008* for testing the pair "Deadlock-Data race", which is less than 0.05, and therefore we can reject the null hypothesis: the fixing time for *Deadlock* and *Data Race* bug types are different. In addition, the A-statistic for the same pair of bug types is about *0.796* (or 0.204 in the second row), which is greater than the significance level of 0.71. We can say that in this case the effect size is "large". We can conclude that fixing time for *deadlock* and *data race* bug types is different with a "large" effect size.

It should however be noted that the likelihood of statistical errors vastly increases when doing multiple tests using the same dataset. The results from the inter-bug-type comparisons are thus less reliable than the results from the comparison between concurrency and non-concurrency bugs.

> *Answer RQ2: Concurrency bugs do require longer fixing time than non-concurrency bugs, but the difference is not very large.*

RQ3: Are concurrency bugs more severe than non-concurrency bugs?

We analyzed the difference between concurrency and non-concurrency bug severity in order to understand if the severity of bugs is differently distributed. Figure 4 shows the severity distributions. In order to statistically compare the severity between concurrency bugs and non-concurrency bugs, we apply a *Two-Sample Kolmogorov-Smirnov* test (also known as two-sample K-S test) to find if the frequency between these two types of bugs is significantly different. Our null hypothesis can be formulated as follows: are the severity level results of concurrency bugs and non-concurrency bugs drawn from the same distribution. In this test, if the *D-value* is larger than the *critical-D-value*, the observed frequency is distributed differently.

Table 4. Kolmogorov-Smirnov test for concurrency and non-concurrency bugs severity

Shade	Non-concurrency bugs			Concurrency bugs			$|f(x) - g(x)|$
	Observed frequency	Observed proportion	Observed cumulative proportion f(x)	Observed frequency	Observed proportion	Observed cumulative proportion g(x)	
Blocker	41	0.185520362	0.185520362	66	0.298642534	0.298642534	0.113122172
Critical	18	0.081447964	0.266968326	20	0.090497738	0.389140271	0.122171946
Major	118	0.533936652	0.800904977	120	0.542986425	0.932126697	0.131221719
Minor	29	0.131221719	0.932126697	15	0.067873303	1	0.067873303
Trivial	15	0.067873303	1	0	0	1	0
Critical D-value $= D_{221,0.05} = \frac{1.36}{\sqrt{221}} = 0.091$				D-value$=$ Sup$|f(x) - g(x)| = 0.131221719 = 1.36\ 221$			

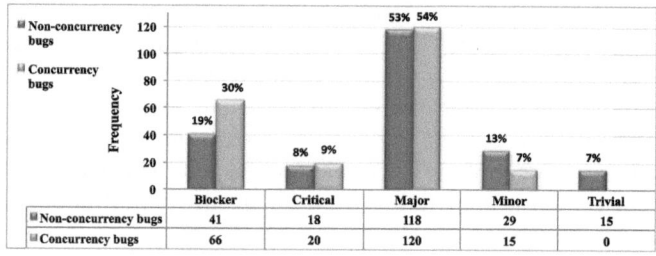

Fig. 4. Concurrency and non-concurrency bug severity

Table 4 shows that the D-value is *0.131*, which is larger than the Critical-D-value of *0.091*. Thus, statistically we have enough evidence to conclude that there is a difference between the concurrency and non-concurrency bug severity distribution. In other words, the concurrency and non-concurrency severity types are distributed differently.

Finally, we are also interested to identify the severity distribution difference between different concurrency bugs classes. The results obtained for this analysis are shown in Fig. 5. The results indicate that the highest severity is observed for the "Blocker" class. We expected that most of the bugs to be of *Deadlock* type. In reality, as shown in Fig. 5, most of the bugs are of *Data race* type. We can interpret this fact in the following way: the *Data race* type might represent the most problematic bug type in terms of severity in the Hadoop project.

On the other hand, after comparing the different type of concurrency bugs we found that most of the bugs categorized as being part of the *Data race* type in terms of severity belongs to the Major class; the highest population of *Deadlock* bugs belong to Critical class; the highest population of bugs categorized in the *Suspension* type belongs to Critical class; the highest population of bugs corresponding to *Atomicity violation* type belongs to Major and Minor class; the highest population of *Order violation* bugs belongs to Minor class and the

highest population of *Starvation* bugs belong to Major class. We can interpret
that the *Deadlock* and *Suspension* bugs have higher severity.

> *Answer RQ3: Concurrency bugs are considered to be more severe than non-concurrency bugs, but the difference is not that large.*

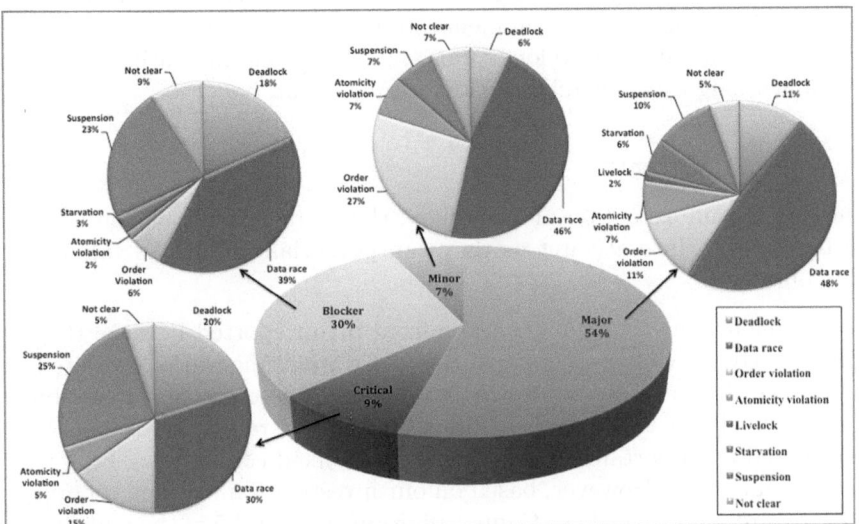

Fig. 5. Concurrency bugs severity

5   Discussion

In our study, we found a much smaller share of concurrency bugs than the one
found by other similar studies. This could possibly be due to the different time
span of our study and that of other similar studies. An interesting observation
is that 70 % of the bugs that we found were reported in the five-year interval
of 2006–2010, and the remaining 30 % were reported in the five-year interval of
2011–2015.

Similarly, the fixing time found by other studies is much larger for concurrency bugs than for non-concurrency bugs. We find a difference, but it is relatively small. This could be due to a large portion of fixing time in other studies
relate to reproducing the bugs using the bug scenario in the bug description. In
our study we found surprisingly few reports stating difficulties in reproducing
the bug.

The involvement of more than one thread cause a concurrency bug. For this
reason we predicted to find that concurrency bugs were more severe than non-concurrency bugs. However, we expected most of the "Blocker" bugs to *deadlock*

type due to its characteristic and properties but this was not the case. In our study *Data race* was the biggest portion of "Blocker". We can interpreter that *Data race* is the most problematic bug to fix in Hadoop project.

Moreover, our investigation shows that about half of the concurrency bugs are of *Data race* type. The reason could be that *Data race* is more severe than other type of bugs (as shown in Fig. 5) and it would be normal if it takes longer time to fix. About 15 % of the bugs belongs to the *Suspension* type. By investigating the bug reports' description and comments we noticed that most of the *Suspension* bugs occurred when the developer put a block of code in waiting mode for an unnecessary long time, thereby causing a *Suspension* bug.

5.1   Validity Threats

In the design and execution of this study, there are several considerations that need to be taken into account as they can potentially limit the validity of the results obtained.

- Some concurrency bugs might go unfixed or unreported because they occur infrequently, only on certain platforms/software configurations, or are hard to reproduce. It would be interesting to consider these kinds of bugs, but they are not likely to have detailed discussions. As a result, these bugs are not considered as important as the reported and fixed concurrency bugs that are used in our study. However, based on our investigation , 81 bug reports out of 4872 bug reports tagged as "Cannot reproduce" while 25 of them mentioned at least one of the concurrency keywords (listed in Sect. 2.2) in their description or comments.
- The reports with other status (i.e., "In Progress" -this issue is being actively worked on at the moment by the assignee - or "Open" -This issue is in the initial 'Open' state, ready for the assignee to start work on it-) were not considered in this study and there is a chance that we did not include the relevant reports.
- Even if the obtained results (for RQ1, RQ2 and RQ3) are based on data samples from a single project, these results might apply to other software as well. More analysis is required to confirm whether this is in fact the case.

6   Related Work

A series of related studies on debugging, predicting and fixing concurrent software have been conducted. In particular, there is a large body of studies on prediction [13–16] and propagation [17,18] of bugs in source code.

Most of these studies strive to identify the components or source code files, that are most prone to contain bugs. Fault prediction partially focuses on understanding the behavior of programmers and its effects on software reliability. This work is complementary to the study conducted in this research, which is concentrated on a specific type of bugs (i.e., concurrency bugs) and on understanding their consequences.

In [19], Vandiver et al. analyzed the consequences of bugs for three database systems. This work is focused on presenting a replication architecture, instead of on studying bugs. The authors did not distinguish between concurrency and non-concurrency bugs, and only evaluated whether they caused crash or Byzantine faults.

Three open-source applications bug databases (Apache web server, GNOME desktop environment and MySQL database) are investigated by Chandra and Chen [20], with a slightly different focus than ours. The authors analyzed all types of bugs (only 12 of them were concurrency bugs) to determine the effectiveness of generic recovery techniques in tolerating the bugs. Concurrency bugs are only one possible type of bug that affects their results. In contrast, based on our main objective we focus on a more narrow type of bugs by limiting ourselves to concurrency bugs, but provide a broader analysis (comparing concurrency and non-concurrency bugs) taking into consideration several types of these bugs.

Farchi et al. [21] analyzed concurrency bugs by creating such bugs artificially. They asked programmers to write codes which have concurrency bugs. We believe that artificially creating bugs may not lead to bugs that are representative of the real-world software bugs. We, on the other hand, analyze the bug database of an open-source software, which is well maintained, and widely used software.

Lu et al. examined concurrency bug patterns, manifestation, and fix strategies of 105 randomly selected real-world concurrency bugs from four open-source (MySQL, Apache, Mozilla and OpenOffice) bug databases [1]. Their study concentrated on several aspects of the causes of concurrency bugs, but the study of their effects was limited to determining whether they caused deadlocks or not. We use the same study methodology to find relevant bug reports but we provide a complementary angle by studying the effects of recent concurrency bugs not limited to deadlock and not-deadlock bugs. In other words, according to our objective we used other classification(s) for our study.

7   Conclusion and Future Work

This paper provides a comprehensive study of 4872 fixed bug reports from a widely used open source storage designed for big-data applications. The study covers the fixed bug reports from the last ten years, with the purpose of understanding the differences between concurrency and non-concurrency bugs. Two aspects of these reports are examined: fixing time and severity. Based on a structured selection process, we ended up with 221 concurrency bugs and 221 non-concurrency bugs (sampled). By analyzing these reports we have identified the frequencies of concurrency and non-concurrency bugs. The study also helped us to recognize the most common type of concurrency bugs in terms of severity and fixing time. The main results of this study are: (1) Only a small share of bugs is related to concurrency while the vast majority are non-concurrency bugs. (2) Fixing time for concurrency and non-concurrency bugs is different but this difference is relatively small. (3) Concurrency and non-concurrency bugs are different in terms of severity, while concurrency bugs are more severe than non-concurrency bugs. These findings could help software designers and developers to understand how to address concurrency bugs, estimate the most time-consuming ones, and prioritize them to speed up the debugging and bug-fixing processes.

Acknowledgment. This research is supported by Swedish Foundation for Strategic Research (SSF), SYNOPSIS project and the Swedish Knowledge Foundation (KKS), TOCSYC project.

References

1. Lu, S., Park, S., Seo, E., Zhou, Y.: Learning from mistakes: a comprehensive study on real world concurrency bug characteristics. In: ACM Sigplan Notices, vol. 43, pp. 329–339. ACM (2008)
2. Peri, R.: Software development tools for multi-core/parallel programming. In: 6th Workshop on Parallel and Distributed Systems: Testing, Analysis, and Debugging, p. 9. ACM (2008)
3. Zhang, W., Sun, C., Lim, J., Lu, S., Reps, T.: Conmem: detecting crash-triggering concurrency bugs through an effect-oriented approach. ACM Trans. Softw. Eng. Methodol. (TOSEM) **22**(2), 10 (2013)
4. Desouza, J., Kuhn, B., De Supinski, B.R., SamDofalov, V., Zheltov, S., Bratanov, S.: Automated, scalable debugging of MPI programs with Intel message checker. In: Proceedings of the Second International Workshop on Software Engineering for High Performance Computing System Applications, pp. 78–82. ACM (2005)
5. Godefroid, P., Nagappan, N.: Concurrency at Microsoft: an exploratory survey. In: CAV Workshop on Exploiting Concurrency Efficiently and Correctly (2008)
6. Süß, M., Leopold, C.: Common mistakes in OpenMP and how to avoid them. In: Mueller, M.S., Chapman, B.M., de Supinski, B.R., Malony, A.D., Voss, M. (eds.) IWOMP 2005 and IWOMP 2006. LNCS, vol. 4315, pp. 312–323. Springer, Heidelberg (2008)
7. Fonseca, P., Li, C., Singhal, V., Rodrigues, R.: A study of the internal and external effects of concurrency bugs. In: 2010 IEEE/IFIP International Conference on Dependable Systems and Networks (DSN), pp. 221–230. IEEE (2010)
8. Polato, I., Ré, R., Goldman, A., Kon, F.: A comprehensive view of hadoop research? a systematic literature review. J. Netw. Comput. Appl. **46**, 1–25 (2014)
9. What is an Issue - Atlassian Documentation (2015). https://confluence.atlassian.com/jira063/what-is-an-issue-683542485.html
10. Asadollah, S.A., Hansson, H., Sundmark, D., Eldh, S.: Towards classification of concurrency bugs based on observable properties. In: 1st International Workshop on Complex Faults and Failures in Large Software Systems, Italy (2015)
11. Qi, S., Otsuki, N., Nogueira, L.O., Muzahid, A., J. Torrellas.: Pacman: tolerating asymmetric data races with unintrusive hardware. In: 2012 IEEE 18th International Symposium on High Performance Computer Architecture, pp. 1–12. IEEE (2012)
12. Vargha, A., Delaney, H.D.: A critique and improvement of the CL common language effect size statistics of McGraw and Wong. J. Educ. Behav. Stat. **25**(2), 101–132 (2000)
13. Neuhaus, S., Zimmermann, T., Holler, C., Zeller, A.: Predicting vulnerable software components. In: Proceedings of the 14th ACM Conference on Computer and Communications Security, pp. 529–540. ACM (2007)

14. Nagappan, N., Ball, T.: Static analysis tools as early indicators of pre-release defect density. In: 27th International Conference on Software Engineering, pp. 580–586. ACM (2005)
15. Rahman, F., Khatri, S., Barr, E.T., Devanbu, P.: Comparing static bug finders and statistical prediction. In: Proceedings of the 36th International Conference on Software Engineering, pp. 424–434. ACM (2014)
16. Lewis, C., Lin, Z., Sadowski, C., Zhu, X., Ou, R., Whitehead, E.J.: Does bug prediction support human developers? findings from a google case study. In: 2013 35th International Conference on Software Engineering (ICSE), pp. 372–381. IEEE (2013)
17. Voinea, L., Telea, A.: How do changes in buggy Mozilla files propagate? In: Proceedings of the 2006 ACM Symposium on Software Visualization, pp. 147–148. ACM (2006)
18. Pan, W.-F., Li, B., Ma, Y.-T., Qin, Y.-Y., Zhou, X.-Y.: Measuring structural quality of object-oriented softwares via bug propagation analysis on weighted software networks. J. Comput. Sci. Technol. **25**(6), 1202–1213 (2010)
19. Vandiver, B., Balakrishnan, H., Liskov, B., Madden, S.: Tolerating byzantine faults in transaction processing systems using commit barrier scheduling. ACM SIGOPS Operating Syst. Rev. **41**(6), 59–72 (2007)
20. Chandra, S., Chen, P.M.: Whither generic recovery from application faults? a fault study using open-source software. In: Proceedings International Conference on Dependable Systems and Networks, DSN 2000, pp. 97–106. IEEE (2000)
21. Farchi, E., Nir, Y., Ur, S.: Concurrent bug patterns and how to test them. In: Parallel and Distributed Processing Symposium, p. 7. IEEE (2003)

A Bayesian Belief Network for Modeling Open Source Software Maintenance Productivity

Stamatia Bibi[1](✉), Apostolos Ampatzoglou[2], and Ioannis Stamelos[3]

[1] Department of Informatics and Telecommunications,
University of Western Macedonia, Kozani, Greece
sbibi@uowm.gr
[2] Department of Computer Science,
University of Groningen, Groningen, Netherlands
a.ampatzoglou@rug.nl
[3] Department of Computer Science,
Aristotle University of Thessaloniki, Thessaloniki, Greece
stamelos@csd.auth.gr

Abstract. Maintenance is one of the most effort consuming activities in the software development lifecycle. Efficient maintenance within short release cycles depends highly on the underlying source code structure, in the sense that complex modules are more difficult to maintain. In this paper we attempt to unveil and discuss relationships between maintenance productivity, the structural quality of the source code and process metrics like the type of a release and the number of downloads. To achieve this goal, we developed a Bayesian Belief Network (BBN) involving several maintainability predictors and three managerial indices for maintenance (i.e., duration, production, and productivity) on 20 open source software projects. The results suggest that maintenance duration depends on inheritance, coupling, and process metrics. On the other hand maintenance production and productivity depend mostly on code quality metrics.

Keywords: Maintenance · Productivity · Software metrics · Bayesian networks

1 Introduction

Software maintenance is, according to van Vliet [27], one of the most effort and time intensive activities in the software lifecycle, since it consumes 50–75 % of the overall project resources. According to ISO 14764-2006 the most common maintenance activities include the adaptation of a system to new environments, the implementation of additional requirements, the improvement of run- or design-time quality properties, or the identification of latent defects. It is expected that the worse the internal quality of a system is, the more difficult to maintain the software will be [2]. However, there are several precautionary actions that managers can take (e.g., software refactorings [10]) so as to improve the structural quality of the software, which in turn will lead to decreased maintenance effort and cost. Nevertheless, the time budget that is usually

© IFIP International Federation for Information Processing 2016
Published by Springer International Publishing Switzerland 2016. All Rights Reserved
K. Crowston et al. (Eds.): OSS 2016, IFIP AICT 472, pp. 32–44, 2016.
DOI: 10.1007/978-3-319-39225-7_3

allocated on such maintenance activities is usually limited. Thus, it should be cautiously allocated to the modules that suffer from the most important bad smells [10].

In this study we focus on the relationship between structural software quality characteristics (expressed through metrics), maintenance production (i.e., software units maintained) and duration. Although we acknowledge the fact that structural quality is not the only parameter that should be used in such a model (i.e., a complete model should consider the number of changing requirements, number of defects, etc.), we isolate software structure, in order to explore its influence exclusively. In classical economics production and duration are combined through the measure of productivity, which is defined as an average measure of production in the unit of time [6]. In this line of thought, we define maintenance productivity as the average lines of code that are being maintained (*software units maintained*) in a given time unit. Although the exploration of the relationship between software units maintained and structural quality measures is not novel (see Sect. 2), to the best of our knowledge this is the first study that considers maintenance productivity. To achieve this goal we used a Bayesian Belief Network (BBN) to model the relationships between the input (*structural software metrics*) and output parameters (*maintenance production, maintenance duration, and maintenance productivity*). The network has been trained through a case study on 454 versions of 20 Open Source Software (OSS). The rest of the paper is organized as follows: Sect. 2 presents research efforts on studies related to maintenance production; Sect. 3 presents background information on BBN and the metrics that have been used in the developed network; Sect. 4 presents the case study design; in Sect. 5, we present and discuss our results and the implications to the researchers and practitioners; in Sect. 6 we present threats to validity and finally, and in Sect. 7 we conclude the paper.

2   Related Work

Research on software maintenance effort can be categorized into two groups: (a) development of effort estimation models, and (b) development of methods that improve the maintenance outcomes.

Among popular effort estimation models we can find Estimation by Analogy (EbA) and estimation based on Regression. Shepperd et al. [24] suggested EbA for allocating staff in software maintenance projects based on similar completed historical maintenance projects. De Lucia et al. [16] use multiple regression analysis to construct corrective maintenance effort estimation models. The results show that the performance of the model is improved when the different types of maintenance tasks are included. The use of function points are proposed for estimating the effort of software maintenance projects [1]. Bayesian Networks are also used in Software Maintenance [26]. Van Koten and Gray [26] use Bayesian Networks to predict the maintainability measured as the change in software lines of code between subsequent releases. The results are improved compared to regression models. In [19] BBNs aim to predict delays in software maintenance tasks. Bayesian Networks have been also applied in software fault prediction [9] and cost estimation [25]. The application of the method indicated certain advantages regarding their ability to be combined with expert judgement and provide flexible and informative estimates.

On the other hand there are studies found in literature that examine the factors that affect software maintenance effort. System size, system age, number of input/output data items, application type, and programming language are among the parameters that can affect software maintenance effort according to [1, 12]. Also there is a vast literature on code metrics that affect the maintainability of software and consequently the corresponding effort required. According to Riaz et al. [22] the metric suites proposed by Li and Henry [15] and Chidamber and Kemerer [8] are the most accurate ones for assessing software maintainability. On the other hand there are studies that explore the specific parameters that affect open source project development, quality and evolution [14, 20, 21]. Developer participation, core team size, code ownership, productivity, defect density, and problem resolution intervals were examined in these studies leading to the conclusion among others that defect density and productivity benefit from the large open source community of testers and bug fixers. Speed of releases seems to require highly modularized software. To the best of our knowledge this is the first study that considers maintenance productivity.

3   Background Information

In this section we present some background information that is needed to comprehend this study. In particular, we provide information related to *Bayesian Belief Networks*, and *structural quality metrics* associated to maintainability.

Bayesian Belief Networks are Directed Acyclic Graphs (DAGs), which are causal networks that consist of a set of nodes and a set of directed links between them, in a way that they do not form a cycle [13]. Each node represents a random variable that can take mutually exclusive values according to a probability distribution, which can be different for each node. Each link expresses probabilistic cause-effect relations among the linked variables and is depicted by an arc starting from the influencing variable (parent node) and terminating on the influenced variable (child node). The relation between the two nodes is based on Bayes' Rule:

$$P(A|B) = \frac{P(B|A)P(A)}{P(B)} \tag{1}$$

A simple BBN example is presented in Fig. 1. The model consists of two nodes. The first node (NOC) represents the number of classes in a software package and the second node (Maintenance Effort) represents the effort required for package maintenance measured in Person-Months widely reported in literature as Man-Months (MMs). We consider that the values of these two nodes fall into two discrete categories (Low and High). For the node NOC, let's suppose that *Low values* range between 1 class and 10 classes (Similarly for Maintenance Effort values). For example the first column of the Node Probability Table states that if the number of classes is low then there is 70 % probability that the maintenance effort will be low and 30 % percent probability that the maintenance effort will be high. The algorithm used for learning Bayesian Networks is analytically presented in [7].

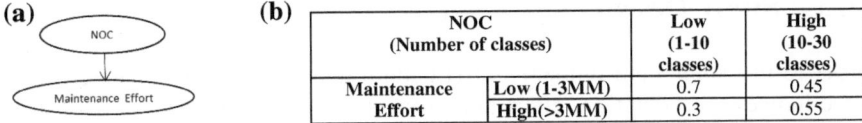

(a)

(b)

NOC (Number of classes)		Low (1-10 classes)	High (10-30 classes)
Maintenance Effort	Low (1-3MM)	0.7	0.45
	High(>3MM)	0.3	0.55

Fig. 1. a. A BBN for maintenance effort b. Node probability table for Fig. 1a

The tool used for constructing the networks and the classifier can be found in the web (http://www.cs.ualberta.ca/~jcheng/bnpc.htm).

Maintainability Predictors: In this study we focus on metrics that are the most accurate software maintainability predictors. According to Riaz et al. [22] the metric suites proposed by Li and Henry [15] and Chidamber and Kemerer [8] are the most accurate ones, while the model of van Koten and Gray [26] is the most stable one [22]. The metric suite that is used from the aforementioned study is presented in Table 1. In order to automate the calculation of software quality metrics we used Percerons Client (http://www.percerons.com), i.e., a tool developed in our research group.

Table 1. Maintainability predictors

Metric/Description	Phase	Quality attribute (QA)
Depth of Inheritance Tree (DIT). Inheritance level number, 0 for the root class	Design	Inheritance
Number of Children Classes (NoCC). Number of sub-classes that the class has	Design	Inheritance
Message Passing Coupling (MPC). Number of send statements defined in the class	Code	Coupling
Response For a Class (RFC). Number of local methods plus the number of methods called by local methods in the class	Code	Coupling
Lack of Cohesion of Methods (LCOM). Number of disjoint sets of methods (number of sets of methods that do not interact with each other), in the class	Code	Cohesion
Data Abstraction Coupling (DAC). Number of abstract types defined in the class	Design	Coupling
Weighted Method per Class (WMC). Average cyclomatic complexity of all methods	Code	Complexity
Number of Methods (NOM). Number of methods in the class	Design	Size
Lines of Code (SIZE1/LoC). Number of semicolons in the class	Code	Size
Number of Properties (SIZE2). Number of attributes and methods in the class	Design	Size
Coupling Between Objects (CBO). Number of classes that one class depends on	Design	Coupling
Average Method Size (AMS). Avereage number of semicolons in a method	Code	Complexity

4   Case Study Design

In order to investigate the influence of structural quality in several managerial maintenance indices (i.e., duration, effort and productivity), we performed a case study on 20 open-source software (OSS) projects. The case study is designed and reported according to the guidelines of Runeson et al. [23].

4.1   Objectives and Research Questions

The objective of this study is to analyze software metrics and investigate their influence on the maintenance production, duration and productivity. In particular we investigate three research questions:

RQ_1: *Which quality metrics are related to the duration of maintenance among two successive releases?*

This question aims at identifying the metrics that mostly influence the time required for developing a new version of an OSS project measured in days elapsed from one release to another. Quick successive releases may indicate the level of readiness of the project community, the tendency to launch quick releases, and short time to fix bugs or add functionality.

RQ_2: *Which quality metrics are related to the production of maintenance among two successive releases?*

The objective of this question is to reveal which quality metrics are more associated to the production of the maintenance in OSS, measured as the number of lines of code added from previous release. The target of this analysis is to identify the quality characteristics whose levels enable a substantial change in a single version. We expect that low values of coupling and complexity, and high values of cohesion, will yield for projects in which maintenance production is large and efficient.

RQ_3: *Which quality metrics are related to the productivity of maintenance among two successive releases?*

This research question is relevant to productivity. Productivity is calculated as the ratio between production and duration. We note that this calculation of productivity deviates from the typical one, because duration in OSS development might include idle time, when developers are inactive. However, to the best of our knowledge, the actual development time cannot be retrieved from source code repositories. The objective is to confirm if high levels of quality lead to increased productivity, and to some extent eliminate the bias caused by change load.

4.2   Case Selection and Data Processing

To collect subjects for our case study we retrieved a set of popular and active OSS projects. In particular, we selected only projects that were active in 2014 (i.e., published at least one version), and when sorted by popularity (based on the default sourceforge. net measure) they were among the top ranked ones. Additionally, we selected projects containing more than 300 classes to ensure that sufficient units of analysis will participate in the study and that toy-applications would be excluded. Therefore, we downloaded and collected metrics data from 20 popular OSS projects so as to build a dataset that is adequate for statistical analysis. Some demographics for these projects are presented in Table 2.

Table 2. Case study subjects

Name	NOC	Versions	Cases	Name	NOC	Versions	Cases
AoI	749	31	27	iText	645	22	20
Azureus	3,888	24	22	Java game library	654	40	33
Checkstyle	1,186	32	16	ZDF MediaThek	617	40	33
Dr Java	3,464	55	43	Pixelator	827	33	33
File bot	7,466	20	17	Mondrian	1,471	32	25
FreeCol	794	40	33	Open rocket	3,018	26	21
FreeMind	443	41	35	Subsonic	4,688	40	11
Hibernate	3,821	48	31	Sweet home 3D	341	24	17
Home player	457	30	25	UMS	5,499	50	9
Html unit	920	27	25	Tux guitar	745	17	11

The case study is an embedded multiple-case study, in the sense that for every OSS project (i.e., *case*), we analyze every transition between two versions (i.e., *units of analysis*) [23]. For each release of the projects presented in Table 2, we collected three sets of data: the structural quality metrics presented in Table 1 (see Sect. 3), the targeted maintenance managerial indices (see Sect. 4.1), and some process metrics. The obtained process metrics include the *date* each release was uploaded, the sequential *number of release* that indicates the maturity of the project (i.e., if we are in the beginning of the project lifecycle or not), and the *number of downloads* recorded for each release (considering the previous version each time) from the date launched to 01/01/2015. At this point the resulting project releases were further filtered to exclude releases that presented negative values in the production variable (deletion of functionality) and releases that presented zero duration time (releases uploaded all at once). After this pre-processing phase the remaining project releases were selected for analysis. Descriptive statistics for all dependent variables of our analysis are presented in Table 3.

Table 3. Descriptive statistics for maintenance indices

Maintenance index	N	Mean	Minimum	Maximum	Std. Dev.
Production (Δ_{LOC})	454	2629.16	1	162429	10748.11
Duration (in days)	454	79.85	1	1055	91.6
Productivity	454	76.03	0.01	9962	522.47

To apply the BBN analysis we had to further process the gathered metrics, since quality metrics present continuous arithmetic values. In particular, continuous values had to be transformed to categorical ones, so as to be utilized in BBN analysis. The transformation method used was the *equal frequency binning* [28]. This method automatically sets the boundaries of each bin (category), so as to ensure that all of them have an equal number of observations. Each metric that is represented in a categorical form has five distinct categories (VL—Very Low, L—Low, A—Average, H—High, and VH—Very High).

4.3   Data Analysis

On the completion of the aforementioned process we applied the Bayesian Network analysis and utilized heatmaps to graphically represent our data. Our goal was to better depict the influence of the independent variables on the dependent ones.

The first step of the analysis includes the selection and tuning of the variables that affect the structure of the BBN. In this step expert input is required to set the order of the variables that will affect the causal relationships that the model will define. Metrics order was selected taking into account two considerations: (a) the *development phase*, when the values of the metrics will be available in the sense that we first define certain design metrics, while some time afterwards certain source code metrics are available, and (b) the *relatedness* of metrics, based on their calculation method. For example coupling metrics like CBO and MPC are closely related. In the model CBO precedes MPC, in the sense that the value of CBO "includes" the value of MPC.

After extracting the model we employed heatmaps to visualize the obtained outcome. Heatmaps are graphical representations that use color intensity in order to denote occurrence frequency. While applying heatmaps to our results set, we developed a matrix, in which row represents a value of the dependent variable (e.g., *low maintenance duration*) and a column a value of the independent variable (e.g., *systems with a very low level of polymorphism*). Each cell is a percentage that shows the probability that the independent variable will present a certain value according to the value of the dependent variable (e.g., *10 % of the cases with a very low level of polymorphism are maintained very quickly—low maintenance duration*).

5   Results and Discussion

In this section we present the results obtained from the BBN analysis, organized by research question. The extracted network including all structural quality metrics, process measures, and managerial maintenance indices is presented in Fig. 2. We note that since this study aims to investigate the interdependencies between the nodes of the graph, the estimation accuracy of the network is not explored. A discussion/interpretation of the most important relationships presented in the network is provided later in this section, while answering each research question.

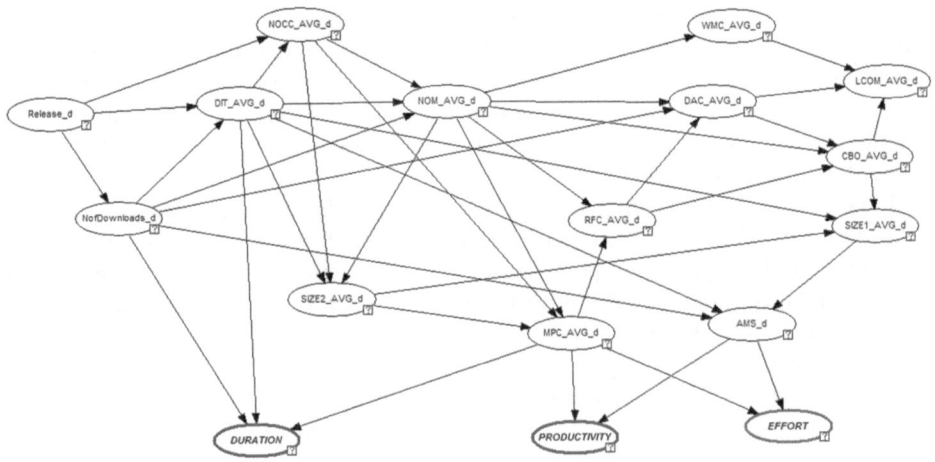

Fig. 2. Maintenance indices Bayesian belief network

5.1   Duration

In this section we identify the structural properties that are related to maintenance duration (RQ_1). From Fig. 2, we can observe that variables that are directly connected to *DURATION* are *Number of downloads, Depth of Inheritance Tree* (DIT), and *Message Passing Coupling* (MPC). The heatmaps visualizing the relationships of these variables to the duration of the maintenance activities is presented in Table 4.

Table 4. Parameters influencing maintenance duration

Duration	#Downloads					DIT					MPC				
	VS	S	A	H	VH	VS	S	A	H	VH	VS	S	A	H	VH
Very Small	28	23	18	16	15	19	16	24	17	20	22	19	22	21	16
Small	21	21	18	21	18	18	18	24	21	18	17	19	25	20	19
Average	15	24	22	20	19	22	23	19	21	19	18	24	17	21	18
High	18	17	22	21	23	23	22	18	18	20	19	24	17	19	23
Very High	18	15	20	22	25	18	21	15	23	23	24	14	19	19	24

By interpreting the left-most part of the heatmap, we can observe that as the **number of downloads** *increases,* the **maintenance duration** becomes *larger.* This result can be intuitively interpreted by the fact that projects with many downloads are expected to serve larger communities, leading to the creation of more feature requests and bug fixing activities. The number of extra requirements that are requested in each maintenance cycle increases their duration. Based on the central part of the heatmap, our results suggest that an *average* **depth of inheritance tree** offers *shorter* **maintenance cycles**. On the other hand, *extensive or limited* **inheritance** leads to *larger* **maintenance cycles**. Again, this can be characterized as an expected result, in the sense that: (a) using very large inheritance trees decreases software understandability since the full list of accessible variables and metrics from a class can spread to many classes, and (b) using limited inheritance does not make use of one of the most important benefits from using the object-oriented paradigm, and at the same time hinders the applicability of well-known object-oriented principles (e.g., open-closed principle [17]) and design patterns (e.g., template method, state/strategy, etc. [11]) that have been reported as beneficial to maintainability.

Finally, *very high* **coupling** leads to *high* or *very high* **maintenance duration** (see right-most part of the heatmap). This result is expected in the sense that according to the high coupling principle [17] dense inter-connection of classes reduces their understandability, increases the probability of initiating a ripple effect, and reduces their changeability. On the other hand, by focusing on *very small* **coupling** we get interesting results. Intuitively one would expect that very small coupling would increase modularity (low ripple effect, increase changeability) and therefore be connected to quick maintenance cycles, but this is the 2nd most frequent event. The most frequent event is that very small coupling is connected to large maintenance cycles. This result, although initially surprising, can be interpreted by the inherent relationship/trade-off between coupling and cohesion (as it is confirmed by the network of Fig. 2). Specifically, it is expected that low coupling can also lead to bad design, in cases that specific classes are growing so large that they do not need to call methods from other classes (they are self-contained). This leads to reduced coupling, but probably these classes are assigned to more than one responsibility. This decision overrules the Single Responsibility Principle, which according to Martin [17], in turn leads to maintainability problems, especially focused on understandability and change proneness.

5.2   Production

In this section, we explore the BBN for mining relationship related to RQ$_2$, i.e., metrics that are related to maintenance production, measured as lines of code added from one version to the other. Similarly to Sect. 5.1, in Table 5, we present the heatmap for the two variables that are directly related to maintenance production. Interestingly, we can observe that the two most important parameters are: one complexity metric (namely AMS) and the same coupling metric as in Table 4 (namely MPC). This is considered important from two perspectives:

(a) **Average Method Size (AMS)** has, until now, not been explored as a possible maintainability predictor, although it appears to be related to maintenance production. However this result can be considered intuitive, in the sense that the size of the method is related to one the most persistent and frequently occurring bad smells, namely *Long Method* [10]. According to the literature methods of large size are very difficult to understand, modify and extend, leading to difficulties in increasing maintenance production.

(b) **Message Passing Coupling (MPC)** is consistently the coupling metric that can be used as the optimal maintainability index. The superiority of MPC with regard to assessing ripple effects (a significant aspect of maintainability) compared to the other examined coupling metrics is also discussed by Arvanitou et al. [5]. In particular MPC is the only (among the investigated metrics) that captures both coupling volume (number of relationships) and coupling intensity (how closely connected the two classes are). An additional important characteristic of MPC is that it counts coupling intensity using the discrete count function, and therefore is not biased from the number of times one method is being called [4].

Table 5. Parameters influencing maintenance production

Production	AMS					MPC				
	VS	S	A	H	VH	VS	S	A	H	VH
Very Small	16	27	25	20	13	15	22	23	17	22
Small	21	23	18	21	17	25	20	25	14	17
Average	21	17	15	21	26	23	21	19	21	16
High	24	15	17	22	22	20	19	15	23	24
Very High	19	16	24	20	20	18	18	19	24	21

5.3   Productivity

Similarly to RQ_1 and RQ_2, in Table 6, we present the heatmap that visualizes the parameters that are more closely related to maintenance productivity. By comparing the results of Table 6, with those of Tables 4 and 5, we can observe that productivity is more closely related to maintenance production rather than maintenance duration.

Table 6. Parameters influencing maintenance productivity

Productivity	AMS					MPC				
	VS	S	A	H	VH	VS	S	A	H	VH
Very Small	19	26	21	20	14	16	27	22	13	23
Small	19	22	19	19	21	23	23	22	14	18
Average	23	20	14	22	20	19	17	24	18	22
High	17	12	16	28	27	27	15	13	28	17
Very High	25	16	28	14	17	15	18	22	28	18

In particular we observe that the only metric that is consistently among the optimal maintenance predictors is MPC, whereas AMS is only related to maintenance production and productivity. Concerning the range of values for these variables we can reach the following conclusions: According to Martin [23], the average method size should not exceed 5 lines of code. Based on the findings of this case study, very small methods provide a maximum productivity in 42 % of the cases, which is a rather intuitive result. The counter point, as discussed by Fowler [10] (i.e., long methods are hard to maintain) cannot be discussed based on our results, since in order for such an investigation to be possible, it would be required to count the number of long method bad smells and not an aggregated/average measure. Concerning MPC, we can observe that tightly coupled systems are exhibiting small and very small productivity rates—a result that is expected based on the negative effect of coupling on maintainability.

5.4   Implications to Practitioners and Researchers

The results of our case study have provided some interesting insights and implications to both practitioners and researchers. Concerning practitioners, our study provides evidence that indeed structural quality metrics are affecting maintenance indices. However, from the vast amount of metrics that are available, only a limited number of them are highly influential. As expected the most significant metrics cover the most frequently quantified quality attributes, directly or indirectly, i.e., complexity, cohesion, coupling, and inheritance. In particular, the study pointed out that practitioners should pay attention on balancing the values of the following metrics: Average Method Size (AMS), Message Passing Coupling (MPC), and Depth of Inheritance Tree (DIT). Thus, practitioners should not only include these metrics in their quality dashboards, but also manage their natural trade-off (e.g., optimizing coupling on the expense of cohesion).

Furthermore, the outcome of this study indicated some interesting future research directions. First a replication of the case study can be performed including metrics of different categories and suites (e.g., architecture level) and also metrics that describe the communication and message exchange of the OSS developers' community. Secondly, the development of a complete estimation model that additionally takes into account factors other than software structure is expected to fully capture and predict all aspects of software maintenance productivity. Finally, tailoring the proposed model in an industrial context is necessary for the adoption of such approaches in closed source software development.

6   Threats to Validity

In this section we discuss the threats to validity of our case study, based on the categorization described by Runeson et al. [23]. With regard to *internal validity*, we need to clarify that the relationships obtained through the network are influenced by some confounding factors. For example, the load of high-level changes from one version of the system to another (e.g., new features, number of fixed bugs, etc.) is not considered in this study. However, we believe that the large size of our dataset imposed a normal distribution of actual changes that minimizes the effect of the confounding factor. Additionally, we remind that the investigation of the strength of relationships is out of the scope of this study, since it only aims at their identification.

Concerning *external validity*, we have identified two threats to generalization. First, since all the examined projects come from one source code repository the results cannot be generalized to the OSS population. Second, since we only explored Java projects (due to the limitation of the used tool) the results cannot be generalized to other programming languages. However, we believe that projects popularity and size are indicative factors of successful OSS projects.

Regarding *reliability*, based on the fact that our study is purely quantitative and the developed protocol (see Sect. 4) is thoroughly described, we believe that the process is easily replicable by other researchers. Though, concerning *construct validity*, Bayesian network model construction includes by its nature many subjective decisions made by the modeler. The parameters of the model such as the selection of the binning method for the discretization of the values of the continuous variables and the ordering of the independent variables may also affect the model extracted. This provides an interesting direction for future studies that could include additionally sensitivity analysis regarding the parameters of the model.

7   Conclusions

Long-term monitoring of maintenance effort requires a measurement process of respective attributes that affect software maintenance and a model to represent the interrelations of the attributes gathered. Open source software is a suitable paradigm of continuous, sustainable maintenance efforts. Understanding why each system requires more or less maintenance effort is necessary for better monitoring software maintenance process and releases launch. In this study we have performed an empirical study on the factors that affect software maintenance duration, production and productivity on 20 open source software projects. We suggest Bayesian Networks as a tool to model all attributes and factors that can affect maintenance efforts. The created model included structural quality and process metrics, and managerial indices. The results indicate that maintenance *duration* is affected by the popularity of a project and *DIT* (a design metric) and *MPC* (a source code metric). On the other hand Production and Productivity are solely affected by quality metrics *AMS* and *MPC*.

References

1. Abran, A., Nguyenkim, H.: Measurement of the maintenance process from a demand-based perspective. J. Softw. Maintenance: Res. Pract. **5**(2), 63–90 (1993)
2. Ampatzoglou, A., Ampatzoglou, A., Chatzigeorgiou, A., Avgeriou, P.: The financial aspect of managing technical debt: a systematic literature review. Inf. Softw. Technol. **64**(8), 52–73 (2015). Elsevier
3. Ampatzoglou, A., Michou, O., Stamelos, I.: Building and mining a repository of design pattern instances: practical and research benefits. Entertainment Comput. **4**(2), 131–142 (2013). Elsevier
4. Ampatzoglou, A., Chatzigeorgiou, A., Charalampidou, S., Avgeriou, P.: The effect of GoF design patterns on stability: a case study. Trans. Softw. Eng. **41**(8), 781–802 (2015). IEEE Computer Society
5. Arvanitou, E.M., Ampatzoglou, A., Chatzigeorgiou, A., Avgeriou, P.: Introducing a ripple effect measure: a theoretical and empirical validation. In: 9th International Symposium on Empirical Software Engineering and Measurement (ESEM 2015), Beijing, China. IEEE Computer Society, 22–23 October 2015
6. Boehm, B.W.: Software Engineering Economics, 1st edn. Prentice Hall PTR, Upper Saddle River (1981)
7. Cheng, J., Greiner, R.: Learning Bayesian belief network classifiers: algorithms and system. In: 14th Canadian Conference on Artificial Intelligence (AI 2001) (2001)
8. Chidamber, S.R., Darcy, D.P., Kemerer, C.F.: Managerial use of metrics for object oriented software: an exploratory analysis. Trans. Softw. Eng. **24**(8), 629–639 (1998). IEEE Computer Society

9. Fenton, N., Neil, M., Marsh, W., Hearty, P., Marquez, D., Krause, P., Mishra, R.: Predicting software defects in varying development lifecycles using Bayesian nets. Inf. Softw. Technol. **49**(1), 32–43 (2007)

10. Fowler, M., Beck, K., Brant, J., Opdyke, W., Roberts, D.: Refactoring: Improving the Design of Existing Code, 1st edn. Addison-Wesley Professional, Boston (1999)

11. Gamma, E., Helms, R., Johnson, R., Vlissides, J.: Design Patterns: Elements of Reusable Object-Oriented Software. Addison-Wesley Professional, Boston (1995)

12. Ghods, M., Nelson, K.M.: Contributors to quality during software maintenance. Decis. Support Syst. **23**(4), 361–369 (1998)

13. Jensen, F.: Bayesian Networks and Decision Graphs. Springer, Heidelberg (2002)

14. Koch, S., Neumann, C.: Exploring the effects of process characteristics on product quality in open source software development. In: Principle Advancements in Database Management Technologies: New Applications and Frameworks, p. 132 (2009)

15. Li, W., Henry, S.: Object-oriented metrics that predict maintainability. J. Syst. Softw. **23**(2), 111–122 (1993). Elsevier

16. de Lucia, A., Pompella, E., Stefanucci, S.: Assessing effort estimation models for corrective software maintenance through empirical studies. Inf. Softw. Technol. **47**(1), 3–15 (2005). Elsevier

17. Martin, R.C.: Agile Software Development: Principles, Patterns and Practices. Prentice Hall, Upper Saddle River (2003)

18. Martin, R.C.: Clean Code: A Handbook of Agile Software Craftsmanship, 1st edn. Prentice Hall PTR, Upper Saddle River (2008)

19. de Melo, A.C.V., de J. Sanchez, A.: Bayesian networks in software maintenance management. In: Vojtáš, P., Bieliková, M., Charron-Bost, B., Sýkora, O. (eds.) SOFSEM 2005. LNCS, vol. 3381, pp. 394–398. Springer, Heidelberg (2005)

20. Midha, V., Bhattacherjee, A.: Governance practices and software maintenance: a study of open source projects. Decis. Support Syst. **54**(1), 23–32 (2012)

21. Mockus, A., Fielding, R., Herbsleb, J.: Two case studies of open source software development: Apache and Mozilla. Trans. Softw. Eng. Methodol. **11**(3), 309–346 (2002). ACM

22. Riaz, M., Mendes, E., Tempero, E.: A systematic review on software maintainability prediction and metrics. In: 3rd International Symposium on Empirical Software Engineering and Measurement (ESEM 2009), USA, pp. 367–377. IEEE Computer Society (2009)

23. Runeson, P., Host, M., Rainer, A., Regnell, B.: Case Study Research in Software Engineering: Guidelines and Examples. Wiley, Hoboken (2012)

24. Shepperd, M., Schofield, C., Kitchenham, B.: Effort estimation using analogy. In: 18th International Conference on Software Engineering (ICSE 1996), pp. 170–178. ACM (1996)

25. Stamelos, I., Angelis, L., Dimou, P., Sakellaris, E.: On the use of Bayesian Belief Networks for the prediction of software productivity. Inf. Softw. Technol. **45**, 51–60 (2002). Elsevier

26. van Koten, A., Gray, A.R.: An application of Bayesian network for predicting object-oriented software maintainability. Inf. Softw. Technol. **48**(1), 59–67 (2006). Elsevier

27. van Vliet, H.: Software Engineering: Principles and Practice. Wiley, Hoboken (2008)

28. Witten, I., Frank, E.: Data Mining: Practical Machine Learning Tools and Techniques. Morgan Kaufmann, Burlington (2005)

Core-Periphery Communication
and the Success of Free/Libre Open Source
Software Projects

Kevin Crowston[1](✉) and Ivan Shamshurin[2]

[1] Syracuse University School of Information Studies,
348 Hinds Hall, Syracuse, NY 13244–4100, USA
crowston@syr.edu
[2] Syracuse University School of Information Studies,
337 Hinds Hall, Syracuse, NY 13244–4100, USA
ishamshu@syr.edu

Abstract. We examine the relationship between communications by core and peripheral members and Free/Libre Open Source Software project success. The study uses data from 74 projects in the Apache Software Foundation Incubator. We conceptualize project success in terms of success building a community, as assessed by graduation from the Incubator. We compare successful and unsuccessful projects on volume of communication by core (committer) and peripheral community members and on use of inclusive pronouns as an indication of efforts to create intimacy among team members. An innovation of the paper is that use of inclusive pronouns is measured using natural language processing techniques. We find that core and peripheral members differ in their volume of contribution and in their use of inclusive pronouns, and that volume of communication is related to project success.

1 Introduction

Community-based Free/Libre Open Source Software (FLOSS) projects are developed and maintained by teams of individuals collaborating in globally-distributed environments [8]. The health of the developer community is critical for the performance of projects [7], but it is challenging to sustain a project with voluntary members over the long term [4, 11]. Social-relational issues have been seen as a key component of achieving design effectiveness [3] and enhancing online group involvement and collaboration [15]. In this paper, we explore how community interactions are related to community health and so project success.

Specifically, we examine contributions made by members in different roles. Members have different levels of participation in FLOSS development and so taken on different roles [5]. A widely accepted models of roles in community-based FLOSS teams is the core-periphery structure [1, 3, 12]. For example, Crowston and Howison [7] see community-based FLOSS teams as having an onion-like core-periphery structure, in which the core category includes core developers and the periphery includes co-developers and active users. Rullani and Haefliger [17] described periphery as a "cloud" of members that orbits around the core members of open source software development teams.

K. Crowston et al. (Eds.): OSS 2016, IFIP AICT 472, pp. 45–56, 2016.
DOI: 10.1007/978-3-319-39225-7_4

Generally speaking, access to core roles is based on technical skills demonstrated through the development tasks that the developer performs [13]. Core developers usually contribute most of the code and oversee the design and evolution of the project, which requires a high level of technical skills [7]. Peripheral members, on the other hand, submit patches such as bug fixes (co-developers), which provides an opportunity to demonstrate skills and interest, or just provide use cases and bug reports or test new releases without contributing codes directly (active users), which requires less technical skill [7].

Despite the difference in contributions, both core and peripheral members are important to the success of the project. It is evident that, by making direct contributions to the software developed, core members are vital to project development. On the other hand, even though they contribute only sporadically, peripheral members provide bug reports, suggestions and critical expertise that are fundamental for innovation [17]. In addition, the periphery is the source of new core members [10, 20], so maintaining a strong periphery is important to the long-term success of a project. Amrit and van Hillegersberg [1] examined core-periphery movement in open source projects and concluded that a steady movement toward the core is beneficial to a project, while a shift away from the core is not. But how communication among core and periphery predicts project success has yet to be investigated systematically, a gap that this paper addresses.

2   Theory and Hypotheses

To develop hypotheses for our study, we discuss in turn the dependent and independent variables in our study.

The dependent variable for our study is project success. Project success for FLOSS projects can be measured in many different ways, ranging from code quality to member satisfaction to market share [6]. For the community-based FLOSS projects we examine, success in building a developer community is a critical issue, so we chose building a developer community as our measure of success.

To identify independent variables that predict success (i.e., success in building a developer community), we examine communication among community members. A starting hypothesis is that more communication is predictive of project success:

H1: Successful projects will have a higher volume of communication than unsuccessful projects

More specifically, we are interested in how members in different roles contribute to projects. As noted above, projects rely on contributions from both core and peripheral members. We can therefore extend H1 to consider roles. Specifically, we hypothesize that:

H2a: Successful projects will have a higher volume of communication by core members than unsuccessful projects.
H2b: Successful projects will have a higher volume of communication by peripheral members than unsuccessful projects.

Prior research on the core-periphery structure in FLOSS development has found inequality in participation between core and peripheral members. For example, Luthiger Stoll [14] found that core members make greater time commitment than peripheral members: core participants spend an average of 12 h per week, with project leaders averaging 14 h, and bug-fixers and otherwise active users, around 5 h per week. Similarly, using social network analysis, Toral et al. [19] found that a few core members post the majority of messages and act as middlemen or brokers among other peripheral members. We therefore hypothesize that:

H3: Core members will contribute more communication than will peripheral members.

Prior research on the distinction between core-periphery has mostly focused on coding-related behaviour, as project roles are defined by the coding activities performed [3]. However, developers do more than just coding [3]. Both core and peripheral members need to engage in social-relational behaviour in addition to task-oriented behaviour such as coding. Consideration of these non-task activities is important because effective interpersonal communication plays a vital role in the development of online social interaction [16].

Scialdone et al. [18] and Wei et al. [21] analyzed group maintenance behaviours used by members to build and maintain reciprocal trust and cooperation in their everyday interaction messages, e.g., through emotional expressions and politeness strategies. In this paper, we examine one factor they identified, investigating how core and peripheral members use language to create "intimacy among team members" thus "building solidarity in teams". Specifically, Scialdone et al. [18] found that core members of two teams used more inclusive pronouns (i.e., pronouns referring to the team) than did peripheral members. They interpreted this finding as meaning that "peripheral members in general do not feel as comfortable expressing a sense of belonging within their groups". We therefore hypothesize that:

H4: Core members will use more inclusive pronouns in their communication than will peripheral members.

Scialdone et al. [18] further noted that one team they studied that had ceased production had exhibited a greater gap between core and periphery in usage of inclusive pronouns. Such a situation could indicate that the peripheral members of the group do not feel ownership of the project, with negative implications for their future as potential core members. Scialdone et al. [18] noted that such use of inclusive pronouns is "consistent with Bagozzi and Dholakia [2]'s argument about the importance of we-intention in Linux user groups, i.e., when individuals think themselves as 'us' or 'we' and so attempt to act in a joint way". A similar argument can be made for the importance of core member use of inclusive pronouns. We therefore hypothesize that:

H5a: Successful projects will have a higher usage of inclusive pronouns by core members than unsuccessful projects.
H5b: Successful projects will have a higher usage of inclusive pronouns by peripheral members than unsuccessful projects.

3   Methods

3.1   Setting

Scialdone et al. [18] and Wei et al. [21] studied only a few projects and noted problem making comparison across projects that can be quite diverse. To address this concern, in this paper we studied a larger number of projects (74 in total) that all operated within a common framework at a similar stage of development. Specifically, we studied projects in the Apache Software Foundation (ASF) Incubator. The ASF is an umbrella organization including more than 60 free/libre open source software (FLOSS) development projects. The ASF's apparent success in managing FLOSS projects has made it a frequently mentioned model for these efforts, though often without a deep understanding of the factors behind that success.

The ASF Incubator's purpose is to mentor new projects to the point where they are able to successfully join the ASF. Projects are invited to join the Incubator based on an application and support from a sponsor (a member of the ASF). Accepted projects (known as Podlings) receive support from one or more mentors, who help guide the Podlings through the steps necessary to become a full-fledged ASF project.

The incubation process has several goals, including fulfillment of legal and infrastructural requirements and development of relationships with other ASF projects, but the main goal is to develop effective software development communities, which Podlings must demonstrate in order to graduate from the Incubator. The Apache Incubator specifically promotes diverse participation in development projects to improve the long-term viability of the project community and ensure requisite diversity of intellectual resources. The time projects spend in incubation varies widely, from as little as two months to nearly five years, indicating significant diversity in the efforts required for Podlings to become viable projects. The primary reason that projects are retired from the Incubator (rather than graduated) is a lack of community development that stalls progress.

3.2   Data Collection and Processing

In FLOSS settings, collaborative work primarily takes place by means of asynchronous computer-mediated communication such as email lists and discussion fora [5]. ASF community norms strongly support transparency and broad participation, which is accomplished via electronic communications, such that even collocated participants are expected to document conversations in the online record, i.e., the email discussion lists. We therefore drew our data from messages on the developers' mailing list for each project.

A Perl script was used to collect messages in html format from the site http://markmail.org. We discarded any messages sent after the Podling either graduated or retired from the ASF Incubator, as many of the projects apparently used the same email list even after graduation. After the dataset was collected, relevant data was extracted from the html files representing each message thread and other sources.

3.2.1 Dependent Variable: Success

The dependent variable, project success in building a community, was determined by whether the project had graduated (success) or been retired (not success) based on the list of projects maintained by the Apache Incubator and available on the Apache website. The dataset includes email messages for 24 retired and 50 graduated Podlings. The data set also included messages for some projects still in incubation and some with unknown status; these were not used for further analysis.

As a check on this measure of successful community development, we examined the number of developers active in the community (a more successful community has more developers). We considered as active members of the projects those who sent an email to the developer mailing list during incubation.

3.2.2 Core Vs. Periphery

Crowston et al. [9] suggested three methods to identify core and peripheral members in FLOSS teams: relying on project-reported formal roles, analysis of distribution of contributions based on Bradford's Law of Scatter, and core-and-periphery analysis of project social network. Their analysis showed that relying on project-reported roles was the most accurate. Therefore, in this study, we identified a message sender as a core member if the sender's name was on the list of project committers on the project website. If we did not find a match, then the sender was labeled as non-committer (peripheral member). we developed a matching algorithm to take into account the variety of ways that names appear in email message.

3.2.3 Inclusive Pronouns

As noted above, we examined the use of inclusive pronouns as one way that team members build a sense of belong to the group. Inclusive pronouns were defined as:

reference to the team using an inclusive pronoun. If we see "we" or "us" or "our", and it refers to the group, then it is Inclusive Reference. Not if "we" or "us" or "our" refer to another group that the speaker is a member of.

That is, the sentences were judged on two criteria: (1) whether there are language cues for inclusive reference (a pronoun), as specified in the definition above and (2) if these cues refer to the current group rather than another group. To judge the second criteria may require reviewing the sentence in the context of the whole conversation. This usage is only one of the many indicators studied by Scialdone et al. [18] and Wei et al. [21], but it is interesting and tractable for analysis.

To handle the large volume of messages drawn from many projects, we applied NLP techniques as suggested (but not implemented) by previous research. Specifically, we used a machine-learning (ML) approach, where an algorithm learns to classify sentences from a corpus of already coded data. Sentences were chosen as the unit of coding instead of the thematic units more typically used in human coding, because sentences can be more easily identified for machine learning. Training data was obtained from the SOCQA (Socio-computational Qualitative Analysis) project at the Syracuse University (http://socqa.org/) [22, 23]. The training data consists of 10,841 sentences drawn from two Apache projects, SpamAssassin and Avalon. Trained annotators manually coded each sentence as to whether it included an inclusive pronoun (per the above definition) or not. The distribution of the classes in the training data is shown in Table 1 ("yes" means the sentence has an inclusive pronoun). Note that the sample is unbalanced.

Table 1. Distribution of classes in the training data

	#	%
"yes"	1395	12.9
"no"	9446	87.1
Total	10841	

As features for the ML, we used bag of words, experimenting with unigrams, bigrams and trigrams. Naïve Bayes (MNB), k Nearest Neighbors (KNN) and Support Vector Machines (SVM) algorithms (Python LibSVM implementation) were trained and applied to predict the class of the sentences, i.e., whether a sentence has inclusive pronoun or not. We expected that the NLP would have no problem handling the first part of the definition, but that the second (whether the pronoun refers to the project or some other group) would pose challenges.

10-fold cross-validation was used to evaluate the classifier's performance on the training data. Results are shown in Table 2. The results show that though all three approaches gave reasonable performance, SVM outperformed other methods. The Linear SVM model was therefore selected for further use. We experimented with tuning SVM parameters such as minimal term frequency, etc. but did not find settings that affected the accuracy, so we used the default settings.

Table 2. Results of 10-fold cross-validation on the training data

	Unigram	Bigram	Trigram
MNB	0.86	0.81	0.75
KNN	0.89	0.89	0.88
SVM (LinearSVC)	0.97	0.97	0.97

The random guess baseline for a binary classification task would give an accuracy of 0.5; a majority vote rule baseline (classify all examples to the majority class) provides an accuracy of 0.87. The trained SVM model significantly outperforms both. To further evaluate model performance, it was applied to new data and the results checked by a trained annotator (one of the annotators of the training data set). Specifically, we used the model to code 200 sentences (10 sentences randomly selected from 5 projects each in the "graduated", "in incubator", "retired" and "unknown" classes of projects). The annotator coded the same sentences and we compared the results. The Cohen kappa (agreement corrected for chance agreement) for the human vs. machine coding was 88.6 %, which is higher than the frequently applied threshold of 80 % agreement. In other words, the ML model performed at least as well as a second human coder would be expected to do.

Examining the results, somewhat surprisingly, we found no cases where a predicted "inclusive reference" refers to another group, suggesting that the ML had managed to learn the second criterion. Two sentences that the model misclassified are illustrative of limitations of the approach:

It looks like it requires work with "our @patterns" in lib/path.pmI looked at the path.pm for www.apache.org *and it is a clue.*

The actual class is "no" but the classifier marked it as "yes" because the inclusive pronoun "our" was included in the sentence, though in quotes.

Could also clarify download URLs for third-party dependencies wecan't ship.

The actual class is "yes" but the model marked the sentence as "no" due to the error in spelling (no space after "we"). The human annotator ignored the error, but there were not enough examples of such errors for the ML to learn to do so. Despite such limitations, the benefit of being able to handle large volumes of email more than makes up for the possible slight loss in reliability of coding, especially considering that human coders are also not perfectly reliable.

4   Findings

In this section we discuss in turn the findings from our study, first validating the measure of success, then examining support for each hypothesis.

4.1   Membership

As a check on our measure of success (graduation from the Incubator), we compared the number of developers in graduated and retired projects (active developers were those who had participated on the mailing list). The results are shown in Table 3. As the table shows, graduated projects had more than twice as many developers active on the mailing list as did retired projects. The differences are so large than a statistical test of significance seems superfluous (for doubters, a Kruskal-Wallis test, chosen because the data are not normally distributed, shows a statistically significant difference in the number of developers between graduated and retired projects, $p = 0.001$). This result provides evidence for the validity of graduation as a measure of project community health.

Table 3. Mean number of developers by project status and developer role

Project status	Core	Peripheral
Graduated	31.6 (19.4)	82.2 (102.4)
Retired	13.9 (9.3)	25.4 (18.3)

N = 74. Standard deviations in parentheses.

Hypothesis 1 was that successful projects would have more communication. As shown in Table 4, this hypothesis is strongly supported, as graduated projects have many times more messages sent than retired projects during the incubation process (p = 0.0001).

Table 4. Mean number of project messages by project status and developer role

	Core	Peripheral
Graduated	8265 (8878)	7306 (8908)
Retired	1791 (1805)	1652 (2058)

N = 74. Standard deviations in parentheses.

Hypotheses 2a and 2b were that core and peripheral members respectively would communicate more in successful projects than in unsuccessful projects. The differences in Tables 4 and 5 show that these hypotheses are supported (p = 0.0001 for core and p = 0.0001 for peripheral members for overall message count in graduated vs. retired projects, and p = 0.0011 and p = 0.0399 for messages per developer).

Table 5. Mean number of messages sent per developer by project status and developer role

	Core	Peripheral
Graduated	239 (191)	109 (119)
Retired	107 (200)	47 (92)

N = 74. Standard deviations in parentheses.

Hypothesis 3 was that core members would communicate more than peripheral members. From Table 4, we can see that in fact in total core and peripheral members send about the same volume of messages in both graduated and retired projects. However, there are fewer core members, so on average, each sends many more messages on average, as shown in Table 5 (p = 0.0001).

Table 6. Mean number of messages including an inclusive pronoun sent per developer by project status and developer role

	Core	Periphery
Graduated	22 (18)	6 (5)
Retired	12 (8)	4 (5)

N = 74. Standard deviations in parentheses.

Hypothesis 4 was that core members would use more inclusive pronouns than peripheral members. Table 6 shows the number of messages sent by developers that included an inclusive pronoun. The table shows that core developers do send more messages with inclusive pronouns in both graduated and retired projects (p = 0.0001).

Table 7. Mean percentage of messages that include an inclusive pronoun per developer by project status and developer role

	Core	Periphery
Graduated	7.6 (3.4)	5.5 (2.2)
Retired	9.3 (5.)	5.3 (3.2)

N = 74. Standard deviations in parentheses.

To control for the fact that core developers send more messages in general, we computed the percentage of messages that include an inclusive pronoun, as shown in Table 7. From this table, we can see that the mean percentage of messages sent by core developers that include an inclusive pronoun is higher than for peripheral members (p = 0.001).

Hypotheses 5a and b were that there would be more use of inclusive pronouns by core and peripheral members respectively in successful projects. From Table 6, this hypothesis seems supported for core members at least, but note that successful projects have more communication overall. Examining Table 7 suggests that there is in fact slightly more proportional use of inclusive pronouns by core members in unsuccessful projects, but no difference in use by peripheral members. However, neither difference is significant using a KW test, meaning that Hypothesis 5 is not supported.

Finally, to assess which of the factors we examined are most predictive of projects success, we applied a stepwise logistic regression, predicting graduation from the various measures of communication developed (e.g., total number of message by developer role, mean number, percentage of message with inclusive pronouns). Our first regression identified only one factor as predictive, the number of core members. This result can be expected, as we argued above that the number of core members can also be viewed as a measure of community health. A regression without counts of members identified the total number and the mean number of messages sent by core members as predictive, with mean having a negative coefficient. (The R^2 for the regression was 33 %.) This combination of factors does not provide much insight as it is essentially a proxy for developer count: greatest when there are a lot of messages but not many messages per developer, i.e., when there are more developers.

5   Discussion

In general, our data suggest that successful projects (i.e., those that successfully built a community and graduated from incubation) have more members and a correspondingly large volume of communication, suggesting an active community. As expected, core members contribute more, but overall, the message volume seems almost evenly split between core and peripheral members, suggesting that both roles play an important part in projects. These results demonstrate the importance of interaction between and the shared responsibilities of core and peripheral members.

As expected, core members do display somewhat greater ownership of the project, as expressed in the use of inclusive pronouns, but counter to our expectations, the use of inclusive pronouns did not distinguish successful and unsuccessful projects. A possible explanation for this result is a limitation in our data processing: we determined developer status (core or periphery) based on committer lists from the project website collected at the time of analysis. This process does not take into account the movement of developers from periphery to core (or less frequently, from core to periphery). It could be that in successful projects, active peripheral members (i.e., those using more inclusive pronouns) are invited to join the core, thus suppressing the average for peripheral members.

6 Conclusions

The work presented here can be extended in many ways in future work. First, as noted, developers may change status during the project. The results would be more accurate if they took into account the history of when developers became committers to correctly assign their status over time. Obtaining such historical data is challenging but not impossible. Second, the ML NLP might be improved with a richer feature set [24], though as noted, the performance was already as good as would be expected from an additional human coder. Third, it would be interesting to examine the first few months of a project for early signs that are predictive of its eventual outcome. Fourth, it might similarly be possible to predict which peripheral members will become core members from their individual actions. Fifth, we can consider the effects of additional group maintenance behaviours from Wei et al. [21]. The Syracuse SOCQA project has had some success applying ML NLP techniques to these codes, suggesting that this analysis is feasible. Sixth, it is necessary to consider limits to the hypothesized impacts. For example, we hypothesized that more communication reflects a more developed community, but it could be that too much communication creates information overload and so has a negative impact. Finally, in this paper we have considered only communication behaviours. A more complete model of project success would take into account measure of development activities such as code commits or project topic, data for which are available online.

Despite its limitations, our research offers several advances over prior work. First, it examines a much large sample of projects. Second, it uses a more objective measure of project success, namely graduation from the ASF Incubator, as a measure of community development. Finally, it shows the viability of the application of NLP and ML techniques to processing large volumes of email messages, incorporating analysis of the content of messages, not just counts or network structure.

Acknowledgements. We thank the SOCQA Project (Nancy McCracken PI) for access to the coded sentences for training and Feifei Zhang for checking the coding results. SOCQA was partially supported by a grant from the US National Science Foundation Socio-computational Systems (SOCS) program, award 11–11107.

References

1. Amrit, C., van Hillegersberg, J.: Exploring the impact of socio-technical core-periphery structures in open source software development. J. Inf. Technol. **25**(2), 216–229 (2010)
2. Bagozzi, R.P., Dholakia, U.M.: Open source software user communities: a study of participation in Linux user groups. Manage. Sci. **52**(7), 1099–1115 (2006)
3. Barcellini, F., Détienne, F., Burkhardt, J.-M.: A situated approach of roles and participation in open source software communities. Hum.-Comput. Interact. **29**(3), 205–255 (2014)
4. Bonaccorsi, A., Rossi, C.: Why F/OSS can succeed. Res. Policy **32**, 1243–1258 (2003)
5. Crowston, K., Wei, K., Howison, J., Wiggins, A.: Free/Libre open source software development: what we know and what we do not know. ACM Comput. Surv. **44**(2), Article 7 (2012)
6. Crowston, K., Howison, J., Annabi, H.: Information systems success in free and open source software development: theory and measures. Softw. Process Improv. Pract. **11**(2), 123–148 (2006)
7. Crowston, K., Howison, J.: Assessing the health of open source communities. IEEE Comput. **39**(5), 89–91 (2006)
8. Crowston, K., Li, Q., Wei, K., Eseryel, U.Y., Howison, J.: Self-organization of teams for Free/Libre open source software development. Inf. Softw. Technol. **49**(6), 564–575 (2007)
9. Crowston, K., Wei, K., Li, Q., Howison, J.: Core and periphery in Free/Libre and open source software team communications. In: Proceedings of the Hawai'i International Conference on System System (HICSS-39) (2006)
10. Dahlander, L., O'Mahony, S.: Progressing to the center: coordinating project work. Organ. Sci. **22**(4), 961–979 (2011)
11. Fang, Y., Neufeld, D.: Understanding sustained participation in open source software projects. J. Manage. Inf. Syst. **25**(4), 9–50 (2009)
12. Jensen, C., Scacchi, W.: Role migration and advancement processes in OSSD projects: a comparative case study. In: Proceedings of the 29th International Conference on Software Engineering (ICSE), pp. 364–374 (2007)
13. Jergensen, C., Sarma, A., Wagstrom, P.: The onion patch: migration in open source ecosystems. In: Proceedings of the 19th ACM SIGSOFT Symposium and the 13th European Conference on Foundations of Software Engineering, pp. 70–80 (2011)
14. Luthiger Stoll, B.: Fun and software development. In: Proceedings of the First International Conference on Open Source Systems, Genova, Italy, 11–15 July 2005
15. Park, J.R.: Interpersonal and affective communication in synchronous online discourse. Libr. Q. **77**(2), 133–155 (2007)
16. Park, J.-R.: Linguistic politeness and face-work in computer mediated communication, part 2: an application of the theoretical framework. J. Am. Soc. Inf. Sci. Technol. **59**(14), 2199–2209 (2008)
17. Rullani, F., Haefliger, S.: The periphery on stage: the intra-organizational dynamics in online communities of creation. Res. Policy **42**(4), 941–953 (2013)

18. Scialdone, M.J., Heckman, R., Crowston, K.: Group maintenance behaviours of core and peripheral members of Free/Libre open source software teams. In: Proceedings of the IFIP WG 2.13 Working Conference on Open Source Systems, Skövde, Sweden, 3–6 June 2009
19. Toral, S.L., Martínez-Torres, M.R., Barrero, Federico: Analysis of virtual communities supporting OSS projects using social network analysis. Inf. Softw. Technol. **52**(3), 296–303 (2010)
20. von Krogh, G., Spaeth, S., Lakhani, K.R.: Community, joining, and specialization in open source software innovation: a case study. Res. Policy **32**(7), 1217–1241 (2003)
21. Wei, K., Crowston, K., Li, N.L., Heckman, R.: Understanding group maintenance behaviour in Free/Libre open-source software projects: the case of fire and gaim. Inf. Manage. **51**(3), 297–309 (2014)
22. Yan, J.L.S., McCracken, N., Crowston, K.: Design of an active learning system with human correction for content analysis. Paper Presented at the Workshop on Interactive Language Learning, Visualization, and Interfaces, 52nd Annual Meeting of the Association for Computational Linguistics, Baltimore, MD, June 2014. http://nlp.stanford.edu/events/illvi2014/papers/mccracken-illvi2014.pdf
23. Yan, J.L.S., McCracken, N., Crowston, K.: Semi-automatic content analysis of qualitative data. In: Proceedings of the iConference, Berlin, Germany, 4–7 Mar 2014
24. Yan, J.L.S., McCracken, N., Zhou, S., Crowston, K.: Optimizing features in active machine learning for complex qualitative content analysis. Paper Presented at the Workshop on Language Technologies and Computational Social Science, 52nd Annual Meeting of the Association for Computational Linguistics Baltimore, MD, June 2014

On Involvement in Open Standards: How Do Organisations Contribute to W3C Standards Through Editorship?

Jonas Gamalielsson[(✉)] and Björn Lundell

University of Skövde, Skövde, Sweden
{jonas.gamalielsson,bjorn.lundell}@his.se

Abstract. Over the years, a number of open standards have been developed and implemented in software for addressing a number of challenges, such as lock-in, interoperability and longevity of software systems and associated digital artefacts. Understanding organisational involvement and collaboration in standardisation is important for informing any future policy and organisational decisions concerning involvement in standardisation. The overarching goal of the study is to establish how organisations contribute to open standards development through editorship. Specifically, the focus is on open standards development in W3C. Through an analysis of editorship for all W3C recommendations we contribute novel findings concerning organisational involvement and collaboration, and highlight contributions from different types of organisations and countries for headquarter of each organisation. We make three principal contributions. First, we establish an overall characterisation of organisational involvement in W3C standardisation. Second, we report on organisational involvement in W3C standardisation over time. Third, we establish organisational collaboration in W3C standardisation through social network analysis.

1 Introduction

Over the years, a number of ICT standards have been developed and deployed for addressing a number of challenges in the area of software systems, including interoperability and longevity of systems (Lundell 2012). In the area of ICT standardisation there are a number of efforts and different (sometimes conflicting) interests amongst stakeholders involved. Previous research shows that "companies are the most important and typically the most powerful stakeholders in (ICT) standards setting" (Jakobs 2014a). Further, it has also been argued that "the absence of important players may lead to inadequate standards" (Jakobs 2006). In addition, previous research reports that some companies "aim to control the strategy of" a standardisation organisation, whereas other merely participate (Jakobs 2014a).

Many ICT standards are implemented in software (including several open source implementations), and in some cases open source implementations have evolved into standards (e.g. Behlendorf 2009; Allman 2011). However, previous research shows that some standards may not be implemented in open source software due to inability to

K. Crowston et al. (Eds.): OSS 2016, IFIP AICT 472, pp. 57–70, 2016.
DOI: 10.1007/978-3-319-39225-7_5

clarify conditions for use of standard essential patents which are controlled by some of the organisations contributing to development of those specific standards (Lundell and Gamalielsson 2015).

Challenges for ICT standardisation have also been recognised by policy makers and organisations developing standards. For example, the ICT rolling plan is an ongoing effort within the EU which recognises the importance of organisational involvement in standardisation for innovation (EC 2015) and there are also policy initiatives within the EU which recognise the importance of open standards (EC 2013). Similarly, there are a number of national policy initiatives, such as the national policy for open standards in the UK (2012, 2015). Further, amongst organisations developing standards there are also efforts for how to improve ICT standardisation such as initiatives for considering open source work practices in standardisation addressed in a recent ETSI workshop[1].

From this it is evident that understanding organisational involvement and collaboration in standardisation is a challenge and is important for informing any future policy and organisational decisions on involvement in standardisation. To address this challenge the ***overarching goal*** of the study is to establish how organisations contribute to open standards development through editorship. Specifically, the focus is on standards development in W3C. Through an analysis of editorship for all W3C standards we investigate organisational involvement and collaboration, and highlight involvement in development of standards by different types of organisations and countries for headquarter of each organisation. We make three principal contributions. ***First***, we establish an overall characterisation of organisational involvement in W3C standardisation. ***Second***, we report on organisational involvement in W3C standardisation over time. ***Third***, we establish organisational collaboration in W3C standardisation.

We focus on W3C standardisation since it has been claimed that W3C standards constitute an exemplar of open standards (Friedrich 2011) and are widely deployed in software systems. All W3C standards are written in English and all communication is in English. In fact, W3C has adopted a work practice inspired by OSS development (Lundell et al. 2014; Gamalielsson et al. 2015), and work according to an open model with respect to intellectual property rights. This, in turn, facilitates participation from different types of companies and other organisations. There is limited knowledge concerning details on organisational involvement and collaboration in open standards development. To the best of our knowledge, this study contributes novel findings from the first comprehensive analysis of organisational involvement (through editorship) in all standards provided by W3C.

The rest of this paper is organised as follows. We present a background on W3C and previous research (Sect. 2). Thereafter we present research approach (Sect. 3), results (Sect. 4), analysis (Sect. 5), followed by conclusions (Sect. 6).

---

[1] For an overview of outcomes from the ETSI summit, see conclusions from the ETSI general chair (Hicks 2015) and a position statement presented during the summit by the W3C Legal counsel (Wenning 2015).

2 Background

2.1 W3C

W3C (World Wide Web Consortium) is "an international community where Member organizations, a full-time staff, and the public work together to develop Web standards" (W3.org 2016). Individuals and all types of organisations can become members (including commercial, educational, and governmental entities). Funding stems from membership fees, research grants and other types of public and private funding, sponsorship, and donations. There are some key components in the organisation of the standardisation process. One of these is the advisory committee, which has one representative from each W3C member and performs different kinds of reviews in the process of standardisation, and also elects an advisory board and the technical architecture group (which primarily works on web architecture development and documentation). Further, the W3C director and CEO assess consensus for decisions of W3C-wide impact. There is also a set of charted groups (working groups, interest groups, and coordination groups) consisting of member representatives and invited experts, which assist in the creation of web standards, guidelines, and supporting materials. W3C standards evolve through different stages through work in these charted groups (working draft, candidate recommendation, proposed recommendation, and W3C recommendation). "W3C recommendation" represents the most mature development stage, and indicates that the standard is ready for deployment and widespread use.

Development of web standards and their implementations have been characterised by 'openness' in terms of development, use, and provision of such technology. In the words of Bekkers and Updegrove (2013):

> "Early in the development and deployment of the Web, and partly as a result of Berners-Lee's decision not to patent its underlying technology, a culture of free license rights for Web infrastructure developed and took firm hold. Concurrently, open source software became increasingly commonly used to provide the software 'stack' supporting the servers that enable the Web's existence. The result was the adoption by W3C in 2003 of an extremely license fee intolerant Patent Policy." (p. 27)

Further, the W3C is seen as a "prime example for how Open Standards can boost innovation are the internet and the world wide web." (Friedrich 2011, p. 6). It is also argued that such standards constitute "a major driver for growth – both on the global scale but also regarding the many small and medium sized enterprises everywhere that prosper because of the internet and because of implementing the standards. Included are web hosting shops, web design shops, web shops themselves, etc. Open Standards are at the core of this. They promoted the biggest boost in innovation we have seen in the last decades." (Friedrich 2011, p. 6).

2.2 Previous Research

There are studies that address organisational involvement in open source projects but without addressing standards or their implementations. One such study explored organisational contributions to source code repositories over time for the open source modelling tools Topcased and Papyrus (Gamalielsson et al. 2011) and a different study reported results on organisational contributions to mailing lists for the open source project Nagios through analysis of email address subdomains (Gamalielsson et al. 2010). There are also studies focused on organisational aspects, for example addressing different motivations for firms to participate in open source projects (e.g. Bonaccorsi and Rossi 2006), community building aspects in communities sponsored by organisations (e.g. West and O'Mahony 2008), and emerging involvement of professional and commercial organisations in OSS (Fitzgerald 2006). However, none of these studies explicate how the actual organisational participation occurs in concrete cases.

There are a few closely related studies. One of these explored Drupal and its use of the software standards RDFa, CMIS and OpenID (Gamalielsson et al. 2013) without considering organisational influences. Further, another study focused on influences between implementations of the PDF format and PDF standardisation (Gamalielsson and Lundell 2013). Further, one study investigated influences between W3C RDFa and the Drupal implementation of RDFa through use of issue trackers (Lundell et al. 2014). There is also an in-depth study of organisational influences in the W3C RDFa standard and its implementation in Drupal (Gamalielsson et al. 2015). However, none of these studies present an overall picture of organisational involvement in all standards for a major standardisation organisation. Hence, this motivates a comprehensive investigation of organisational involvement in W3C standards.

3   Research Approach

By conduct of a systematic investigation of editorship for all W3C standards that had reached the status "W3C recommendation" at time of data collection (1 Oct. 2015), we analysed organisational involvement and collaboration in W3C.

As the *first* part of our approach we establish an overall characterisation of organisational involvement in W3C standardisation using fundamental statistical metrics. In a *second* part, we report (using a similar approach) on organisational involvement in W3C standardisation over time. *Third*, we establish organisational collaboration in W3C standardisation by undertaking social network analysis involving fundamental network metrics. A social network (represented as an undirected graph) at organisational level is gradually derived by, for each standard, creating an edge between all organisations that editors are affiliated with for the standard, and increasing the weight of each of these edges by one. Similarly, networks at the level of organisation type and country of headquarter are derived by connection (for each standard) of the mapped organisation type and country for each organisation, and by increase of edge weight by one. For all three parts, we highlight involvement in development of standards by different organisations, types of organisations and countries for headquarter of each organisation.

Data for standards (standard name, date of release, and editors & associated organisations) were manually collected from the W3C website[2]. Mapping of organisation type and country of headquarter for each organisation was established through a

---

[2] http://www.w3.org/TR/tr-date-stds.

systematic manual search for organisation names by use of LinkedIn[3], Wikipedia[4], or (as a last resort) Google search[5]. Custom made scripts were used to parse and analyse the data and derive results. Prior to data processing, collected data were manually cleansed in order to remove redundancy and inconsistency. Social networks were visualised and analysed through use of the Gephi software package[6].

4 Results

4.1 Characterisation of Organisational Involvement in W3C Standardisation

There are (at time of data collection) 248 specific W3C standards which have reached "W3C recommendation" status. The first of these standards was published 14 Jan. 1997 and the latest 24 Sep. 2015. 230 organisations in total have contributed to W3C standardisation through editorship in standards during these 19 years. There are on average 3,3 organisations contributing through editorship to each of these standards (with a minimum of one organisation and a maximum of 22 organisations). Further, 83 % of the standards (205 of the 248 standards) have more than one organisation represented in the editorial board.

Table 1 shows the number (and proportion) of standards for the 15 organisations that through editorship are involved in the largest number of standards (O1 through O15). An organisation has been mapped to one of the following organisation types: Micro Enterprise (MiE, an enterprise with 1–9 employees), Small and Medium-sized Enterprise (SME, an enterprise with 10–250 employees), Larger Enterprise (LE, an enterprise with more than 250 employees), Research Institute (RI), University (Uni), Standardisation Organisation (SO), Non-profit Organisation (NPO), Public Broadcasting Service (PBS), and Hospital (H). The same mapping scheme was used in Gamalielsson et al. (2015). Further, the country of the organisation's headquarter is also stated in the table (according to the ISO 3166-1 alpha-2 character scheme). In Table 1, it can be observed that the vast majority of contributing organisations (11 out of 15) are larger enterprises. Further, we note that amongst the top 15 organisations there are 12 from countries where the majority of citizens are native English speakers[7] (United States, Great Britain, and Ireland). In particular, the United States is clearly dominating in terms of involvement in number of standards.

The number (and proportion) of standards for different organisation types is shown in Table 2. It can be noted that large enterprises are clearly involved in the largest number of standards. An interesting observation is that small & medium sized enterprises and micro enterprises are involved in a relatively large number of standards (55 and 46, respectively).

---

[3] https://www.linkedin.com/.

[4] https://en.wikipedia.org.

[5] https://www.google.com.

[6] https://gephi.org/.

[7] According to https://en.wikipedia.org/wiki/English-speaking_world.

Table 1. Number (and proportion) of standards for the top 15 organisations

Org	O1	O2	O3	O4	O5	O6	O7	O8	O9	O10	O11	O12	O13	O14	O15
Type	SO	LE	LE	LE	LE	LE	LE	LE	LE	RI	LE	LE	Uni	Uni	LE
Country	US	US	US	US	US	US	US	US	FI	IE	US	NO	GB	GB	JP
# std	72	60	43	31	26	19	15	14	13	11	11	11	10	10	9
% std	29	24	21	13	10	8	6	6	5	4	4	4	4	4	4

Table 2. Number (and proportion) of standards for organisation types

Type	LE	Uni	SO	SME	MiE	RI	NPO	Other	H	PBS
# std	182	79	72	55	46	30	24	15	6	2
% std	73	32	29	22	19	12	10	6	2	1

Table 3 shows the number and proportion of standards for the top 15 countries involved in W3C standardisation through editorship. In total there are 26 countries involved (in descending order in terms of involvement these countries are United States, Great Britain, Germany, Canada, Ireland, Japan, France, Finland, Norway, Netherlands, Spain, Sweden, Austria, Italy, Switzerland, Australia, Belgium, South Korea, Thailand, Chile, China, Russia, Czech Republic, Greece, Israel, and United Arab Emirates). Of the remaining 11 (of the 26) countries (excluded from Table 3) Australia is involved in four standards; Belgium, South Korea, and Thailand are involved in three; Chile, China, and Russia are involved in two; and Czech Republic, Greece, Israel, and United Arab Emirates are involved in only one standard. Another observation from Table 3 is that Unites States is clearly dominating overall and involved in the vast majority of all W3C standards. It can also be noted that of the 26 countries involved, the majority of citizens are native English speakers in 4 of the top 5 countries. We also note that for the remaining 22 countries (except Australia), English is not an official language.

Table 3. Number (and proportion) of standards for the top 15 countries

Country	US	GB	DE	CA	IE	JP	FR	FI	NO	NL	ES	SE	AT	IT	CH
# std	223	52	27	21	17	16	15	14	13	12	9	7	6	6	5
% std	90	21	11	8	7	6	6	6	5	5	4	3	2	2	2

4.2   Characterisation of Organisational Involvement Over Time

Table 4 shows involvement in number of standards released over time for the top 15 organisations. We note that only the top organisation has been continuously involved in standards released since the beginning of W3C standardisation. It can also be observed that organisations amongst the top 15 have been involved in standards released during a varying number of the total 19 years of W3C standardisation[8] (for O1 through O15 for

---

[8] We acknowledge that due to time of data collection, three months remain for 2015.

standards released during 19, 16, 15, 9, 9, 8, 7, 6, 8, 4, 8, 6, 6, 2, and 5 years, respectively) and with a varying amount of involvement and degree of continuity.

Table 4. Involvement in number of standards released over time for the top 15 organisations

O\Y	97	98	99	00	01	02	03	04	05	06	07	08	09	10	11	12	13	14	15
O1	1	1	2	4	1	4	1	4	4	1	8	6	2	4		4	6	11	4	4
O2			3	1	1	1	7	2	1	6	1	4	6	10	5		5	5	2
O3			1	2		3	1	4	5	5	1	3	3	5	1		5	1	3
O4								2	1		3		6	9	5		3	1	1
O5		2	1			3	3	3	3	5	2		4						
O6								8			2	1	2	1			2	2	1
O7											2		1		2	1	4	2	3
O8								2			2		1			7		1	1
O9		1					1	1	1		2	1					5		1
O10											1					3	4	3	
O11			3				1	1		2	1				1		1	1	
O12											2		1		3	1	2	2	
O13								2		1			1	3		2	1		
O14													1			9			
O15								2		4	1				1			1	

Involvement in number of standards released over time for the different organisation types is shown in Table 5 (listed in the same order as in Table 2). We note that large enterprises have initially been involved in W3C standardisation for standards released in 1998 and continuously since year 2000. Further, it can be observed that organisations of different organisation types have been involved in standards released during a varying number of the total 19 years of W3C standardisation (for organisation type from top to bottom in Table 5 for standards released during 17, 16, 19, 15, 15, 11, 14, 9, 4, and 2 years, respectively) and with a varying amount of involvement and degree of continuity.

Table 5. Involvement in number of standards released over time for organisation types

T\Y	97	98	99	00	01	02	03	04	05	06	07	08	09	10	11	12	13	14	15
LE		1		5	4	2	5	20	8	6	15	9	8	18	16	19	20	18	8
Uni		1	2	1	1	2	1	8		1		3	3	4	5	17	20	8	2
SO	1	1	2	4	1	4	1	4	4	1	8	6	2	4	4	6	11	4	4
SME			1	2	1	3	1	3		1	6	6		6	3	3	6	9	4
MiE			3	2			1	4	1	2	1	4	1	7	1	7	1	8	3
RI		1						2	2		1	1	1		1	8	5	7	1
NPO		1	1			1	2	1	1	1		2		1	1	1	4	5	2
other							1	1	1		3	1	1	1	1	5			
H		1									1	1					3		
PBS																1	1		

Table 6 shows involvement in number of standards released over time for the top 15 countries. We note that only the top country (the United States) has been continuously involved in standards released since the beginning of W3C standardisation. Further, it can be observed that countries amongst the top 15 have been involved in standards released during a varying number of the total 19 years of W3C standardisation (for countries from top to bottom in Table 6 during 19, 13, 7, 12, 6, 9, 7, 8, 6, 9, 7, 7, 3, 6 and 4 years, respectively) and with a varying amount of involvement and degree of continuity.

Table 6. Involvement in number of standards released over time for the top 15 countries

C\Y	97	98	99	00	01	02	03	04	05	06	07	08	09	10	11	12	13	14	15
US	1	1	4	6	4	5	5	21	9	6	17	9	10	17	16	24	32	23	13
UK			1			2	6	1	1	1		3	8	1	11	7	8		2
DE			2				1			6		2				6	6	4	
CA			3	1	2		1		2	2	2			1		1	4	1	1
IE					2						1	3				3	5	3	
JP		1						1	3		4	2		1	1		1	2	
FR		1							1			3			1	7	1	1	
FI		1					1		1	1		2	1				6		1
NO												2		1	3	1	4	2	
NL		1					1	2	1			1				3	1	1	1
ES	1	1	1				1				1	2				2			
SE							1				1	1		1		1		1	1
AT																1	1	4	
IT					1						1	1	1		1	1			
CH		1							1			2				1			

4.3   Organisational Collaboration in W3C Standardisation

Figure 1 shows a social network representing W3C collaboration at organisational level. There are 1205 edges[9] between 226 different organisations[10], which reflects the degree of diversity in collaboration overall. The degree d of a node represents number of other organisations an organisation has collaborated with. The weight w of an edge represents number of standards that two organisations (represented by the connected nodes) have collaborated in through editorship. The top 15 organisations in terms of collaboration (measured by node degree) are (in descending order) a SO (d = 132), a LE (d = 98), a LE (d = 69), a LE (d = 52), a LE (d = 48), a LE (d = 47), a RI

---

[9] A fully connected network would comprise 25425 edges.

[10] Four of the 230 organisations reported in Sect. 4.1 have not collaborated with other organisations and therefore the network contains 226 nodes.

(d = 44), a Uni (d = 40), a Uni (d = 37), a LE (d = 30), a RI (d = 29), a LE (d = 27), a LE (d = 27), a Uni (d = 25), and a LE (d = 25). The top five pairs of organisations collaborating most extensively are a LE and another LE (w = 22) followed by a LE and a SO (w = 14), a LE and another LE (w = 13), a SO and a LE (w = 13), and a SO and a LE (w = 11). The remaining 1200 edges have a weight of 8 or less. In fact, 78 % (940) of all edges have a weight of one, which means that such organisational collaboration has only taken place for one single standard.

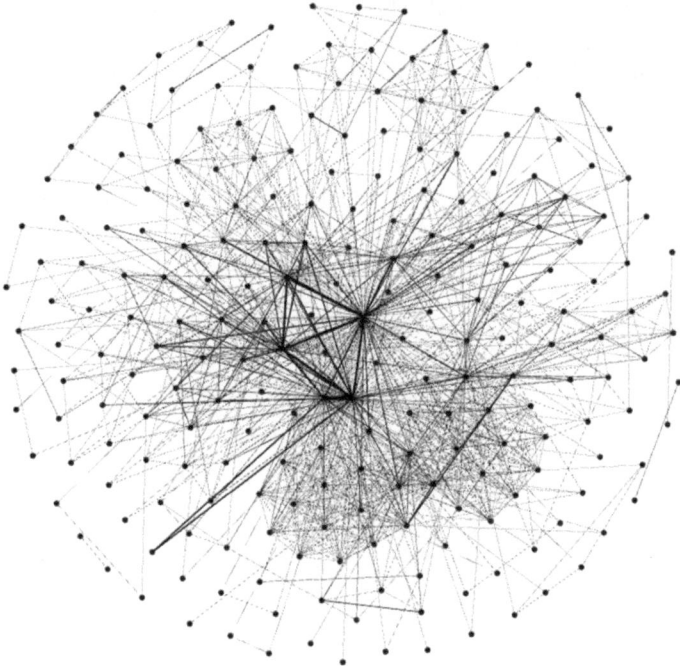

Fig. 1. W3C collaboration at organisational level

A social network representing W3C collaboration at organisation type level is shown in Fig. 2. There are in total 40 edges[11] between the 10 different organisation types, which indicates a diversified collaboration overall at this level. The degree d of a node represents number of other organisation types an organisation type has been associated with during organisational collaboration through editorship. The weight w of an edge represents number of standards that organisations of two organisation types (represented by the connected nodes) have collaborated in through editorship. The rank

---

[11] A fully connected network would comprise 45 edges.

order of the 10 organisation types in terms of collaboration (measured by node degree) are (in descending order) SO (d = 9), Uni (d = 9), LE (d = 9), RI (d = 9), SME (d = 9), NPO (d = 8), MiE (d = 7), PBS (d = 7), H (d = 6), and other (d = 6). The top five pairs of organisation types collaborating most extensively are LE and Uni (w = 169) followed by LE and SME (w = 156), LE and SO (w = 129), LE and MiE (w = 87), and RI and Uni (w = 85). The remaining 35 edges have a weight of 58 or less. Further, 7 edges have a weight of three or less, and one edge has a weight of one.

Figure 3 shows a social network representing W3C collaboration at country level. There are in total 129 edges[12] between 26 different countries, which reflects the degree of diversity in collaboration overall. The degree d of a node represents number of other countries a country has been associated with during organisational collaboration through editorship. The weight w of an edge represents number of standards that two countries (represented by the connected nodes) have collaborated in through editorship. The top 15 countries in terms of collaboration (measured by node degree) are (in descending order) a US (d = 25), FR (d = 18), DE (d = 18), GB (d = 16), CH (d = 15), SE (d = 14), NL (d = 14), NO (d = 13), ES (d = 13), JP (d = 12), CA (d = 12), IE (d = 12), FI (d = 12), AT (d = 11), and KR (d = 10). The top five pairs of countries collaborating most extensively are GB and US (w = 166) followed by DE and US (w = 104), US and FR (w = 62), US and CA (w = 56), and US and JP (w = 54). The remaining 124 edges have a weight of 43 or less. In fact, 86 edges have a weight of three or less, and 39 edges have a weight of one.

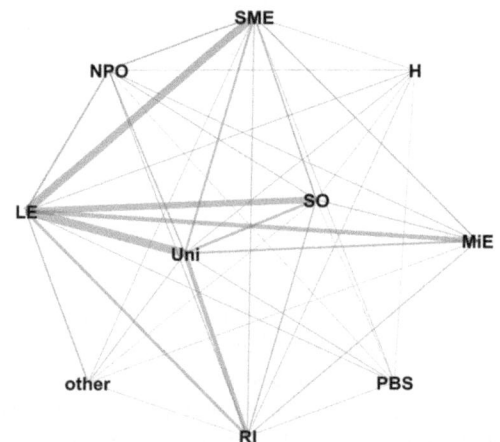

Fig. 2. W3C collaboration at organisation type level

---

[12] A fully connected network would comprise 325 edges.

Fig. 3. W3C collaboration at country level

5   Analysis

First, from the results it is clear that a standardisation organisation and larger enterprises are dominating involvement in W3C standards overall with respect to editorship. The observation that small & medium sized enterprises and micro enterprises are involved in a relatively large number of standards indicates that participation in standardisation in W3C is open and inclusive. This is in-line with earlier findings which suggest that "contributions to W3C standards have a low barrier for entry and participation" (Gamalielsson et al. 2015).

We note that the United States and other countries where the majority of citizens are native English speakers dominate involvement in W3C standards with respect to editorship. Further, our results show rather limited involvement in W3C standardisation through editorship from Asian organisations compared to involvement from US and Europe, something which is in contrast with their corresponding involvement in IETF standardisation (Contreras 2014, p. 915). Amongst Asian countries, Japanese organisations are the most actively involved in W3C standardisation, whereas related research shows that Chinese authors of IETF documents are more active than Japanese (Contreras 2014, p. 926). Further, it has been reported that China is extensively involved in development of ITU-T standards, whereas there is limited involvement in development of IETF, OASIS, and W3C standards (Jakobs 2014b) despite a large number of users.

Second, from the results it is evident that a standardisation organisation and the United States have been continuously involved in standards released since the beginning of W3C standardisation. Other organisations, organisation types, and countries have been involved in standards released during a varying number of the total 19 years of W3C standardisation. In these results it should be noted that involvement in development of a standard in many cases takes place over several years before the year for the release of the W3C recommendation.

Third, from the results it is clear that there is extensive collaboration between different organisations, types of organisations, and countries. Further, by comparison of the top 15 organisations in terms of involvement (Sect. 4.1) and the top 15 organisations in terms of collaboration (Sect. 4.3) we note that 9 out of 15 organisations are in the intersection with similar rankings. This indicates that the majority of organisations with extensive involvement also have extensive collaboration. Similarly, by comparison of the top 15 countries concerning involvement and collaboration it can be noted that 14 out of 15 countries are in the intersection with similar rankings, which indicates that the vast majority of countries with extensive involvement also have extensive collaboration. Further, by comparing metric values for involvement and collaboration for the organisation types we note that rankings are similar (LE, Uni, SO, and SME are top four types in both cases).

6   Conclusions

Findings from the study show that the vast majority of W3C standards have involvement from more than one organisation (often involving collaboration between smaller and larger organisations) with respect to editorship, which is a strong indication of the open and inclusive nature of W3C standardisation. Further, findings show that involvement and collaboration in many cases include international participation from organisations with headquarters in a variety of different countries.

The study also shows that involvement stems from organisations from countries with a majority of native English speaking citizens, something which may be unsurprising given that all standards are written in English. We acknowledge that only editorship has been considered in our study. Accounting for working group participation in W3C standards development could provide for a richer picture of involvement and collaboration.

In conclusion, our study establishes novel details on, and promotes understanding of, organisational involvement and collaboration in open standards development. The findings from our study make a contribution important for informing any future policy and organisational decisions concerning involvement in standardisation.

References

Allman, E.: The robustness principle reconsidered: seeking a middle ground. Commun. ACM **54** (8), 40–45 (2011)

Behlendorf, B.: How open source can still save the world. In: Boldyreff, C., Crowston, K., Lundell, B., Wasserman, A.I. (eds.) OSS 2009. IFIP AICT, vol. 299, p. 2. Springer, Heidelberg (2009)

Bekkers, R., Updegrove, A.: IPR policies and practices of a representative group of standards-setting organizations worldwide. Commissioned by the Committee on Intellectual Property Management in Standard-Setting Processes, National Research Council, Washington, May 2013

Bonaccorsi, A., Rossi, C.: Comparing motivations of individual programmers and firms to take part in the open source movement: from community to business. Knowl. Technol. Policy **18** (4), 40–64 (2006)

Contreras, J.L.: Divergent patterns of engagement in Internet standardization: Japan, Korea and China. Telecommun. Policy **38**(10), 914–932 (2014)

EC: European Commission: Press Release, Digital Agenda: Open standards would save public sector €1 billion a year, Brussels, 25 June 2013. http://europa.eu/rapid/press-release_IP-13-602_en.htm

EC: Rolling plan for ICT standardisation 2015. European Commission (2015)

Fitzgerald, B.: The transformation of open source software. MIS Q. **30**(4), 587–598 (2006)

Friedrich, J.: Making innovation happen: the role of standards and openness in an innovation-friendly ecosystem. In: 2011 7th International Conference on Standardization and Innovation in Information Technology (SIIT), pp. 1–8. IEEE, Piscataway (2011)

Gamalielsson, J., Lundell, B.: Experiences from implementing PDF in open source: challenges and opportunities for standardisation processes. In: Jakobs, K. (ed.) Proceedings of the 8th IEEE Conference on Standardization and Innovation in Information Technology (SIIT 2013), pp. 39–49. IEEE, Piscataway (2013). ISBN 3-86130-802-9

Gamalielsson, J., Lundell, B., Lings, B.: The Nagios Community: An Extended Quantitative Analysis. In: Ågerfalk, P., Boldyreff, C., González-Barahona, J.M., Madey, G.R., Noll, J. (eds.) OSS 2010. IFIP AICT, vol. 319, pp. 85–96. Springer, Heidelberg (2010)

Gamalielsson, J., Lundell, B., Mattsson, A.: Open source software for model driven development: a case study. In: Hissam, S.A., Russo, B., de Mendonça Neto, M.G., Kon, F. (eds.) OSS 2011. IFIP AICT, vol. 365, pp. 348–367. Springer, Heidelberg (2011). ISBN 978-3-642-24417-9

Gamalielsson, J., Lundell, B., Grahn, A., Andersson, S., Feist, J., Gustavsson, T., Strindberg, H.: Towards a reference model on how to utilise open standards in open source projects: experiences based on Drupal. In: Petrinja, E., Succi, G., El Ioini, N., Sillitti, A. (eds.) OSS 2013. IFIP AICT, vol. 404, pp. 257–263. Springer, Heidelberg (2013). ISBN 978-3-642-38928-3

Gamalielsson, J., Lundell, B., Feist, J., Gustavsson, T., Landqvist, F.: On organisational influences in software standards and their open source implementations. Inf. Softw. Technol. **67**, 30–43 (2015). doi:10.1016/j.infsof.2015.06.006

Hicks, R.: Conclusions on ETSI workshop on standardization and open source. In: ETSI Summit on Standardization and Open Source, Sophia Antipolis, France, 19 November 2015

Jakobs, K.: ICT standards research – Quo Vadis? Homo Oeconomicus **23**(1), 79–107 (2006)

Jakobs, K.: Managing corporate participation in international ICT standards setting. In: Proceedings of the International Conference on Engineering, Technology and Innovation (ICE 2014), pp. 1–12. IEEE (2014a)

Jakobs, K.: The (future) role of China in ICT standardisation – a European perspective. Telecommun. Policy **38**(10), 863–877 (2014b)

Lundell, B.: Why do we need open standards? In: Orviska, M., Jakobs, K. (eds.) Proceedings 17th EURAS Annual Standardisation Conference 'Standards and Innovation'. The EURAS Board Series, Aachen, pp. 227–240 (2012). ISBN 978-3-86130-337-4

Lundell, B., Gamalielsson, J.: On implementation of open standards in open source software: under what conditions can formal and open standards be used? In: Bergh-Skriver, K. et al. (eds.) Proceedings 20th EURAS Annual Standardisation Conference: The Role of Standards in Transatlantic Regulation. EURAS Contributions to Standardisation Research, vol. 9, pp. 235–252 (2015). ISBN 978-3-95886-053-3

Lundell, B., Gamalielsson, J., Grahn, A., Feist, J., Gustavsson, T., Strindberg, H.: On influences between software standards and their implementations in open source projects: experiences from RDFa and its implementation in Drupal. In: Proceedings of the 10th International Symposium on Open Collaboration, OpenSym 2014, article 3, p. 3:1. ACM, New York (2014). ISBN 978-1-4503-3016-9

UK: Open Standards Principles: For software interoperability, data and document formats in government IT specifications, HM Government, UK (2012). https://www.gov.uk/government/uploads/system/uploads/attachment_data/file/183962/Open-Standards-Principles-FINAL.pdf

UK: Open Standards Principles: For software interoperability, data and document formats in government IT specifications, HM Government, UK (2015). https://www.gov.uk/government/uploads/system/uploads/attachment_data/file/459075/OpenStandardsPrinciples2015.pdf

W3.org: About W3C (2016). http://www.w3.org/Consortium/. Accessed 12 Jan 2016

Wenning, R.: Standards that help converge open source. In: ETSI Summit on Standardization and Open Source, Sophia Antipolis, France, 19 November 2015

West, J., O'Mahony, S.: The role of participation architecture in growing sponsored open source communities. Ind. Innov. **15**(2), 145–168 (2008)

Combining FOSS and Kanban:
An Action Research

Annemarie Harzl[(✉)]

Institute for Software Technology, Inffeldgasse 16b/II, 8010 Graz, Austria
aharzl@ist.tugraz.at

Abstract. Even though Free and Open Source Software (FOSS) and
Agile Software Development (ASD) have been recognized as important
ways to develop software, share some similarities, and have many success
stories, there is a lack of research regarding the comprehensive integration
of both practices. This study attempts to consolidate these methods
and to answer if FOSS and ASD can be combined successfully. Action
Reseach (AR) is conducted with one sub-team of a large FOSS project.
We performed two action research cycles based on the Kanban method.
This paper has two main contributions; first, it describes a real world
situation, where Kanban is applied to a FOSS project, and second, it
suggests two new Kanban practices. These two methods are targeted
specifically at FOSS projects and their characteristics.

Keywords: Free Open Source Software · Agile Software Development ·
Lean · Kanban · Action Research

1 Introduction

This paper examines the use of Agile Software Development (ASD), namely the
Kanban method [3,19], in the context of Free and Open Source Software (FOSS)
development.

Since the publication of the agile manifesto in 2001 a large body of research
has been published on agile methods [9], e.g. on adopting agile methods [4] and
implementing agile methods in distributed settings [5,22]. FOSS and ASD have
become common software development processes over the last fifteen years [6,9]
and some studies have been done about combining FOSS and ASD [12].

Although Warsta and Abrahamsson [26] and Koch [18] already showed in
2003 and 2004 that FOSS development and the definition of ASD methods are
rather close, research about agile development in the context of open source software was still identified as a future research area in 2009 [1]. In 2013 Gandomani
et al. [12] conducted a systematic literature review on relationships between
ASD and FOSS development. They concluded that the examined studies indicated that ASD can support FOSS development, mainly because they share
several concepts and principles. However, the authors did not find a case study

© IFIP International Federation for Information Processing 2016
Published by Springer International Publishing Switzerland 2016. All Rights Reserved
K. Crowston et al. (Eds.): OSS 2016, IFIP AICT 472, pp. 71–84, 2016.
DOI: 10.1007/978-3-319-39225-7_6

successfully integrating both methodologies. This research tries to comprehensively combine these two for a specific real world case. By doing this we attempt to answer the following research question: "Can FOSS and ASD be comprehensively combined?". This paper describes two action research cycles and proposes two FOSS-related additions to the Kanban practices from the perspective of a real project, therefore making it scientifically and practically relevant.

2   Related Work

Even though the research fields of FOSS and ASD have been of interest for over a decade with a large number of publications, there is to the best of our knowledge no work on comprehensively integrating the two methods. This is supported by the findings of Gandomani et al. [12]. Most studies show only collaboration between the two and most of the time only specific practices are applied to a FOSS project [7,10]. Other studies use Kanban or FOSS for teaching computer science classes [2,21], but never together. Koch [18] compares the methods based on some criteria, but the paper does not include a practical implementation.

3   Background

This section describes some details about the FOSS project under study, my role as a researcher within the project, and reasons for integrating Kanban into a FOSS project.

3.1   The FOSS Project

The project under study is a hybrid student FOSS project. Within the scope of this umbrella project, various teams develop mobile applications for different platforms and purposes. The software development method follows an agile approach with elements of eXtreme Programming (XP) and Kanban. Most of the contributors are participating in the project in the context of their studies (e.g. Bachelor thesis or Master project) and stay with the project between six months and approximately two years (with breaks between the Bachelor thesis and Master project). Unlike usual FOSS projects, where a small number of people develops the majority of the code [15], contributions to this project are more evenly spread. Developers in this project are constantly changing and there are no core developers, who stay with the project for multiple years. Students are often working off-campus and our international contributors are of course working all over the world. Individuals are not assigned to a team, everyone self-selects the team and topic he or she is willing to work on. There are only three distinct roles: contributors, seniors, who are allowed to accept code of others into the main repository and the team coordinator, who is the main contact person for other teams and has a good overview of the team's status. The team coordinator volunteers for this position and the team decides, who is suitable for this position. There exists no central management, only the project head, who is mainly responsible for the overall orientation of the umbrella project and the sub-projects, and one person, who is responsible for organizational activities, e.g. managing accounts and infrastructure. Software development skills of the contributors range from beginner to intermediate and knowledge about agile methods ranges from very little to moderate.

Interesting to note is that this project was not started by "scratching a developer's personal itch" [23], but by a university professor with an idea. The developers of the software are not the target group of the developed software. To foster the understanding of user needs a Usability and User Experience (UX) team works alongside the development teams.

3.2 My Role as a Researcher Within the Project

The study is designed as insider in collaboration with other insiders, but power relations may play a part. In the FOSS project under study I am responsible for organizational and supporting processes, for example creating user accounts and giving a short introduction into the overall project. I am neither programming with other contributors nor am I leading one of the programming teams. However, I am on good terms with the project head and founder, whose word has a lot of bearing in the whole community. He is also the professor grading the students, who do their Bachelor thesis or Master project in the FOSS project. Thus, although I am not in an official hierarchical position, contributors probably see me as someone with informal power within the organization.

3.3 Justification of Kanban

The Kanban method [3,19] is about evolutionary change and strives to establish a culture of continuous improvement (kaizen). It consists of four principles: *start where you are; pursue incremental, evolutionary change; respect the current processes, roles, responsibilities and titles; promote leadership at all levels* and six practices: *visualize the workflow; make policies explicit; manage flow; limit Work In Progress (WIP); implement feedback loops; improve collaboratively, evolve experimentally (using models and the scientific method).* It was mainly chosen for the following three reasons.

First of all, in 2014 Ahmad et al. [2] concluded that Kanban appears to be a good pedagogical tool and useful for teaching inexperienced software developers about software engineering. It appears to have a short learning curve and a low adoption threshold. It further helps students to improve their team work skills, for example communication and collaboration. The project under study is not only a FOSS project, with many inexperienced developers, it serves teaching purposes as well, making Kanban an appropriate and light-weight approach for teaching and FOSS development. Kanban fosters collaboration and keeps the entrance barrier of the project as low as possible, so potential contributors are not scared off.

Another reason was that Kanban is the most adaptive method [17]. It allows for small evolutionary changes, does not require week-long expensive trainings and job titles and responsibilities do not have to be altered. Moreover, small incremental changes do not require positional power, which is not available in a FOSS community anyway. People affected by these changes are not enduring them, but are involved in the process and their participation is an integral part. People are allowed and encouraged to use their own mind. Thus, Kanban is also a good fit for Action Reseach (AR) as research methodology, which is discussed in more detail in Sect. 4.

Last but not least, projects within the umbrella project already used a Kanban-like board. By choosing the Kanban method, the team would be able to keep existing tools and the initial alterations would not be overwhelming.

4   Research Methodology

4.1   Justification of Action Research

To accomplish not only scientific but also practical outcomes was an important part of the motivation to conduct this study. According to Dick [8] AR is well suited for this type of goal, thus, we chose AR as the research method. Researchers and practitioners collaborate to solve real world problems through theoretically informed actions [13]. To achieve outcomes, people affected by those actions have to commit to them. One way to ensure this commitment is through involvement [8], for which AR offers various participatory methods [14]. Another reason for choosing this methodology was that only little research has been done on the integration of ASD and FOSS development [12], suggesting that the theory about this matter is not fully developed. Therefore, according to Edmondson, McManus and Kampenes et al. [11,16], a flexible approach, like AR, would be appropriate.

4.2   Case Selection

The project in question was selected due to the following reasons:

- Personal contact: Direct personal contact to the people involved allows for more detailed observations on group interaction than analysis of e.g. mailing lists. Trust, which is needed to change a work process, is easier established through personal than written contact. Furthermore, it is easier to receive feedback on multiple levels and to refine the research methodology and researcher skills through personal contact.
- Experiments and evaluation: Although the setting with mainly student contributors is rather unusual, students work on many FOSS projects and are not atypical FOSS contributors. Moreover students are often used to research, thus more used to experimenting with different approaches and willing to evaluate them. Other contributors may be more reluctant to do so.

– Time and access: A basic trusting relationship to project members was already established, so the bonding period with the community, which could take a very long time, could be minimized and allowed to conduct the AR within a reasonable time frame. Topics can be discussed in a shorter period of time and one has access to various artefacts, e.g. whiteboards or flipcharts.

While this project should of course not remain the only case studied, in our opinion it is a good starting point to explore Kanban in the context of FOSS projects. We will elaborate on the limitations in Sect. 6.2.

The sub-project was co-selected by the participants of the AR. My supporting role (as described in Sect. 3.2) within the project may have led one team coordinator to ask me for help. The team experienced problems with motivation and their workflow and the team members did not know how to overcome these issues on their own. Therefore, one goal of this research is to achieve practical outcomes, which improve the working situation of the team. This bias for action contributed to the selection of the research methodology.

Asking for help shows some commitment, which is usually needed to achieve action outcomes. Knowing this, we decided to conduct the study with this team. Other factors for the decision were: the team (six to eight people, varying over time) has roughly the average size of teams in this FOSS project (six to twelve team members at the same time), it uses the same agile workflow as the other teams and direct personal contact with the members of the team is possible.

The sub-project develops a mobile application targeted at teenagers, which should enable its users to create small projects without prior domain knowledge. The application has not been released to the public, it is only tested by members of the FOSS project. From the beginning the team used elements of XP and a Kanban board, like all other sub-projects. The applied XP practices included *automated unit tests, pair programming, refactoring, release planning* (occurs in irregular intervals), *short releases, continuous integration, coding standards, collective code ownership, simple design and regular meetings* (weekly). *Visualize the workflow* was the only Kanban practice applied, in the form of an agile board, but members did not know, that this was a Kanban practice.

4.3   Action Research Cycles

A modified version of Susman and Evered's approach [25] was used as a research method. The cyclical model contains the five stages *diagnosing, action planning, action taking, evaluating*, and *specified learning*. One diagnosing phase and two regular AR cycles consisting of action planning, action taking, evaluation and specified learning were realized. An additional cycle zero was added after an observation phase at the beginning of the study. A participatory AR approach was used, all steps were discussed with the study participants and decided jointly.

As already described in Subsect. 3.1 the sub-project uses elements of XP and Kanban. However, an initial questionnaire showed, that team members assess their knowledge about both methods quite differently. While all members think that they have average to very good knowledge about XP only 17 % think that they have very good knowledge about Kanban. The other 83 % think that they possess little to no knowledge about Kanban.

This supported my decision to conduct a Kanban coaching session at the beginning of cycle zero and the second cycle. In these sessions I talked about Kanban in general, its principles and practices, and explained terms like flow and kaizen. These sessions were based on two books [3,19] and one video[1]. It was necessary to provide the participants with some theoretical background about Kanban so they could understand its principles and practices. Furthermore, it was also important to enable them to decide how to integrate Kanban practices into their workflow. Due to observations made during the diagnosing phase, I conducted a cycle zero, including a user analysis and a stakeholder analysis. The first AR cycle was designed to introduce two practices into the team, namely *visualize (the workflow)* and *make policies explicit*. The second AR cycle should then familiarize the team with the principles *limit WIP* and *manage flow*.

4.4   Data Sources

Various types of data sources were used as empirical basis: a questionnaire about the participants knowledge on agile practices, weekly notes from team meetings written by the participants, my notes taken during meetings and discussions, the artefacts produced as part of the user and stakeholder analysis, and the team's Kanban board. Six to eight people participated in the study. Two people joined the team after cycle zero and one person left the team after the second cycle was completed. I had no position in the team but as already discussed in Subsect. 3.2 my role within the umbrella project may result in research bias. I made some suggestions and most of the time the research participants accepted them.

4.5   Data Analysis

Firstly, the questionnaire regarding the agile knowledge of the team was statistically analyzed. Secondly, all researcher notes taken during meetings and discussions, were examined for issues of interest to the research and recurring topics or problems. For this purpose statements were "coded"and grouped together, if they had a theme or problem in common. Thirdly, the results of the team's user analysis and information about the sub-project's target group, retrieved from the project head, were compared. For this purpose statements from the team and the project head were compared one by one and discrepancies identified. Finally, to accomplish a better visualization of the team's workflow, the Kanban board was analyzed for its adherence to Kanban principles and practices, e.g. pull instead of push and limiting work in progress.

---

[1] https://youtu.be/6nOUa6E0250.

5   Action Research

This section explains cycle zero, the two AR cycles and their phases as described in Subsect. 4.3.

5.1   Diagnosing

The sub-project of the FOSS project was inspired by a programming exercise done during a university programming course in 2012. The results showed some promising ideas for a new application, which would fit nicely into the portfolio of the umbrella project. However, the code was neither finished (many functions were only rudimentary implemented) nor was it as structured and neat as it should be, because the course was part of a Bachelor study program and lasted only one semester. Thus, only the ideas remained and the code had to be rewritten.

Some of the students of the programming course decided to do their Bachelor thesis within the scope of the FOSS project. Together with some other students they started to develop the software anew. After a while it became apparent, that the team had been too ambitious and had ignored agile principles, such as working in small iterations and implementing the simplest thing that could possibly work. The team tried to implement too many features in parallel and was overwhelmed by the amount of work necessary to finish it. This situation became even worse when some individuals decided not to use the XP practice pair programming and accomplished most of their work alone, leaving the rest of the team clueless about their contribution to the code. As a result the team ended up with a heap of unfinished code and after around a year the sub-project came to a halt. The team decided to start over again.

The second attempt to restart was not successful either. The application did not meet its usability goals and was abandoned again.

By this time the team members' motivation was understandably very low. They struggled with the code, their workflow and their team spirit. Disillusioned by the failed attempts the team coordinator of this sub-project thought that the team could not solve their problems all by themselves and asked me for help.

The main problems of this team seemed to be: underestimation of the tasks at hand, insufficient adoption of agile practices and the overall workflow resulting in frustration and lack of motivation.

5.2   Cycle Zero: Get to Know Kanban, Your Users and Your Stakeholders

Before starting the AR cycles I regularly attended the weekly team meetings. I observed the interactions in the team and of course got to know the team members. By attending these meetings I got the impression that the team was targeting a different main user group than the project head envisioned. I had of course previously talked with him about the sub-project and its target group. As far as I knew the project head wanted to target beginners in the domain and it seemed to me that the team was targeting people with at least intermediate knowledge in the domain. This assumption led me to add a cycle zero to the study. I wanted to clarify, if there was indeed a misunderstanding between the team and the project head, therefore I moderated a user analysis with the team. This user analysis yielded some unforeseen results and led to a repositioning of the sub-project within the umbrella project with some major changes for the team and its interaction with other teams. Therefore, I performed a stakeholder analysis with the team as well.

Action Planning and Action Taking. The user analysis was done as a simple brainstorming exercise, where we collected all possible user groups team members could think of on a whiteboard. Afterwards, the team chose the main user groups for which they were developing the application.

The stakeholder analysis was conducted according to Leopold and Kaltenecker [19]. First, the team determined all stakeholders and listed them on individual pieces of paper. Each paper was sized differently, reflecting the importance of the stakeholder for the team's long-term success. Then, the pieces were put on a table and arranged around the team's mission, which is at the center of the analysis. Stakeholders, who are affected more by the team's day to day work and possible changes, are placed nearer to the center. Stakeholders, who are affected less, are placed further away. Afterwards, the frequency of relationships between all stakeholders was determined. The stronger the relationship, the more lines were drawn between two stakeholders. At last the quality of these relationships was determined as *friendly, adversarial, love-hate* or *unknown*. For an exemplary stakeholder analysis see Fig. 1.

Evaluating and Specified Learning. The user analysis showed some discrepancy between the main user group the team was targeting and the main user group the project head envisioned. I articulated my impression to the team and we concluded that the team had to talk to the project head. Luckily for us he was available at the time of the user analysis and we asked him to join the

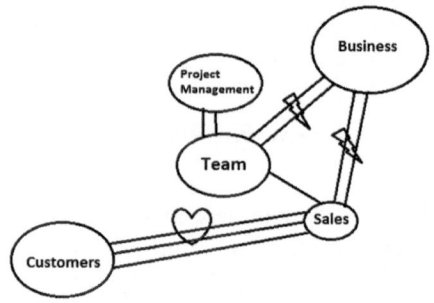

Fig. 1. Exemplary stakeholder analysis, adapted from Leopold and Kaltenecker [19]

discussion. And indeed there was a misunderstanding. He explained to the team which user group they should target and why and it became obvious, that the team had been developing their application for a different target group. This was a very unexpected result for the team and the whole software development came to a halt. The team had to redefine their goals and to rethink their application. Two meetings with the project head followed and the UX team was contacted as well. The project head and the team discussed the goals for their sub-project. The UX team did a user inquiry with four members of the targeted user group. The results of the user inquiry were discussed with the developing team. Based on the input of the four possible users, the developing team and the project head, the UX team designed a digital mockup of the application. This mockup showed an absolutely different Graphical User Interface (GUI) than the current application. It was more intuitive for novice users, but more elaborate to develop. Thus, the team had to reimplement the whole GUI. More importantly the former independent stand-alone application was integrated into another application of the umbrella project. This decision was made jointly by the sub-team, the super-team and the project head. The main reasons for this decision were: the sub-project will extend the functionality of the super-application with some very important features. The sub-project will reach more users as an extension than as a stand-alone application because the super-application is already publicly available and has a steadily growing user base.

As a result of this repositioning from stand-alone application to extension and because it is recommended in Leopold and Kaltenecker [19], I performed a stakeholder analysis with the team. The analysis showed that the intensity and quality of some relationships between stakeholders were unknown to the team and that the team had to work on intensifying some relationships, especially the one with the new super-team.

5.3   First Cycle

Action Planning and Action Taking. The team already used a Jira Kanban board to visualize the workflow. The board contained the following columns: *backlog, in development, done, done and accepted.*

Team policies were determined in an open discussion. Team members collected all policies on a white board and discussed their meaning and importance jointly. After agreeing on a set of policies, they were transferred to the project wiki.

Evaluating and Specified Learning. The main focus in this cycle was *making policies explicit*. We regarded *visualize the workflow* as already finished, because the team already used a board. Additionally, as a consequence of cycle zero the software development was put on hold and the team focused on redefining their goals, hence there was no activity on the board at the time.

Making policies explicit yielded some interesting effects: Team members discussed their unspoken policies for the first time and discrepancies showed. Some were of semantic nature others reflected a different view of processes. During the discussion some problematic habits were identified and immediately discussed. To prevent these habits from reoccuring, new team policies were stipulated jointly and team members agreed to honor those policies.

5.4   Second Cycle

Action Planning and Action Taking. *Limiting work in process* and *managing flow* were introduced to the team during the second Kanban coaching session. Different visualization possibilities were shown and the importance of *limiting WIP* and its effect on transition time, based on Little's Law [20], were explained. It was also discussed how WIP limits could be used to make problems visible and improve flow.

Evaluating and Specified Learning. We revisited the Jira board to limit WIP. In the course of doing so we discovered something we already should have uncovered during the first cycle. The current board did not model a pull system. It was rather a push system. While team members pulled tasks from the backlog into development, the transition from development to code acceptance was a push process. Developers pushed the task from development to done where senior developers had to take them and move them to *done and accepted*. There was not even a state for being *in acceptance*. It was not possible to determine whether a task was already in the process of being accepted, or if it was still simply marked as *done*. I think this oversight can be ascribed to the focus on redefining the goal, which was still in progress during the first cycle.

To repair this, a new state was introduced into the workflow and the column *in acceptance* was added to the board, now reflecting a real pull system. The columns *in development* and *done* were merged into one column. Initially, the team wanted to create two subcolumns for *in development*, but Jira does not offer this functionality. Therefore we experimented with different possibilities of visualization. Figure 2 depicts on the one hand the desired visualization and on the other hand the current visualization, which is realizable within the constraints of Jira.

Afterwards, WIP limits were set and monitored. They soon revealed a bottleneck at the acceptance state. The root cause was quickly identified and team members were working hard to resolve this bottleneck. Due to the merge with the super-project the team now depended on the senior developers of the super-project to accept the sub-team's code. The senior members of the sub-team were and still are working hard to familiarize themselves with the slightly different acceptance process of the super-team and thus dissolving the bottleneck as soon as possible and improving flow. Another positive effect of the focus on the board is, the team now uses their Kanban board during each meeting, which it did not do prior to the AR cycles.

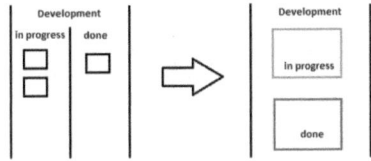

Fig. 2. The desired visualization on the left side and the actual visualization, which is possible in Jira, on the right side

6   Results and Discussion

While this study can not conclusively answer the research question "Can FOSS and ASD be comprehensively combined?" it shows some promising outcomes. Integrating Kanban and FOSS has so far been successful and beneficial for the research participants. New insights, e.g. on the target user group, have been gained and the team's workflow has become more effective. From my point of view, motivation has improved but this remains to be verified in the future.

6.1   Extending the Kanban Practices

Based on the experiences described in Sect. 5, we propose two additional Kanban practices for FOSS projects.

– Conduct regular user interviews or feedback sessions with your users
– Review your assumptions about your current development practices

These recommendations are of course based on a hybrid student FOSS project, but usual FOSS projects could benefit from these additional practices as well. While most companies applying agile and lean practices have a marketing and sales team or even a user focus group, FOSS projects tend not to have this kind of resources. Nowadays, many FOSS solutions are employed by a large number of people, who do not contribute to the code, e.g. Mozilla Firefox or Linux. Thus, FOSS developers are not simply "scratching their own itch" anymore, they serve many people, who must not share the developer's requirements and domain knowledge, all over the world. Therefore, it could be beneficial for FOSS projects to investigate their users' needs. As for the second recommendation: Although, we agree with the Kanban principle "start where you are", we assume it could be beneficial for FOSS projects to review their current development practices before embarking on the endeavor of integrating Kanban, or any other agile or lean method, into their development process. FOSS projects usually do not have SCRUM masters, process experts or in general someone, who controls whether software development practices are exercised correctly. An honest and critical reflection about the current practices can clear some misconceptions, can further a joint understanding of the current situation and it is a first step into the direction of kaizen.

6.2   Limitations

This study is limited to a single case of a hybrid student FOSS project, therefore it has only very limited external validity. Only one team is part of this study therefore the results are not generalizable to other teams or projects without further research.

Another limitation may be my positionality [14] in the setting. Herr and Anderson [14] describe positionality as asking the question, "Who am I in relation to my participants and my setting?". Subsection 3.2 already identified power distance as a possible limitation. The informal power position may result in research bias, since suggestions I make could be accepted due to this perceived power distance and not only because team members agree with these suggestions. In an attempt to counterbalance this bias a bit, whenever possible at least two alternatives were proposed and the final decision was made by the team.

The setting of a hybrid student FOSS project might also be seen as a limiting factor, because some characteristics differ. Teams members contribute to receive course credits and not (only) to earn a reputation among other developers or out of altruistic motives. Student contributors change regularly and there exists no group of core or chief developers, which usually consists of 10 % to 20 % of a team, and which creates around 80 % of the source code [18]. Future research could determine if or how these diverging characteristics impact a FOSS project. Students as main contributors to this project may also be considered a limitation, because they have not finished their studies. But people from different backgrounds contribute to FOSS projects regardless of their formal education and IT students work as normal developers on many FOSS projects. Many FOSS contributors have no formal software engineering education at all. Salman et al. [24] even observed that students and professionals show similar performances in carefully scoped software engineering experiments, when the development approach used is new to both groups.

7   Conclusion

This paper describes a practical integration of Kanban through AR in the context of a hybrid student FOSS project. Based on the findings of this work we proposed additional Kanban practices for FOSS projects. There is a lack of research regarding integration of ASD in the FOSS development context [12]. Thus, this paper contributes by offering some insights on the matter. As future work we plan on conducting more AR cycles with the same team to exercise the practices from the first and second cycle and further introduce the remaining Kanban practices into the workflow. To assure validity of the proposed additions to the Kanban approach, the cycles described in this paper should be conducted with other teams and within other FOSS settings.

References

1. Ågerfalk, P.J., Fitzgerald, B., Slaughter, S.: Introduction to the special issue - flexible and distributed information systems development: state of the art and research challenges. Inf. Syst. Res. **20**(3), 317–328 (2009). http://dx.doi.org/10.1287/isre.1090.0244

2. Ahmad, M.O., Liukkunen, K., Markkula, J.: Student perceptions and attitudes towards the software factory as a learning environment

3. Anderson, D.: Kanban - Successful Evolutionary Change for Your Technology Business. Blue Hole Press, Sequim (2010)

4. Boehm, B.W.: Get ready for agile methods, with care. IEEE Comput. **35**(1), 64–69 (2002). http://doi.ieeecomputersociety.org/10.1109/2.976920

5. Boland, D., Fitzgerald, B.: Transitioning from a co-located to a globally-distributed software development team: a case study at analog devices, inc. In: Proceedings of 3rd Workshop on Global Software Development (2004)

6. Crowston, K., Wei, K., Howison, J., Wiggins, A.: Free/libre open-source software development: what we know and what we do not know. ACM Comput. Surv. **44**(2), 7 (2012). http://doi.acm.org/10.1145/2089125.2089127

7. Deshpande, A., Riehle, D.: Continuous integration in open source software development. In: Russo, B., Damiani, E., Hissam, S.A., Lundell, B., Succi, G. (eds.) Open Source Development, Communities and Quality. IFIP, vol. 275, pp. 273–280. Springer, Boston (2008). http://dx.doi.org/10.1007/978-0-387-09684-1_23

8. Dick, B.: A beginner's guide to action research (2000). http://www.aral.com.au/resources/guide.html

9. Dingsøyr, T., Nerur, S.P., Balijepally, V., Moe, N.B.: A decade of agile methodologies: towards explaining agile software development. J. Syst. Softw. **85**(6), 1213–1221 (2012). http://dx.doi.org/10.1016/j.jss.2012.02.033

10. Düring, B.: Sprint driven development: agile methodologies in a distributed open source project (PyPy). In: Abrahamsson, P., Marchesi, M., Succi, G. (eds.) XP 2006. LNCS, vol. 4044, pp. 191–195. Springer, Heidelberg (2006). http://dx.doi.org/10.1007/11774129_22

11. Edmondson, A.C., McManus, S.E.: Methodological fit in management field research. Acad. Manage. Rev. **32**(4), 1155–1179 (2007)

12. Gandomani, T.J., Zulzalil, H., Ghani, A.A.A., Sultan, A.B.M.: A systematic literature review on relationship between agile methods and open source software development methodology. CoRR abs/1302.2748 (2013). http://arxiv.org/abs/1302.2748

13. Greenwood, D.J., Levin, M.: Introduction to Action Research: Social Research for Social Change. SAGE Publications, Thousand Oaks (2007)

14. Herr, K., Anderson, G.: The Action Research Dissertation - A Guide for Students and Faculty, 2nd edn. SAGE, Thousand Oaks (2015)

15. Kagdi, H.H., Hammad, M., Maletic, J.I.: Who can help me with this source code change? In: 24th IEEE International Conference on Software Maintenance (ICSM 2008), Beijing, China, 28 September–4 October, pp. 157–166. IEEE Computer Society (2008). http://dx.doi.org/10.1109/ICSM.2008.4658064

16. Kampenes, V.B., Anda, B., Dybåa, T.: Flexibility in research designs in empirical software engineering. In: Visaggio, G., Baldassarre, M.T., Linkman, S.G., Turner, M. (eds.) 12th International Conference on Evaluation and Assessment in Software Engineering, EASE 2008, University of Bari, Italy, 26–27 June, Workshops in Computing, BCS (2008). http://ewic.bcs.org/content/ConWebDoc/19536

17. Kniberg, H., Skarin, M.: Kanban and Scrum - making the most of both. C4Media (2010)
18. Koch, S.: Agile principles and open source software development: a theoretical and empirical discussion. In: Eckstein, J., Baumeister, H. (eds.) XP 2004. LNCS, vol. 3092, pp. 85–93. Springer, Heidelberg (2004). http://dx.doi.org/10.1007/978-3-540-24853-8_10
19. Leopold, K., Kaltenecker, S.: Kanban in der IT - Eine Kultur der kontinuierlichen Verbesserung schaffen. Hanser (2013)
20. Little, J., Graves, S.: Little's law. In: Chhajed, D., Lowe, T. (eds.) Building Intuition, International Series in Operations Research & Management Science, vol. 115, pp. 81–100. Springer, US (2008). http://dx.doi.org/10.1007/978-0-387-73699-0_5
21. MacKellar, B., Sabin, M., Tucker, A.: Bridging the academia-industry gap in software engineering: a client-oriented open source software projects course. In: Open Source Technology: Concepts, Methodologies, Tools, and Applications, Chap. 99, pp. 1927–1950. IGI Global (2015)
22. Ramesh, B., Cao, L., Mohan, K., Xu, P.: Can distributed software development be agile? Commun. ACM **49**(10), 41–46 (2006). http://doi.acm.org/10.1145/1164394.1164418
23. Raymond, E.S.: The Cathedral and the Bazaar: Musings on Linux and Open Source by an Accidental Revolutionary. O'Reilly & Associates Inc., Sebastopol (2001)
24. Salman, I., Misirli, A.T., Juzgado, N.J.: Are students representatives of professionals in software engineering experiments? In: 37th IEEE/ACM International Conference on Software Engineering, ICSE 2015, Florence, Italy, 16–24 May, vol. 1, pp. 666–676. IEEE (2015). http://dx.doi.org/10.1109/ICSE.2015.82
25. Susman, G.I., Evered, R.D.: An assessment of the scientific merits of action research. Adm. Sci. Q. **23**(4), 582–603 (1978). http://dx.doi.org/10.2307/2392581
26. Warsta, J., Abrahamsson, P.: Is open source software development essentially an agile method? In: Proceedings of the 3rd Workshop on Open Source Software Engineering, 25th International Conference on Software Engineering, Portland, Oregon, pp. 143–147 (2003)

Who Cares About My Feature Request?

Lukas Heppler, Remo Eckert$^{(\boxtimes)}$, and Matthias Stuermer

University of Bern, Bern, Switzerland
lukas.heppler@students.unibe.ch,
{remo.eckert,matthias.stuermer}@iwi.unibe.ch

Abstract. Previous studies on issue tracking systems for open source software (OSS) focused mainly on requests for bug fixes. However, requests to add a new feature or an improvement to an OSS project are often also made in an issue tracking system. These inquiries are particularly important because they determine the further development of the software. This study examines if there is any difference between requests of the IBM developer community and other sources in terms of the likelihood of successful implementation. Our study consists of a case study of the issue tracking system BugZilla in the Eclipse integrated development environment (IDE). Our hypothesis, which was that feature requests from outsiders have less chances of being implemented, than feature requests from IBM developers, was confirmed.

Keywords: Open source software · Issue tracking system · Feature request · Eclipse · Bugzilla

1 Introduction

Collaboration of core developers with the outside community is an important key to the longevity of an Open Source Software (OSS) project [1]. For users, it is particularly important to have their requirements integrated into future versions of the software product. Issue tracking systems are the main instrument used to integrate the needs of external participants. In an OSS development project, the community can report a bug or feature using issue tracking systems such as Bugzilla [2]. Issue tracking systems have received considerable attention in the OSS literature [3–5]. Due to the open nature of these systems and the ease of data collection, they are an ideal subject for examination when investigating the OSS development process. Issue tracking systems also have various advantages for the community: more problems with the software can be identified, because they are easy to report, and more bugs can be fixed, because there are more developers contributing to solutions. This not only helps to improve the product, but also to tailor a software to the users' needs [6, 7]. Moreover, issue tracking systems are a way to integrate more externals into the OSS community. In the context of the Eclipse IDE, where IBM revealed the source code of its software under an OSS license, their goal was to increase its popularity as a development platform on a larger market, while retaining control over the future path of the software development. The present study examines the area of conflict between the contributors from IBM and the outsiders - people not paid by IBM. Do feature requests from outsiders have less chance of being implemented than those which originate from an IBM employee?

© IFIP International Federation for Information Processing 2016
Published by Springer International Publishing Switzerland 2016. All Rights Reserved
K. Crowston et al. (Eds.): OSS 2016, IFIP AICT 472, pp. 85–96, 2016.
DOI: 10.1007/978-3-319-39225-7_7

To answer this question, this paper is structured as follows: Sect. 2 describes theories on community integration as well as an analysis of previous studies of issue tracking systems. Moreover, the Eclipse IDE is presented in detail. Section 3 describes the method applied to analyse our hypothesis, Sect. 4 presents the results, which are then discussed in Sect. 5.

2   Theory Section

Since Netscape released their source code for the Internet browser Mozilla, an increasing number of business companies have revealed their prior proprietary source code under an OSS license. For the most part, the intention behind such a move is not altruistic, but is based instead on the hope that the community will help to improve and maintain the future code base, in order to reduce internal development efforts [1]. The involvement of a community in an OSS project is a vital factor in the success of the project because the community promotes the project and its development [8, 9]. Moreover, as stated by Grammel et al. [7], integrating the community in the OSS development plays a key role for the success of an OSS project. Ways to involve people in an OSS project include the marketing of the OSS project to attract potential contributors and integrating their efforts into the project. As the project grows, governance structures become necessary [1, 10]. On the technical side, increasing modularity in the source code is one incentive to attract new developers. A modular software makes the software more attractive to outsiders, since the effort required to get to know the code is lower [11]. Another way to integrate a community in an OSS project is to use an issue tracking system; this will be discussed in more detail in the next subsection.

2.1   Issue Tracking Systems

Although there is no strict hierarchical structure in an OSS community, the structure is not completely flat. According to [12], roles and their associated influence can be earned through contributions to the community. The resulting community structure, called the "onion-model" can be shown in a layer where the roles closer to the center (e.g. the project leader and core members) have a greater influence than the roles in the external area (e.g. readers and passive users). Contributions to the community can be made through an issue tracking system, thereby influencing the community structure and the impact each individual has on the OSS project. OSS projects typically have an open issue tracker where developers and users of the software can report bugs and feature requests [3]. Previous studies of issue tracking systems covered topics such as the automatic assignment of bug reports to developers [3, 13, 14], the automatic assignment of priority and severity labels to bug reports [15], the identification of duplicate reports [5, 16], the automatic summarization of reports [17, 18] and the prediction of bug fixing times [19, 20].

Bug fixing times, respectively the speed at which bug reports are processed, are influenced by several factors. Bugs which are critical for the proper functioning of the software (i.e. have a high severity) receive more attention and resources and are therefore fixed faster than more trivial bugs [21]. However, the bug fixing time is also influenced by the characteristics of the person filing the bug report. The popularity of the reporting person within the community reduces the bug fixing time. A bug filed by a reporter whose bugs are usually fixed quickly, has a high chance of any future bugs also being fixed quickly [21].

A study of the issue tracking system BugZilla of the Mozilla Firefox project revealed that bug reports from 'outsiders' tend to be ignored by the developer community. These were processed far more slowly than bugs reported by core developers. Furthermore, the study showed that reports from 'outsiders' tend to be ignored only in the more recent versions of Mozilla Firefox, and not in the earlier stages of development [22].

2.2 Feature Requests in Issue Tracking System

Issue tracking systems are not used only to report bugs, but also serve to request new features or enhancements to the software [3, 23, 24]. Previous research excluded reports containing feature requests or enhancements, despite the fact that these are very interesting for research on OSS communities since they determine the further development of the product, under the influence not only of developers, but also based on the opinions of its users. Other than the famous first lesson by Eric S. Raymond "Every good work of software starts by scratching a developer's personal itch." [25]. Feature requests also allow non-programmers to express their demand for further development of the OSS product. Using issue tracking systems to highlight new functional needs thus allows their ideas and requirements to be integrated.

In this paper we identify measures that influence whether or not a feature request is successful. A key variable indicates whether a feature request was reported by a core developer or by an outsider. Based on the findings of Dalle, den Besten, and Masmoudi [22], we expect that requests from outsiders are less likely to be implemented than feature requests from core developers (IBM developers). Other independent variables included in our analysis will be introduced later in this study.

2.3 Eclipse IDE

The Eclipse IDE project is a longstanding and well-established OSS project, with a wide installation base in both the OSS and in the commercial development field: It presents a large and mature OSS project [20]. While the focus has been on projects such as Linux, Apache or Gnome, the Eclipse IDE was not founded as a "grassroots" community of user-developers [1]. The project was initially owned by IBM and was released as OSS in 2001. By releasing the source code under an OSS license, IBM made a source code available with a value estimated at $40 million [26]. While this seemed a somewhat surprising decision at the time, this step increased its popularity as a development platform across a larger market, attracting more attention to IBM's complementary products. From 2001 until 2004, the control over the development strategy remained in the hands of IBM [27]. In 2004, IBM ceded control over the project and the Eclipse Foundation was established, which now owns the intellectual property rights (IPR). With this decision, IBM allowed other firms to become equal members in the project. Today, the Eclipse Foundation serves as a "steward" of the

Eclipse community. In general, the Eclipse Foundation provides four services to their community: IT-Infrastructure management, IPR-management, development processes and the ecosystem development.

Eclipse was the subject of many studies in the OSS literature [3, 6, 14, 19, 20]. Source code contribution and mailing list activity have already been investigated in terms of participation by IBM developers vs. outsiders. The results indicated that IBM developers initially dominated mailing list and source code contributions, but the participation of outsiders increased over time [27].

3   Method

We obtained a database dump of Eclipse's issue tracking system BugZilla from the website of the MSR Mining Challenge 2011. The dataset included 316'911 reports from 30'230 different reporters for the period from 2001 to 2010. We then used the command line tool Bicho to crawl additional data for the period from 2010 to December 2015 from the Eclipse issue tracking system.

The reports were filtered according to their value for the attribute "severity". Only reports with the severity attribute set to "enhancement" were included in the analysis. "Enhancement" is the label used to tag reports that contain feature requests or enhancements in BugZilla. Our subsample consisted of 24'856 reports.

3.1   Logistic Regression Model

To investigate which factors led to a successful feature request, we included only resolved feature requests and excluded all open feature requests. Furthermore, we investigated only requests marked as "FIXED" or "WONTFIX", because it was only with respect to these issues that a decision was made on whether or not to implement the requested feature. "FIXED" feature requests were considered to be successful and "WONTFIX" were considered unsuccessful. We excluded feature requests with any other resolution such as duplicate reports, invalid requests or requests not related to Eclipse. Therefore, the categories "INVALID", "WORKSFORME", "DUPLICATE" and "NOT ECLIPSE" were omitted from our analysis.

To distinguish IBM developers from outsiders, we used a similar approach as Spaeth, Stuermer, and von Krogh [27]. Reports from users whose e-mail addresses contained @ibm or @oti were classified as IBM developers; all other users were classified as outsiders (early members communicated with @oti e-mail addresses because the initial version of Eclipse was developed by OTI). The original data did not include any e-mail addresses, which made it necessary to crawl the corresponding e-mail address for every user ID from BugZilla via their API interface and merge them into the dataset. Eleven user accounts did not contain any e-mail address, leading to the exclusion of 134 reports. The remaining 11'479 feature requests were included in the analysis.

The following were also included as additional independent variables: the date of the request and the assigned priority (P1 up to P5) of the request; the number of times the request was reassigned to another developer; and the number of times the request was reopened to control for their effect. To measure the attention the feature request received, we counted the number of votes for the feature request and the number of people who had the feature request on their "watch list". Both attributes were visible for anyone working on the request. As a measure of the volume of discussion the feature request generated, we included the number of comments written and the number of separate authors writing comments. To investigate whether an extensively written description had any impact on the success of the feature request, we measured the length of the description in 100s of characters.

In order to include the type of software, we included variables for the three major "products" within the Eclipse SDK: the Java Development Toolkit (JDT), the Plugin Development Environment (PDE) and the Eclipse development platform (Platform) itself. We also included another set of variables for the four most frequent subcomponents: the Core of the product (Core), the User Interface (UI), the Debugging component (Debug) and the Text Editor component (Text).

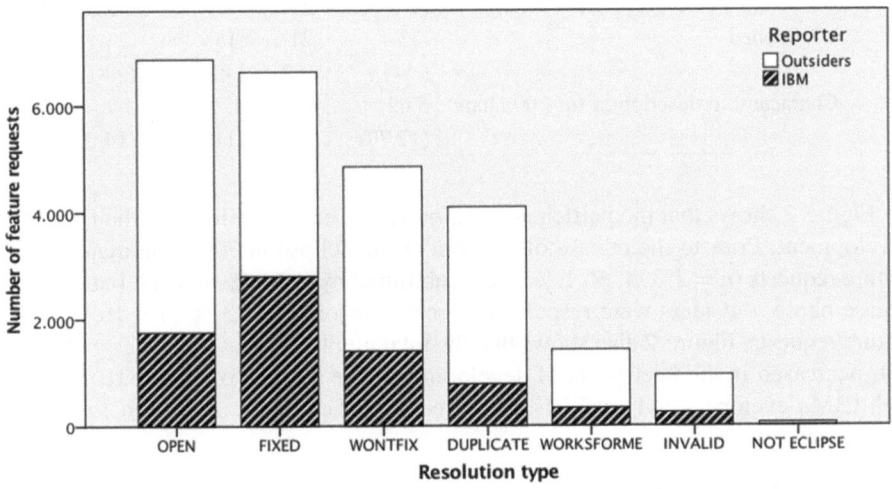

Fig. 1. Number of feature requests from IBM developers and outsiders by resolution type

4   Results

Our dataset consisted of 24'856 feature requests from the period between October 2001 and December 2015. A total of $n = 7'303$ (29.4 %) feature requests were submitted by IBM developers, $n = 17'553$ (70.6 %) were submitted by outsiders.

As Fig. 1 shows, the relative share of feature requests submitted by outsiders varies strongly depending on the resolution type. Outsiders are responsible for over 70 % of all invalid feature requests (INVALID, NOT ECLIPSE, WORKSFORME) and for over 80 % of all duplicate feature requests. The proportion of all feature requests which are later implemented (FIXED) is more balanced. Around 42 % of all implemented feature requests stem from IBM developers and 58 % from outsiders.

Table 1. Mean and SD (in parenthesis) for variables included in the logistic regression model

	FIXED		WONTFIX	
	Outsiders	IBM	Outsiders	IBM
Priority	2.98	3.02	2.81	2.77
	(.47)	(.50)	(.49)	(.55)
# comments	9.83	7.57	4.33	4.29
	(13.11)	(9.03)	(4.41)	(3.67)
# authors	2.88	2.35	2.29	2.18
	(3.30)	(2.12)	(1.45)	(1.34)
# watching	.60	.48	.17	.13
	(2.42)	(1.72)	(.85)	(.83)
Votes	.59	.19	.20	.06
	(3.60)	(1.94)	(.95)	(.33)
# reassignments	1.46	1.27	1.00	1.12
	(1.24)	(1.21)	(1.19)	(1.35)
# reopened	.23	.21	.15	.24
	(.51)	(.52)	(.42)	(.48)
Characters in description (in 100 chars)	5.62	4.69	5.76	5.73
	(12.70)	(7.63)	(11.84)	(14.09)

Figure 2 shows that the participation of outsiders grew rapidly after the first year of development. Prior to the release of version 2.0 of Eclipse in 2002, the majority of all feature requests (n = 1'374, 56.1 %) were submitted by IBM developers. In the post 2.0 release phase, outsiders were responsible for the majority of 73 % (n = 16'477) of all feature requests. Figure 2 also shows that the total number of feature requests filed every year decreased in the later years of development. The number of feature requests from both IBM developers and outsiders decreased after the release of version 3.0 in 2004.

4.1 Logistic Regression

A logistic regression was performed to ascertain the effects on the likelihood that the feature request was successfully implemented of: being an IBM developer vs. outsider; the year the request was submitted; assigned priority; number of characters in the description; number of comments; number of separate authors of comments; number of people watching the request; number of reassignments and times the request was reopened; and the product and component to which the feature request referred. Table 1 shows the mean and standard deviation of variables included in the regression model. The logistic regression model was statistically significant, $\chi^2(17) = 3148.69$, $p < .001$. The model explained 32.2 % (Nagelkerke R^2) of the variance in success rate and correctly classified 72.5 % of all cases (76.6 % of successful and 67 % of unsuccessful requests).

Table 2 indicates feature requests from IBM developers were two times more likely to be successfully implemented than requests from outsiders, $e^\beta = 2.08$, $p < .001$. Feature requests in the later years of development were more likely to be implemented than feature requests in the earlier years of development, $e^\beta = 1.11$, $p < .001$. Increasing priority level by one unit (out of five) doubled the chances of success, $e^\beta = 2.10$, $p < .001$. An increasing number of comments on a feature request was associated with an increased likelihood of the request being successful ($e^\beta = 1.23$, $p < .001$), but an increasing number of separate authors submitting comments on a request was associated with a reduction in the likelihood of success, $e^\beta = .65$, $p < .001$. The number of people watching the feature request slightly increased the likelihood of success, $e^\beta = 1.06$, $p < .05$. While the number of times the feature request was reassigned had a positive effect ($e^\beta = 1.37$, $p < .001$), the number of times the request was reopened ($e^\beta = .74$, $p < .001$) and the length of the description (in 100's of characters) had a minimal negative effect on the likelihood of success, $e^\beta = .99$, $p < .001$. The number of votes slightly increased the likelihood of success, $e^\beta = 1.10$, $p < .001$.

Feature requests concerning the Java development tools (JDT) or Platform yielded noticeably lower likelihoods of success ($e^\beta = .20$, $p < .001$) where there was no significant effect on requests concerning the PDE, $e^\beta = .88$, $p = .723$. Requests concerning the Core of the product ($e^\beta = .79$, $p < .05$) and the Debugging component ($e^\beta = .77$, $p < .01$) were less likely to be successful, whereas feature requests concerning the Text Editor had a significantly higher likelihood of being successful, $e^\beta = 2.33$, $p < .001$. There was no significant effect on the likelihood of success for feature requests concerning the User Interface (UI), all other variables being equal, $e^\beta = .96$, $p = .458$.

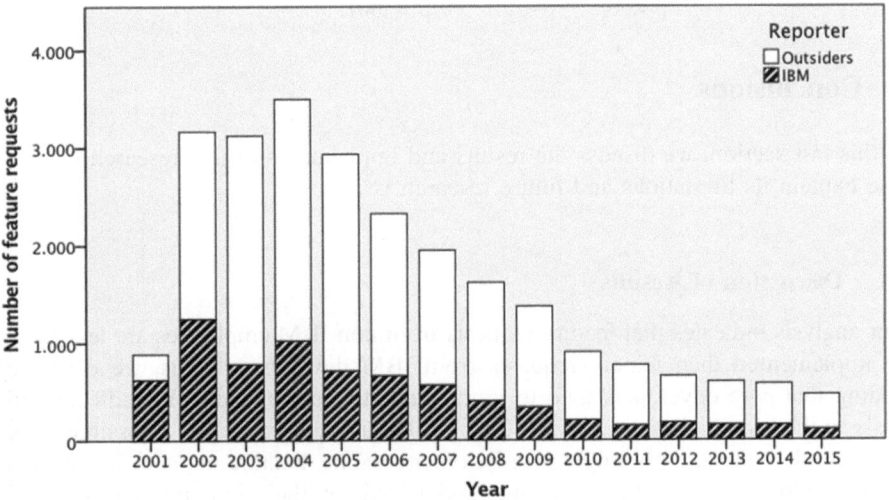

Fig. 2. Number of feature requests from IBM developers and outsiders from 2001 to 2015

Table 2. Summary for logistic regression analysis for variables predicting success of a feature request (n = 11'479)

Variable	B[a]	S.E.	e^β
IBM	.733***	.046	2.08
Year	.108***	.009	1.11
Priority	.742***	.049	2.10
# comments	.210***	.008	1.23
# authors	−.427***	.023	0.65
# watchers	.054*	.023	1.06
Votes	.095***	.026	1.10
# reassignments	.317***	.021	1.37
# reopened	−.298***	.055	0.74
Characters in description	−.012***	.003	0.99
Products			
Plug-in dev. environment	−.133	.374	0.88
Java development tools	−1.614***	.363	0.20
Platform	−1.616***	.361	0.20
Components			
Core	−.235*	.104	0.79
Debug	−.260***	.080	0.77
Text	.845***	.102	2.33
UI	−.044	.060	0.96
Constant	2.993	.397	19.94

[a]. *$p < .05$. **$p < .01$. ***$p < .001$.

5 Conclusions

In this last section, we discuss the results and implications of this research paper. We also explain its limitations and future research issues.

5.1 Discussion of Results

Our analysis indicates that feature requests from non-IBM employees are less likely to be implemented than feature requests from IBM developers. Thus, we confirm the finding that core developers tend to ignore reports from outsiders as indicated previously in the Mozilla Firefox project [22]. While ignorance might be a possible cause of the identified effect, there might also be other reasons. Feature requests formulated by IBM employees might be more qualified based on their in-depth knowledge and experience with the source code and available software features. Feature requests by IBM developers likely target highly relevant areas of improvement within the Eclipse software and, thus, might be implemented more often than feature requests by outsiders. This is somewhat contradictory considering core developers are essentially not required to file feature requests for certain requirements. Through their commit access to the code repository they have the opportunity to implement new functionalities directly into the source code, without going through the feature request process. We assume core developers often file feature reports voluntarily in order to comply with community rules and norms.

The results show that besides IBM affiliation, several other characteristics of feature requests also influence the probability of implementation. Our results suggest the highest positive impact on resolution is induced by the priority level of a feature request. Raising the priority level of a feature request by one doubles the probability that the feature will be implemented. The reason for this might be signaling effects indicating high relevance and demand, thus motivating developers to actually prioritize implementation of a certain feature. Based on this insight, ambitious users might now be tempted to categorize all of their feature requests as high priority. However, issue reporting users in Bugzilla cannot define the priority of their issue. This function is limited to the person to whom the issue is assigned, who can change the priority level, thus inhibiting opportunistic behavior of feature reporters.

Besides reporter origin and feature priority, the number of reassignments also had a strong positive effect on its implementation. Reassignments indicate an issue has been directed to persons with the best skills required to implement the work, following the principle of knowledge specificity [28]. Interestingly, in this context the number of authors involved in a feature request had a negative impact, thus indicating that the mere fact that a large number of people are involved discussing a feature request did not help to implement it. Only when responsibility to resolve the issue changed were the chances of success raised.

In addition the number of comments and the number of votes an issue had received, as well as the number of people watching a feature request positively influenced the probability of its implementation. It is possibly the activity level surrounding a feature request and, thus, the level of interest in the resolution of a certain enhancement that increased the chances of its successful completion.

While we started with a research question concerning the factors influencing implementation probability of a feature request, we coincidentally found the interesting observation of decreasing request numbers over the years. While Eclipse is the leading Java development platform [29] it apparently receives less issues as others researching bug tracking have also found [30]. On the one hand, this might indicate a decreasing level of interest in Eclipse in the long-term. On the other hand, a more mature software solution justifiably receives less feature requests because it already fulfills most user requirements. This unexpected finding raises new questions about software maturity related to community activity and necessitates further research in other OSS projects to test whether their feature request pattern behaves the same, or if it is different - and if so, why.

5.2 Limitations and Future Research

The distinction between IBM developers and outsiders using their e-mail address is one limitation of this empirical research paper. Holders of an IBM e-mail address might not necessarily be core developers, and not all core developers in Eclipse are employed by

IBM. In the Mozilla Firefox study [22] bug reports were differentiated according to their initial state when they enter the issue tracking system. Experienced developers with the "CanConfirm" privilege were able to enter their reports as "NEW", all other reports were initially in the state "UNCONFIRMED". Therefore, reports which entered the issue tracking system in the state "NEW" were considered to come from core developers, whereas reports which entered the issue tracking system in the state "UNCONFIRMED" were considered to come from outsiders. This approach was not applicable to the Eclipse project, because all reports are initially flagged as "NEW", irrespective of the privileges of the reporter. Other methods of identifying core developers in the Eclipse project, such as measuring activity levels in terms of source code contribution, issue tracker and newsgroup activity, could be applied to distinguish between core developers and outsiders.

Future research could analyze if and how differences in the likelihood of success of feature requests from outsiders evolved over time. The effect that reports from outsiders tend to be ignored by the core developers in the Mozilla Firefox project could be shown only for the more recent versions of Firefox and not in the earlier stages of development. Eclipse evolved from being under the strict control of IBM to an independently governed OSS project. The effects of this evolution have already been shown in terms of increased source code contribution and newsgroup activity from outsiders in the Eclipse project [27]. It would be of particular interest to study the effect of governance on the treatment of feature requests from outsiders. Further, a comparison between requirements from IBM developers and outsiders could be made to understand the differences of our quantitative study. Perhaps internal requests are more clear and feasible than those from outsiders and are therefore preferred by the Eclipse IDE developers.

Future research could obtain a dataset of further Eclipse projects or other OSS communities to expand the scope of the analysis. It would allow the reliability of the results of this study to be tested, including the accidently discovered effect of the decreasing number of feature requests. As the issue tracking system keeps record of historical information, it is possible to analyze in-depth the process between the reporting and solving of bugs and feature requests. This represents a reliable and promising source for further studies.

References

1. West, J., O'Mahony, S.: Contrasting community building in sponsored and community founded open source projects. In: Proceedings of the 38th Annual Hawaii International Conference on System Sciences, HICSS 2005 (2005)
2. Scacchi, W.: Understanding the requirements for developing open source software systems. IEE Softw. Proc. **149**, 24–39 (2002)
3. Anvik, J., Hiew, L., Murphy, G.C.: Who should fix this bug? In: Proceedings of the 28th International Conference on Software Engineering, pp. 361–370. ACM, New York (2006)
4. Mockus, A., Fielding, R.T., Herbsleb, J.D.: Two case studies of open source software development: Apache and Mozilla. ACM Trans. Softw. Eng. Methodol. TOSEM **11**, 309–346 (2002)

5. Runeson, P., Alexandersson, M., Nyholm, O.: Detection of duplicate defect reports using natural language processing. In: 29th International Conference on Software Engineering, ICSE 2007, pp. 499–510. IEEE (2007)
6. Anvik, J., Hiew, L., Murphy, G.C.: Coping with an open bug repository. In: Proceedings of the 2005 OOPSLA Workshop on Eclipse Technology eXchange, pp. 35–39. ACM, New York (2005)
7. Grammel, L., Schackmann, H., Schröter, A., Treude, C., Storey, M.-A.: Attracting the community's many eyes: an exploration of user involvement in issue tracking. In: Human Aspects of Software Engineering, pp. 3:1–3:6. ACM, New York (2010)
8. Bagozzi, R.P., Dholakia, U.M.: Open source software user communities: a study of participation in Linux user groups. Manag. Sci. **52**, 1099–1115 (2006)
9. Iivari, N.: Empowering the users? A critical textual analysis of the role of users in open source software development. AI Soc. **23**, 511–528 (2009)
10. Dahlander, L., Magnusson, M.G.: Relationships between open source software companies and communities: observations from Nordic firms. Res. Policy **34**, 481–493 (2005)
11. MacCormack, A., Rusnak, J., Baldwin, C.Y.: Exploring the structure of complex software designs: an empirical study of open source and proprietary code. Manag. Sci. **52**, 1015–1030 (2006)
12. Nakakoji, K., Yamamoto, Y., Nishinaka, Y., Kishida, K., Ye, Y.: Evolution patterns of open-source software systems and communities. In: Proceedings of the International Workshop on Principles of Software Evolution, pp. 76–85. ACM (2002)
13. Kagdi, H., Gethers, M., Poshyvanyk, D., Hammad, M.: Assigning change requests to software developers. J. Softw. Evol. Process. **24**, 3–33 (2012)
14. Rahman, M.M., Ruhe, G., Zimmermann, T.: Optimized assignment of developers for fixing bugs an initial evaluation for Eclipse projects. In: Proceedings of the 2009 3rd International Symposium on Empirical Software Engineering and Measurement, pp. 439–442. IEEE Computer Society (2009)
15. Xuan, J., Jiang, H., Ren, Z., Zou, W.: Developer prioritization in bug repositories. In: 2012 34th International Conference on Software Engineering (ICSE), pp. 25–35 (2012)
16. Wang, X., Zhang, L., Xie, T., Anvik, J., Sun, J.: An approach to detecting duplicate bug reports using natural language and execution information. In: Proceedings of the 30th International Conference on Software Engineering, pp. 461–470. ACM (2008)
17. Mani, S., Catherine, R., Sinha, V.S., Dubey, A.: Ausum: approach for unsupervised bug report summarization. In: Proceedings of the ACM SIGSOFT 20th International Symposium on the Foundations of Software Engineering, p. 11. ACM (2012)
18. Rastkar, S., Murphy, G.C., Murray, G.: Summarizing software artifacts: a case study of bug reports. In: Proceedings of the 32nd ACM/IEEE International Conference on Software Engineering, vol. 1, pp. 505–514. ACM, New York (2010)
19. Giger, E., Pinzger, M., Gall, H.: Predicting the fix time of bugs. In: Proceedings of the 2nd International Workshop on Recommendation Systems for Software Engineering, pp. 52–56. ACM, New York (2010)
20. Panjer, L.D.: Predicting Eclipse bug lifetimes. In: Fourth International Workshop on Mining Software Repositories, ICSE Workshops MSR 2007, p. 29 (2007)
21. Marks, L., Zou, Y., Hassan, A.E.: Studying the fix-time for bugs in large open source projects. In: Proceedings of the 7th International Conference on Predictive Models in Software Engineering, pp. 11:1–11:8. ACM, New York (2011)
22. Dalle, J.-M., den Besten, M., Masmoudi, H.: Channeling Firefox developers: mom and dad aren't happy yet. In: Russo, B., Damiani, E., Hissam, S., Lundell, B., Succi, G. (eds.) Open Source Development, Communities and Quality. IFIP, vol. 275, pp. 265–271. Springer, Boston (2008)

23. Bissyande, T.F., Lo, D., Jiang, L., Reveillere, L., Klein, J., Le Traon, Y.: Got issues? Who cares about it? A large scale investigation of issue trackers from GitHub. In: 2013 IEEE 24th International Symposium on Software Reliability Engineering (ISSRE), pp. 188–197 (2013)
24. Koru, A.G., Tian, J.: Defect handling in medium and large open source projects. IEEE Softw. **21**, 54–61 (2004)
25. Raymond, E.S.: The Cathedral and the Bazaar: Musings on Linux and Open Source by an Accidental Revolutionary. O'Reilly Media, Sebastopol (1999)
26. Fitzgerald, B.: The transformation of open source software. MIS Q. **30**, 587–598 (2006)
27. Spaeth, S., Stuermer, M., Von Krogh, G.: Enabling knowledge creation through outsiders: towards a push model of open innovation. Int. J. Technol. Manag. **52**, 411–431 (2010)
28. Sampler, J.L.: Redefining industry structure for the information age. Strateg. Manag. J. **19**, 343–355 (1998)
29. Rebellabs: Developer Productivity Report 2012: Java Tools, Tech, Devs & Data. Zero Turnaround (2012)
30. Banerjee, S., Helmick, J., Syed, Z., Cukic, B.: Eclipse vs. Mozilla: a comparison of two large-scale open source problem report repositories. In: 2015 IEEE 16th International Symposium on High Assurance Systems Engineering (HASE), pp. 263–270. IEEE (2015)

The Impact of a Low Level of Agreement Among Reviewers in a Code Review Process

Toshiki Hirao[1]([✉]), Akinori Ihara[1], Yuki Ueda[2], Passakorn Phannachitta[1], and Ken-ichi Matsumoto[1]

[1] Nara Institute of Science and Technology, Ikoma, Japan
{hirao.toshiki.ho7,akinori-i,phannachitta-p,matumoto}@is.naist.jp
[2] Interdisciplinary Faculty of Science and Engineering,
Shimane University, Matsue, Japan
s133014@matsu.shimane-u.ac.jp

Abstract. Software code review systems are commonly used in software development. In these systems, many patches are submitted to improve the quality. To verify the quality, voting is commonly used by contributors; however, there still exists a major problem, namely, that reviewers do not always simply reach a broad agreement. In our previous study, we found that consensus is not usually reached, implying that an individual reviewer's final decision usually differs from that of the majority of the other reviewers. In this study, we further investigate the reasons why such situations often occur, and provide suggestions for better handling of these problems. Our analysis of the Qt and OpenStack project datasets allow us to suggest that a patch owner should select more appropriate reviewers who often agree with others' decisions.

Keywords: Modern code review · Software development · Agreement

1 Introduction

Software code review is a process in which reviewers and committers verify patches. In particular, Open Source Software (OSS) projects conduct a review to release higher quality and readability source codes [1]. Endorsed by McIntosh et al. [2], a code review with a sufficient discussion is one of the most useful practices to contribute to a more effective bug detection process. In addition, a code review has proved to be very helpful in providing important feedbacks to developers for future developments [3].

Nowadays, we have various dedicated tools for managing the code review process. For example, Gerrit[1] and ReviewBoard[2] are commonly used by OSS practitioners to improve the quality of their source codes. Technically, conducting a code review process using these tools is done through patch submissions and

---

[1] Gerrit: https://code.google.com/p/gerrit/.
[2] ReviewBoard: https://www.reviewboard.org/.

© IFIP International Federation for Information Processing 2016
Published by Springer International Publishing Switzerland 2016. All Rights Reserved
K. Crowston et al. (Eds.): OSS 2016, IFIP AICT 472, pp. 97–110, 2016.
DOI: 10.1007/978-3-319-39225-7_8

reviews, and voting is known to be one of the most commonly used practices to decide whether or not a patch should be integrated into a version control system (i.e., to be accepted or not). In general situation, a patch with higher quality will more likely be accepted than a patch with lower quality; however, not all submitted patches are of high quality. In such cases, voting results can be varied and thus adding more difficulty in deciding whether or not to use those patches. In other words, a final decision cannot be made unless reviewers and committers have reached a consensus.

In our previous study [4], in practice, consensus is not usually reached through the voting system. As a continuation of our previous study, this study further investigates how often a reviewer disagrees with a review conclusion, and what the impact is of a reviewer with a low level of agreement. Hence, we conduct a case study using Qt and OpenStack project datasets to address the following research questions:

RQ1: How often does a reviewer disagree with a review conclusion?
Results: A more experienced reviewer is likely to have a higher level of agreement than a less experienced reviewer.
RQ2: What is the impact of a reviewer with a low level of agreement in a code review?
Results: A review assigned to a reviewer with a lower level of agreement is more likely to take a longer reviewing time and discussion length.

This paper is arranged as follows. Section 2 describes the background to this paper, related work, and a motivating example. Section 3 provides the design of our two research questions and datasets. Section 4 presents the results with respect to our two research questions. Section 5 discusses a qualitative analysis of our research questions, and addresses the threats to validity. Finally, Sect. 6 concludes this paper and describes our future work.

2   Background

2.1   Modern Code Review (MCR)

In recent years, MCR has become popular and widely used in both proprietary software and open source software [5]. The use of MCR has made the review process more traceable, which in turn, has created opportunities for empirical software engineering researchers to analyze this process [2,3,6–8]. For example, Hamasaki et al. [6,9,10] collected rich code review datasets from a collection of open source projects using the Gerrit and ReviewBoard code review tools.

2.2   Patch-Related Activities in MCR

Jiang et al. noted that a submitted patch is not always merged into a version control system [11]. Examples of abandoned patches include patches with unfixed bugs, irrelevant comments, or duplicate patches [12]. To verify the patches

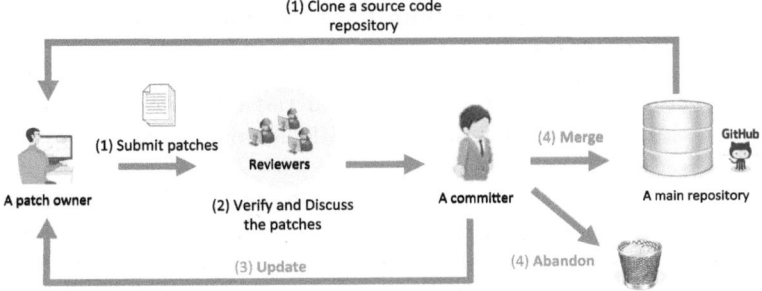

Fig. 1. An overview of modern code review processes

adequately, McIntosh et al. [2] suggested that reviewers discuss the patches carefully and try to reach a consensus in their discussions. In this way, the final decision of whether or not to use a patch can be made simply based on the reviewers' discussions.

Figure 1 provides an overview of a code review process when using a code review tool. In particular [3], the code review process after patch submission acts as follows:

(1) A patch owner clones a source code repository from a web-based version control system service such as GitHub to their local computers. Next, the patch owner creates patches to fix a bug or to enhance patches. After that, the owner submits the patches to a web-based code review tool.
(2) The patch owner requests that reviewers verify the submitted patches. The reviewers verify the changes. Next, the reviewers post an approving positive vote or a disapproving negative vote, and sometimes also post comments.
(3) If the patch owner needs to revise his or her patches, he or she will update the patches.
(4) If the patches are approved by the reviewers and a committer, the committer will **Merge** the patches into the main repository. On the other hand, if the patches are not approved by the reviewers and a committer, the committer will **Abandon** the patches. In this paper, Merge and Abandon are referred to as a final review conclusion.

Weißgerber et al. [13] found that a smaller patch is more likely to be accepted. In addition, Tao et al. [12] investigated reasons why a patch was rejected through quantitative and qualitative analysis. Furthermore, to verify a patch adequately, Thongtanunam et al. [3] and Xia [14] proposed approaches to recommend a appropriate reviewer for patches submitted by a patch owner based on reviewers' experiences.

2.3 A Motivating Example: The Code Review Collaboration Among Reviewers

Based on practical observations explained in the following of this section, we would like to seek a better understanding of disagreements among reviewers and committers.

Tables 1 and 2 show the number of patches in each voting pattern in the two projects when a committer makes the final review conclusion using Qt and OpenStack project data. Each cell has #Merged patches (a value on the left) and #Abandoned patches (a value on the right). These two tables show the patches with less than seven positive votes or negative votes. Then, 91 % of patches in Qt and 91 % of patches in OpenStack are covered in whole patches.

15 % of patches in the Qt and 31 % of patches in the OpenStack of all the patches do not follow the majority rule that selects alternatives which have a majority. For example, in Table 2, 467 patches are abandoned, even though #Positive is greater than #Negative in this case. This indicates that even if a patch received higher #Positive, in practice, the patch is not guaranteed to be accepted. Therefore, we believe that not all reviewers who post a vote, which later be in agreement with the final review conclusion in the code review discussion.

Table 1. The voting patterns made in the final review conclusion in Qt.

	N = 0	N = 1	N = 2	N = 3	N = 4	N = 5	N = 6	N = 7
P = 0	56, 4268	25, 2090	16, 505	3, 93	2, 23	0, 2	0, 0	0, 0
P = 1	40425, 968	1475, 571	135, 122	19, 28	3, 6	0, 1	0, 0	1, 0
P = 2	11748, 247	920, 135	81, 38	20, 12	5, 0	1, 3	0, 0	0, 0
P = 3	2686, 51	316, 29	54, 6	8, 1	1, 0	0, 0	0, 0	0, 0
P = 4	587, 10	79, 8	17, 1	6, 1	1, 0	1, 0	0, 0	1, 0
P = 5	119, 2	36, 1	7, 1	1, 0	0, 0	1, 0	0, 0	0, 0
P = 6	17, 0	3, 0	4, 0	0, 0	1, 0	0, 0	0, 0	0, 0
P = 7	6, 0	2, 0	0, 0	0, 0	0, 0	0, 0	0, 0	0, 0

Table 2. The voting patterns made in the final review conclusion in OpenStack.

	N = 0	N = 1	N = 2	N = 3	N = 4	N = 5	N = 6	N = 7
P = 0	141, 20	4243, 3155	1193, 1214	351, 344	133, 116	47, 47	20, 9	2, 6
P = 1	11964, 1047	3497, 1444	1185, 752	436, 298	157, 122	67, 37	27, 16	8, 10
P = 2	6269, 264	**2254, 467**	865, 302	324, 134	126, 64	54, 25	15, 14	9, 5
P = 3	3069, 90	1317, 211	514, 124	251, 68	85, 31	33, 25	15, 9	11, 2
P = 4	1519, 42	690, 106	303, 55	134, 39	51, 25	24, 7	11, 2	1, 3
P = 5	687, 30	357, 50	146, 37	86, 20	45, 13	13, 5	10, 2	1, 2
P = 6	370, 13	193, 36	91, 25	52, 13	15, 5	17, 5	8, 2	0, 2
P = 7	182, 10	116, 29	60, 17	36, 7	23, 5	4, 3	3, 3	3, 2

Thus, in this paper, we study the impact of a reviewer with a low level of agreement in a code review collaboration.

3   Case Study Design

This study considers two research questions to understand the impact of a reviewer who disagrees with the review conclusion of a patch in a code review collaboration. In the following section, we provide detailed explanations of the case study designed to answer these research questions, and address our experimental Dataset.

3.1   Research Questions

RQ1: How often does a reviewer disagree with a review conclusion?

Motivation. Rigby et al. [15] pointed out that code reviews are expensive because they require reviewers to read, understand, and assess a code change. Thongtanunam et al. [3,14,16] showed that to effectively assess a code change, a patch owner should find an appropriate reviewer who has a deep understanding of the related source codes to closely examine code changes and find defects. In other words, the appropriate reviewer is more likely to assess the patches adequately. However, this reviewer might not always agree with a review conclusion.

Approach. To answer the first research question, we analyze the differences of a reviewer's agreement according to a reviewer's experience (the number of votes in the past). A committer confirms the reviewers' votes to decide a final review conclusion (Merge or Abandon). To analyze the review decision results, we scan comments for the known patterns of automatically generated voting comments in Gerrit as shown in Table 3. Table 3 illustrates five level validating scores ("+2", "+1", "0", "−1", "−2") in Gerrit. A reviewer can vote "+1", "0" and "−1" score. On the other hand, a committer can vote "+2", "+1", "0", "−1" and "−2" for the score [17]. In our study, we use these vote scores "+2", "+1", "0", "−1" and "−2" to analyze assessments by reviewers and committers.

Next, to identify the frequency of votes that disagreed with the review conclusions, we track the voting history of each reviewer. We count the number of times that a reviewer disagreed with the review conclusion of a patch in the past. We need to be careful when calculating the frequency, because some patches have often been updated. In the case where a patch has been updated twice, a reviewer will have two chances to post a vote. In this case, we count the votes twice. Figure 2 shows an example of a voting process. A reviewer X reviews two patches, namely Patch01.java and Patch02.java. As shown in the figure, his or her first positive vote disagrees with the first review conclusion, which was decided upon to be "Updated", because a positive vote implies that this patch does not have any problems. After the patch is updated, his or her second vote is still positive. Finally, the vote of the reviewer X agrees with the final conclusion, which is "Merged". In this case, the rate of agreed upon votes for reviewer X is

Table 3. The patterns of automatically generated voting comments in the Gerrit.

Role	Score	Automatically generated voting comments
Committer	+2	"Looks good to me, approved"
		"Looks good to me"
Reviewer	+1	"Looks good to me, but someone else must approve"
		"Works for me"
		"Code-Review +1"
		"Workflow +1"
		"Verified"
	0	"No score"
	−1	"I would prefer that you didn't submit this"
		"I would prefer that you didn't merge this"
		"Code-Review −1"
		"Workflow −1"
		"Doesn't seem to work"
Committer	−2	"Fails"
		"Do not merge"
		"Do not submit"

Table 4. The definition of agreement and disagreement patterns

		Review conclusion		
		Merge	Abandon	Update
Reviewer's vote	Positive (+2 or +1)	agree	disagree	disagree
	Negative (0, −1 or −2)	disagree	agree	agree

$\frac{1}{2} = 0.5$ (Reviewer X's level of agreement $= 50\%$). Also, a reviewer Y posts a negative vote for only Patch01.java. The rate of agreed votes for the reviewer Y is $\frac{1}{1} = 1.0$ (Reviewer Y's level of agreement $= 100\%$). The level of agreement has a range between 0.0 and 1.0. In summary, Table 4 describes the definition of the agreement and disagreement votes. If a reviewer posts a positive vote (+2 or +1) for a patch and a committer decides to merge this patch, the vote is a vote of agreement. On the other hand, if the committer decides to abandon this patch or a patch owner updates this patch, the vote is a vote of disagreement.

RQ2: What is the impact of a reviewer with a low level of agreement in a code review?

Motivation. In a code review, when a discussion does not always reach a consensus among reviewers and committers, it may take much longer time to completely finish the code review. In addition, it may not be simple to identify which vote a committer should believe. In this second research question, we investigate the

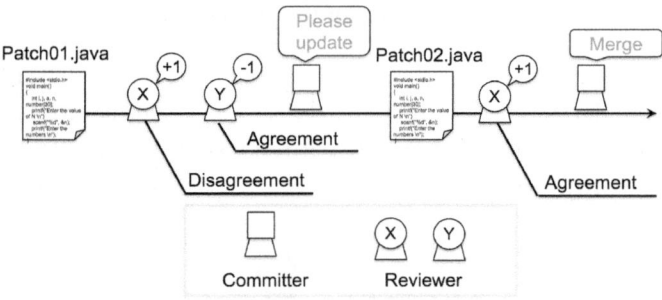

Fig. 2. An example of a voting process.

impact of code review collaboration with a reviewer who often disagrees with a review conclusion using the reviewer's level of agreement measured in the RQ1.

Approach. In this research question, we focus on the minimum level of agreement of reviewers as calculated in each individual review. According to Fig. 2, a minimum level of agreement in this example is the level of agreement of reviewer X's, which is 0.5. The minimum level of agreement has a range between 0.0 and 1.0. When the value of a minimum level of agreement is low, it can be implied that the review has a reviewer who often disagrees with a review conclusion. In our opinion, a lower level of minimum agreement has a negative effect on the code review process. To further analyze the negative effect, we define two technical terms as follows:

Reviewing Time: The time in days from the first patch submission to the final review conclusion. We hypothesize that a reviewer with a lower level of agreement may take much longer time to reach a consensus in the discussion. To reduce the chance of a release postponement, the *Reviewing Time* should be shorter.

Discussion Length: The number of comments which reviewers post into a reviewing board. We hypothesize that a reviewer with a lower level of agreement may disagree more often, so that such a code review needs a much longer discussion period to reach a consensus among reviewers and committers.

3.2 Experimental Dataset

We conduct a case study on two large and successful OSS projects, namely, Qt[3] and OpenStack[4]. These two projects are commonly found in the literature on OSS studies, such as in [2–4,6,9,18] mainly because these projects contains a large amount of reviewing activity using a code review tool.

Table 5 shows that originally Qt and OpenStack had 70,705 and 92,984 review reports, respectively. However, we are concerned that reports consisting of no

---

[3] http://qt.digia.com/.
[4] http://www.openstack.org/.

Table 5. Summary of the studied datasets

	Qt	OpenStack
Original datasets	70,705	92,984
At least 1 vote and without only bot test's vote	61,076	61,642
Without 10% sets	55,523	56,038

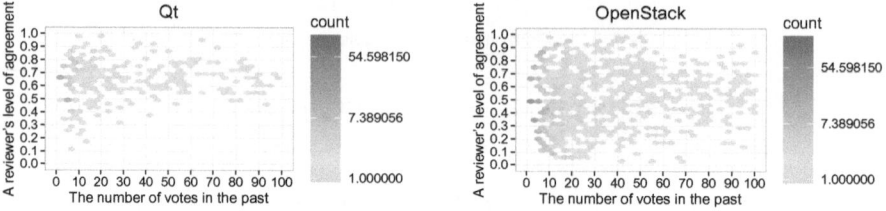

Fig. 3. The relationship between a reviewer's level of agreement and the number of votes.

votes or only bot tests' votes are not useful because we focus on a human reviewer. Therefore, we filter out those review reports prior to our case studies. In more detail, we exclude the earliest (oldest) 10% from the two datasets. Based on our observations, most of the data points falling in this range have insufficient beneficial information for the reviewer's agreement's calculation. The review reports used in this study includes 55,523 review reports in the Qt project and 56,038 review reports in the OpenStack.

4   Case Study Results

4.1   RQ1: How Often Does a Reviewer Disagree with a Review Conclusion?

Figure 3 shows the relationship between a reviewer's level of agreement and the number of votes in the past using a Hexagon binning plot. We define a reviewer who has a lower number of votes than the median of the total votes as a *less experienced reviewer*, and one who has a higher number of votes than this median value as a *more experienced reviewer*, where the median values of the number of votes in Qt and OpenStack are 8 and 11 votes without an outlier, respectively. From this figure, we found that the *more experienced reviewers* are more likely to have a higher level of agreement than the *less experienced reviewers*.

Previous studies [3, 14] suggested identifying an appropriate reviewer based on expertise; however, expertise is not necessarily associated with the agreement of a review conclusion. We therefore suggest one more criteria when choosing an appropriate reviewer based on the results of this experiment. That is, if a patch owner needs the reviewers to reach a consensus for their patches as soon as possible, we suggest that the patch owner invites reviewers with a higher level of agreement.

4.2 RQ2: What Is the Impact of a Reviewer with a Low Level of Agreement in a Code Review?

We begin the investigation for our RQ2 with a quantitative analysis of the reviews disagreed upon among reviewers in the two projects. After that, we further analyze the impact of a reviewer with a low level of agreement in terms of *Reviewing Time* and *Discussion Length*.

Figure 4 shows the rate of the patches disagreed upon according to a minimum agreement of Qt and OpenStack, respectively. In both projects, we found that 11 % of reviews in the Qt and 65 % of reviews in the OpenStack did not reach a consensus among reviewers and a committer. In more detail, when a patch owner invites a reviewer who has a minimum level of agreement between 10 % and 20 %, we found that 64 % of reviews in the Qt and 70 % reviews in the OpenStack did not reach a consensus among reviewers and a committer. Observed by correlation, we found that the rate of disagreed upon reviews and the minimum level of agreement exhibited strongly negative values ($r = -0.79$ in Qt and $r = -0.90$ in OpenStack). This means that a decision made by a reviewer with a lower level of agreement is less likely to reach a consensus among those of the other reviewers.

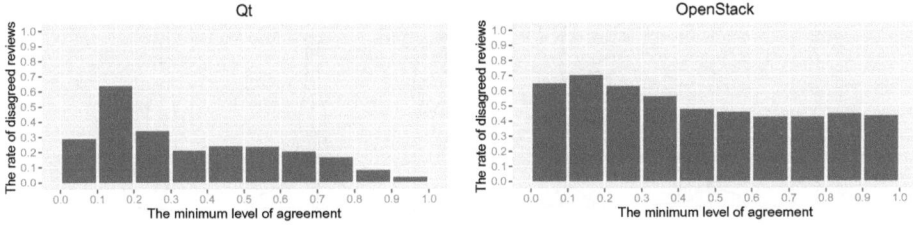

Fig. 4. The rate of review disagreements

Reviewing Time. Figure 5 shows the distribution of reviewing time according to a minimum level of agreement. From this figure, in the Qt project, many patches with a reviewer who has a minimum level of agreement between 70 %– 90 % are more likely to take a much longer reviewing time than others. On the other hand, in OpenStack, the minimum level of agreement appears to be inapplicable to explaining whether or not a reviewer would take a longer reviewing time. Since the features of these distributions seems to be dependent on an individual project, we therefore perform a further analysis of these two projects using a statistical method.

Figure 6 classifies the reviews into two groups, i.e., the Top 50 % and the Remaining 50 % of the population, where the cut-off is determined using the median values of the minimum level of agreement for each project. In Qt, the values of the minimum, the lower quartile, the median, the upper quartile and the maximum are 0.00, 0.78, 0.83, 0.88 and 1.00, respectively, and that of the OpenStack project are 0.00, 0.40, 0.54, 0.70 and 1.00, respectively. We found that the reviews of the Top 50 % are likely to take a shorter reviewing time than those of the Remaining 50 %. Confirmed by the Wilcoxon signed-rank test with a p-value less than 0.01, we found that the difference in the distributions between the Top 50 % and the Remaining 50 % in both Qt and OpenStack are statically significant.

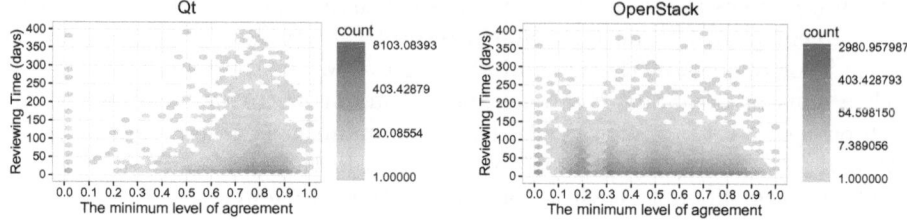

Fig. 5. The distribution of *Reviewing Time*

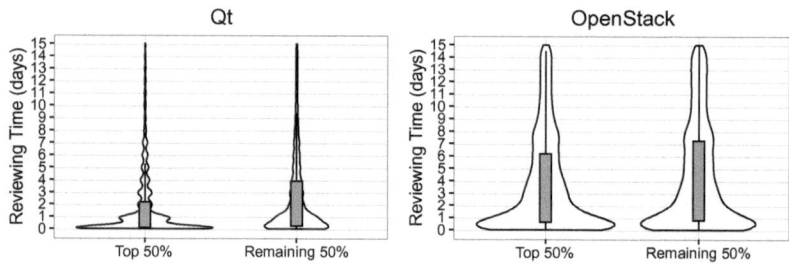

Fig. 6. The difference of the *Reviewing Time* between the Top 50 % and the Remaining 50 %

Discussion Length. Figure 7 shows that the distribution of discussion length (the number of comments in a review) according to the minimum level of agreement. From this figure, in Qt, many patches with a reviewer who has a minimum level of agreement between 60 %–90 % more likely to take a much longer time for discussion than others. On the other hand, in OpenStack, many patches with a reviewer who has a minimum level of agreement with less than 20 % more likely to take a much longer time for discussion than others. Similar to the *Reviewing Time*, we found that the features of these distributions also depend on an individual project. Hence, we further perform an analysis based on statistical method as done when we observed the *Reviewing Time*. Figure 8 shows that the Top 50 % are more likely to take a shorter *Discussion length*. These results were also confirmed by Wilcoxon signed-rank test as being statistically significant with a p-value less than 0.01.

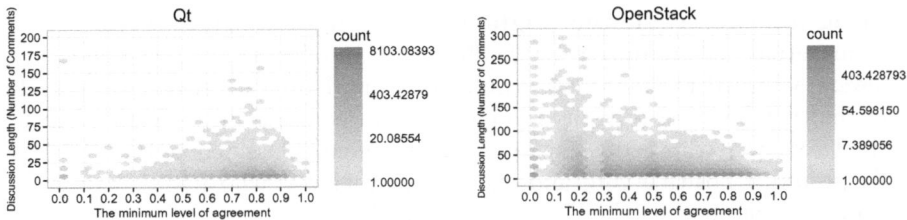

Fig. 7. The distribution of the *Discussion Length*

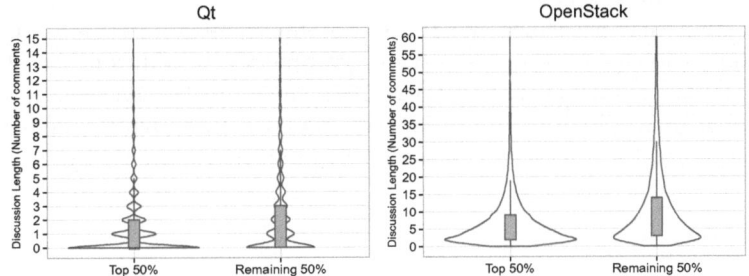

Fig. 8. The difference of the *Discussion Length* between the Top 50 % and the Remaining 50 %

5   Discussion

In this section, we conduct a qualitative analysis to better understand why the reviewers with a low level of agreement often disagrees with a review conclusion and make the review process longer by reading actual review discussions. In addition, this section also discloses the threats to validity of this study.

5.1   A Qualitative Analysis

A reviewer with a lower level of agreement is more likely to overlook problems of source codes. We read an actual review report ID 8141[5] and found that a reviewer named Claudio had overlooked the problem of the test cases, and we found that he disagreed with the final review conclusion (Abandon) of the review. To prove that our approach can explain this case, we calculated the level of agreement of this reviewer and found that the level of agreement of this reviewer was low (classified as Remaining 50 %). In addition, we also found similar cases[6,7] as being in agreement with the analysis result of the review ID 8141.

---

[5] https://codereview.qt-project.org/#/c/8141.
[6] https://review.openstack.org/#/c/10363.
[7] https://review.openstack.org/#/c/10305.

Inviting another reviewer might take a longer discussion period. We read an actual review report ID 28,257[8] and found that a record saying that reviewers assigned to this review could not complete this review and therefore asked another reviewer to verify the patches. For example, in a review ID 28,257, the first reviewer who had a low level of agreement (classified as the Remaining 50 %) posted a positive vote and the second reviewer who had a high level of agreement (classified as the Top 50 %) posted a negative vote. Therefore, this discussion did not reach a consensus among reviewers. In the detailed record of this review, we found that the second reviewer said that "*I recommend asking JsonDb maintainer / developers to review this change before rubber stamping it*", indicating that it seemed not to be easy for the second reviewer to make a review conclusion using the first reviewer's review. In addition, we also found cases similar to this review report ID 28,257, which are[9,10]. We therefore suggest that a patch owner invites an appropriate reviewer (i.e., with a higher level of agreement) in order to reach a final review conclusion more easily.

5.2 Threats to Validity

External validity. We found that a reviewer with a lower level of agreement takes a longer reviewing time and discussion length. We might obtain new findings if we investigate another project with different characteristics than Qt and OpenStacks. Nonetheless, as our results were subject to a robust statistically significant test, we believe that the results probably would not be much different than what we did found in this study.

Internal validity. Not all disagreed upon reviews have problems. It is possible that a reviewer might disagree with a committer's decision, but the both opinions could be correct. This situation might express a valuable discussion. We will investigate deeply the disagreed upon discussion process to determine whether or not a disagreed upon discussion is valuable for a patch integration.

In addition, we should also take into consideration the rank of the reviewer's role in the Gerrit system. A maintainer and committer have stronger rights compared to a reviewer, so that a reviewer is likely to agree with their opinions. Therefore, we would like to investigate the level of agreement by considering the rank of the reviewer's role.

6   Conclusion

In this study, we have investigated the impact of reviewers with a low level of agreement using Qt and OpenStack. In our research questions, we found that a more experienced reviewer is more likely to have a higher level of agreement than those who have less experience, and a review assigned to a reviewer with a lower

---

[8] https://codereview.qt-project.org/#/c/28257.

[9] https://codereview.qt-project.org/#/c/1048.

[10] https://codereview.qt-project.org/#/c/7375.

level of agreement is more likely to take a longer reviewing time and discussion length. In our discussion, we found that a reviewer with a lower level of agreement often overlooks problems presented in source codes. From the findings of this study, we suggest that a patch owner should invite an appropriate reviewer to review the patch, where appropriateness is to be determined by using the level of agreement calculated in the entire project. In the future, we will propose a more sophisticated method to invite an appropriate reviewer based on additional important criteria. We believe that this future direction will contribute to a more efficient code review process.

Acknowledgment. This work has been conducted as part of our research under the Program for Advancing Strategic International Networks to Accelerate the Circulation of Talented Researchers.

References

1. Kochhar, P.S., Bissyande, T.F., Lo, D., Jiang, L.: An empirical study of adoption of software testing in open source projects. In: Proceedings of the 13th International Conference on Quality Software (QSIC 2013), pp. 103–112 (2013)
2. McIntosh, S., Kamei, Y., Adams, B., Hassan, A.E.: The impact of code review coverage, code review participation on software quality: a case study of the Qt, VTK, and ITK projects. In: Proceedings of the 11th Working Conference on Mining Software Repositories (MSR 2014), pp. 192–201 (2014)
3. Thongtanunam, P., Tantithamthavorn, C., Kula, R.G., Yoshida, N., Iida, H., Matsumoto, K.-I.: Who should review my code? a file location-based code-reviewer recommendation approach for modern code review. In: Proceedings of the 22nd International Conference on Software Analysis, Evolution, and Reengineering (SANER 2015), pp. 141–150 (2015)
4. Hirao, T., Ihara, A., Matsumoto, K.-I.: Pilot study of collective decision-making in the code review process. In: Proceedings of the Center for Advanced Studies on Collaborative Research (CASCON 2015) (2015)
5. Bacchelli, A., Bird, C.: Expectations, outcomes, and challenges of modern code review. In: Proceedings of the 35th International Conference on Software Engineering (ICSE 2013), pp. 712–721 (2013)
6. Bosu, A., Carver, J.C.: Peer code review in open source communities using review-board. In: Proceedings of the 4th Workshop on Evaluation and Usability of Programming Languages and Tools (PLATEAU 2012), pp. 17–24 (2012)
7. Rigby, P.C., Bird, C.: Convergent contemporary software peer review practices. In: Proceedings of the 9th Joint Meeting on Foundations of Software Engineering (ESEC/FSE 2013), pp. 202–212 (2013)
8. Morales, R., McIntosh, S., Khomh, F.: Do code review practices impact design quality? a case study of the Qt, VTK, and ITK projects. In: Proceedings of the 22nd International Conference on Software Analysis, Evolution, and Reengineering (SANER 2015), pp. 171–180 (2015)
9. Hamasaki, K., Kula, R.G., Yoshida, N., Cruz, A.E.C., Fujiwara, K., Iida, H.: Who does what during a code review? datasets of OSS peer review repositories. In: Proceedings of the 10th Working Conference on Mining Software Repositories (MSR 2013), pp. 49–52 (2013)

10. Mukadam, M., Bird, C., Rigby, P.C.: Gerrit software code review data from android. In: Proceedings of the 10th Working Conference on Mining Software Repositories (MSR 2013), pp. 45–48 (2013)
11. Jiang, Y., Adams, B., German, D.M.: Will my patch make it? how fast?: case study on the linux kernel. In: Proceedings of the 10th Working Conference on Mining Software Repositories (MSR 2013), pp. 101–110 (2013)
12. Tao, Y., Han, D., Kim, S.: Writing acceptable patches: an empirical study of open source project patches. In: Proceedings of the International Conference on Software Maintenance and Evolution (ICSME 2014), pp. 271–280 (2014)
13. Weißgerber, P., Neu, D., Diehl, S.: Small patches get in! In: Proceedings of the 5th International Working Conference on Mining Software Repositories (MSR 2008), pp. 67–76 (2008)
14. Xia, X., Lo, D., Wang, X., Yang, X.: Who should review this change?: putting text and file location analyses together for more accurate recommendations. In: Proceedings of the 31st International Conference on Software Maintenance and Evolution (ICSME 2015), pp. 261–270 (2015)
15. Rigby, P.C., Storey, M.-A.: Understanding broadcast based peer review on open source software projects. In: Proceedings of the 33rd International Conference on Software Engineering (ICSE 2011), pp. 541–550 (2011)
16. Aurum, A., Petersson, H., Wohlin, C.: State-of-the-art: software inspections after 25 years. Softw. Test. Verification Reliab. 12(3), 133–154 (2002)
17. Milanesio, L.: Learning Gerrit Code Review. Packt Publishing (2013)
18. Thongtanunam, P., McIntosh, S., Hassan, A.E., Iida, H.: Investigating code review practices in defective files: an empirical study of the Qt system. In: Proceedings of the 12th Working Conference on Mining Software Repositories (MSR 2015), pp. 168–179 (2015)

Certification of Open Source Software – A Scoping Review

Eirini Kalliamvakou[1], Jens Weber[1], and Alessia Knauss[2(✉)]

[1] Department of Computer Science, University of Victoria,
3800 Finnerty Rd, Victoria V8P5C2, Canada
{ikaliam,jens}@uvic.ca
[2] Department of Computer Science and Engineering,
Chalmers University of Technology,
Hörselgången 5, 41296 Gothenburg, BC, Sweden
alessia.knauss@chalmers.se

Abstract. Open source software (OSS) systems are being used for increasingly critical functions in modern societies, e.g., in health care, finance, government, defense, and other safety and security sensitive sectors. There is an increasing interest in software certification as a means to assure quality and dependability of such systems. However, the development processes and organizational structures of OSS projects can be substantially different from traditional closed-source projects. The distributed, "bazaar-style" approach to software development in OSS systems is often perceived incompatible with certification. This paper presents the results of a scoping review on certification in OSS systems in order to identify and categorize key issues and provide a comprehensive overview of the current evidence on this topic.

1 Introduction

As the use of software expands to an increasing number of domains and products, it is also entering areas where, either by law or best practice, software must conform to certain rules and standards. Examples of such domains are healthcare, defense, and the increasingly important domain of transportation (e.g., self-driving vehicles). Due to the criticality of the systems and the high risk associated with software malfunctions in such domains, high standards in terms of the software's security, reliability, and safety have to be maintained [26]. Additionally, domains such as government and public administration, although not necessarily operating critical systems, have in many countries requirements in place that ask for some guarantee of the software's reliability and proper licensing before OSS can be used. The European Union, for example, introduced the OSEPA project (Open Source software usage for European Public Administration, http://osepa.eu) in order to systematically discuss issues related to OSS adoption in public administration. Their list of deliverables includes case studies and surveys regarding the successful adoption of OSS in public administration and the critical factors behind it. Technical characteristics that OSS must fulfill, software quality, and licensing are high on the list of priorities.

© IFIP International Federation for Information Processing 2016
Published by Springer International Publishing Switzerland 2016. All Rights Reserved
K. Crowston et al. (Eds.): OSS 2016, IFIP AICT 472, pp. 111–122, 2016.
DOI: 10.1007/978-3-319-39225-7_9

A common misconception regarding software certification is that it ensures the absence of defects [18]. This is not part of a certification's goal and it is also far from its reach. At most, software certification can attest, through a series of evaluation activities, that certain properties exist in the software, and that it conforms to specified standards. These properties can be associated with the end product or the process that lead to it, or both. The properties are assessed and verified against standards that must be met, and an awarded certificate is equivalent to assuring that the software has these properties. Today, software is mostly certified based on the process used in its development, which seems insufficient to verify software used as part of critical systems and devices [26]. The product needs to possess certain properties too, and therefore should be certified based on evidence that comes from the software code.

Open Source Software (OSS) is a special category of software in terms of distribution and licensing. The Open Source Initiative (OSI, http://opensource.org) provides the open source definition, which essentially lists the characteristics that software must possess to be considered open source. OSS started based on the idea that software should be openly accessible to all, and by people who practiced this principle of creating software that they released through the Internet visibly and openly. As a side effect, communities of like-minded developers started forming around OSS projects, a fact that has received much academic attention [3, 13, 27]. Today, OSS development is considered mainly community-driven and sustained through the volunteers that create and maintain the software. With the increasing adoption of OSS and the piling evidence of the high quality of OSS [1, 22, 28], the ability to adopt OSS instead of proprietary software in critical domains often hinges on issues of software certification.

The objective of this paper is to study existing literature systematically and present a comprehensive overview on experiences and issues related to the certification of OSS systems. We present the results of a scoping review of the literature on this topic. Our findings include 17 relevant papers on the topic of certification of OSS systems.

This paper is organized as follows: First we present our method, questions, and protocol for searching the literature regarding software certification in the OSS domain. We then present and discuss our findings. Finally, we will draw conclusions and acknowledge potential limitations of this study.

2 Research Method

We use a systematic scoping review method to gather published evidence on certification issues in OSS systems. According to Rumrill et al. scoping reviews "focus on examining the range and nature of a particular research area" [21]. Scoping reviews are often used as a pre-cursor to generate more specific research questions, which could be addressed by more in-depth Systematic Literature Reviews on a particular issue or hypothesis [17]. Both methods have in common that they follow a well-defined methodology that minimizes bias and allows repeatability. This includes the definition of a research protocol that specifies the research questions, search strategy, inclusion/exclusion criteria, and the information to be extracted from the retrieved literature. The search and review methods are documented to allow the reader assessing rigor and repeatability of the study [16].

2.1 Objective and Research Questions

The objective behind conducting this scoping review is to gain an overview of the research and discussion in the field of software certification related to the cases of open source software projects. The research questions in scoping reviews are generally more abstract, aiming to give an overview of existing literature. Hence, we focus on identifying the amount of research activity, who is leading the research, the topics covered and the approaches or solutions used in OSS certification.

We formulate our research questions as follows:

RQ1: How much research activity is there in the area of OSS certification?
RQ2: Who is leading the research on certification of OSS systems?
RQ3: What issues/topics of certification for OSS have been identified and studied?
RQ4: What approaches or solutions have been proposed to address these issues?

To answer these questions and conduct the scoping review we devised a search protocol defined as follows.

2.2 Sources and Keywords

We performed our search by using digital collections of publishers and organizations relating to software engineering and computer science. We used the following databases to acquire the primary studies:

- IEEE Xplore
- ACM Digital Library
- Wiley InterScience (Computer Science section)
- Science Direct (Computer Science section)
- SpringerLink

These digital libraries are widely used and well established in the software engineering and computer science domains. A consultation with a subject librarian for computer science at the University of Victoria confirmed that this was a sufficiently comprehensive list of digital libraries to be used for our study. Meta search engines such as Google Scholar and CiteseerX were used as validity checks in an attempt to retrieve any relevant publications not covered by the above collections.

The following query was used in our study, targeting both title and abstract of the publication: "open source OR FLOSS OR (Libre AND software OR project) OR (Free AND software OR project) AND (certification OR certify)".

2.3 Search and Selection

Our search includes all publications that have been added to the publishers' digital collection up to April 2013. The following inclusion and exclusion criteria were applied to filter the query results:

In order to be considered for *inclusion*, papers were required to fulfill all the following requirements:

- Abstract and/or title contain the keywords as defined in our search string.
- Papers are published in journals, conference proceedings, or are book chapters. We also included papers that are part of grey literature (technical reports, white papers etc.), although our search did not yield any. We did not include magazine papers unless they had academic references and were peer-reviewed.
- Software certification is the main theme of the paper and refers to OSS projects. Being the main theme is evidenced by the certification mentioned in more than one third of the pages of the publication.
- Publications are in English.
- The full paper content is available in the collection (not just its abstract).

In turn, papers were *excluded* if they failed to fulfill at least one of the above criteria.

Papers that met all above inclusion criteria were reviewed in full text to make a final decision on their relevance to this scoping review. We included papers that discuss the process and activities of obtaining some form of third party certification for any type of OSS. We also included papers that discuss or propose the use of tools, methods, approaches, and frameworks in OSS projects that seek certification. Another type of paper we were interested in would discuss possible changes and extensions in the way assessment is carried out for software certification in the case of OSS. Papers that offer positions or debate on how certification affects OSS and vice versa are also accepted, even when the proposed solutions are not fully validated since certification issues in OSS are a relatively recent issue and the status of the research is still formed.

We did not include papers that use the term certification in any other context than software receiving an assurance from a certification authority or body, based on conformance to specified standards. For example, we do not include papers that discuss certification in the context of network security and related tokens or certificates.

When reviewing the full text, we attempted to extract the issue discussed and the solutions proposed. If the issues and the solutions genuinely link to software certification and not just the general software engineering domain, we include the paper. This criterion is reinforced by the assessment of how central the software certification theme is in the paper.

3   Results

In this section we present the findings of our study for each research question defined above.

RQ1: How much research activity is there in the area of OSS certification?

Querying the online libraries with the search string defined in our protocol resulted in 114 papers after removing duplicate entries. Based on our inclusion and exclusion criteria, 11 of the identified papers were classified as relevant giving an inclusion rate of 9.6 %. After performing the validity checks using meta search engines defined in our protocol, we identified an additional source that was not indexed in the selected digital libraries. This was an open access journal, the Electronic Communications of the

European Association of Software Science and Technology (ECEASST), which hosts for publication some of the papers included in the proceedings of the International Workshop on Foundations and Techniques for Open Source Software Certification (OpenCert). We used the journal's search function to repeat our search protocol. The search through this additional source yielded 11 papers, 6 of which met our inclusion criteria. As a result, the final number of papers yielded by queries was 125, with 17 selected primary studies (inclusion rate 13.6 %).

There were a few cases of relevant papers that refer to studies being part of the same research. Authors of the 17 primary studies have multiple publications on the same research and refer to them in some of the 17 papers. For now, we have included them in our list of relevant primary studies. However, in our refinement steps, we will carry out cross-referencing of the included papers, and we will categorize these sub-studies as secondary papers.

The results of our study show that the earliest (one) publication was in 2008. 4 out of the 17 papers were published in 2009, 6 papers in 2010, 5 papers in 2011, and 1 paper in 2012. Of the 17 included papers, 11 appeared in conference or workshop proceedings (64.7 %) and 6 were journal articles (35.3 %).

RQ2: Who is leading the research on certification in OSS systems?

Although with not a substantially higher number of publications, USA is leading the research efforts regarding certification in OSS. USA has 5 out of the 17 relevant publications. Interestingly, 4 out of the 5 publications involve at least one common author. Italy and the UK are the next in line with 4 and 2 publications respectively, out of the list of included papers. The distribution of publications among the leading countries is shown in Table 1.

Table 1. Leading countries in OSS certification research

Country	# of Papers	Paper ID
U.S.A.	5	P6, P8, P9, P10, P11
Italy	4	P1, P3, P13, P16
U.K.	2	P5, P7

Ten of the primary studies originated in a particular safety critical domains, while seven are not domain specific. Most domain-specific papers target healthcare (5 out of 17 papers), followed by transportation (4 out of 17 papers).

RQ3: What issues of certification for OSS have been studied?

OSS certification compared to closed source. Several researchers have studied the differences of certifying OSS compared to the certification of closed source software. Fusani and Marchetti [10] point out that the stakeholder groups involved in the two kinds of software are different and gain confidence in the software through different sources of information and in different ways. The authors discuss the different factors that impact the closed source and open source environments and how they should be taken into account in the certification process. They observe that the evolution of OSS is much more dynamic and not as linear as in closed systems. Fabbrini et al. make similar observations but also present two concrete process scenarios for OSS certification, the first being developer-initiated and the second being client- (i.e., adopter-) initiated [8].

Kakarontzas et al. point out that OSS is more amenable to product-focused certification than to process-focused certification, because the development processes of OSS are often less tightly controlled than in closed source systems [11]. Moreover, the availability of the source code provides a better basis for product-focused evaluation. Feuser and Peleska [9] make similar argument, suggesting that the openness of OSS provides opportunities for open proofs that certification objectives are met. Moreover, extensive peer reviewing by a large community may improve quality assurance. Organizing this "crowd-sourced" review and certification process is a challenge. Khoroshilov suggests integrating it in the educational process of software engineering trainees [14]. Cerone and Settas propose the concept of a community-driven process of generating anti-patterns to be used for quality assurance [5].

Morasca et al. discuss the specific differences between the testing processes of OSS in contrast to closed source systems. For example, OSS testing processes can be guided by metrics such as code coverage and the results of static analyses, e.g., potential defect density, data and control flow analysis, program slicing etc. [19].

Certification economics. Comar et al. raise several common challenges with the certification process of safety critical software [6]. Certification commonly happens in discrete and costly steps and, once certified, the system is commonly closed to changes and adaptation to avoid the need for recertification. This effect is referred to as the "Big Freeze". To overcome this problem, they propose an approach to continuous certification, called the Open-DO process. Properly implemented the Open-Do process ensures that a system is certifiable at any time. Open-Do is supported by a suit of open source tools.

Cotroneo et al. consider economic aspects of certification from a different perspective, namely from an adopter's point of view [7]. The challenge here is to select and certify the best open source product from a potentially larger set of available systems. They propose definition and use of a pre-certification kit (PK) to filter out suitable candidates. A PK is generated in a two-step process, by firstly specifying a reference model that captures the requirements on the type of system to be certified (e.g., an operating system, a health record, etc.), and secondly selecting software metrics to be extracted from candidate systems, indicative of whether or not the specified requirements are being met.

Development process. Bertrand and Fuhrman discuss the suitability of OpenUP, an OSS development process adapted from the Unified Process, as a foundation for developing certifiable software [4]. They specifically attempt to align OpenUP with DO-178B, a certification standard used in avionics, and point out arising challenges, e.g., with respect to the use of different terminologies. Kakarontzas et al. introduce the OPEN-SME process, which emphasizes activities that prepare OSS for software reuse and focuses on generating trustworthy, product-focused evidence on software quality attributes [11].

OSS for evolving complex standards. Several authors have highlighted the role of OSS as an enabler for the development of standards in inherently complex application domains. Sethi et al. discuss interoperability and standardization issues in community tele-medicine [23]. They argue that a commonly accessible OSS interoperability framework may be more effective in enabling industry to produce certifiably interoperable technologies than a set of abstract standard specifications. Van der Leest uses an OSS prototype to study design alternatives and implementation trade-offs of the ARINC 653 standard used in the avionics domain [25].

OSS security. The certification of software security is an issue discussed by a number of authors. Smith et al. criticize the "security by checklist" approach commonly used in certifying closed source systems [24]. They expose security vulnerabilities in open source Electronic Health Record (EHR) software that would have been undetected by current certification programs. Similar studies have been published by Austin et al. [2], Helms and Williams [12], and King et al. [15].

RQ4: What approaches or solutions have been proposed to address these issues?

The previous section discussed major common themes of issues discussed in the selected primary studies. Table 2 gives a comprehensive overview of these issues and summarizes the proposed approaches or solutions for each paper.

Table 2. Summary of issues and solutions per paper covered in primary studies

Paper	Issues	Solutions
P1 – [19]	Selecting **testing processes for OSS** vs. closed source software	**Evaluate maturity** stage of project testing process, improvements based on OSS characteristics
P2 – [6]	*"Big freeze"* **effect** after certification, to avoid need for re-certification	**Continuous integration**, software certifiable at all times, use of open tools and standards for certification-relevant material
P3 – [7]	Producing evidence for **certification is costly**, specific focus on operating system software	Use a **pre-certification kit** to evaluate properties the OS, including metrics and acceptable values
P4 – [4]	**Government-set standards** for civil avionics software (**DO-178B**)	**OpenUP process framework** as a checklist to prepare for certification, project can customize processes on top
P5 – [1]	Standard compliance checking, specific focus on CASE tools	**Compliance test generation** from standards specification
P6 – [25]	**Studying design alternatives for ARINC 653 certification is difficult** because platforms are closed & proprietary	**OSS prototype implementation** allows examination of benefits and weaknesses of design and architectural alternatives in using virtualization to achieve ARINC 653

(Continued)

Table 2. (*Continued*)

Paper	Issues	Solutions
P7 – [23]	Difficulty of **developing interoperability standards in complex domains**, e.g., telecare	**Open source framework** for designing communication standards
P8 – [24] P9 – [2]	**"Security by checklist"** fails to detect implementation level vulnerabilities	Enhancing existing test scripts to **include implementation level vulnerabilities**. Source code required
P10 – [12]	**Certification of access control** in secure software, focus on medical information systems	**Systematic method for product-focused assessment** based on access control criteria compiled from different standards
P11 – [15]	**Certification of secure audit mechanisms**, focus on medical information systems	**Systematic method for product-focused assessment** based on auditing criteria compiled from different standards
P12 – [11]	**OSS component reuse** without assurances	**Component-based certification of OSS** to increase confidence. **OpenSME process**
P13 – [8]	**Inputs for certifying for OSS** vs closed source	**Stakeholder-driven scenarios** for the certification process
P14 – [14]	**Who undertakes certification-related activities** in OSS communities?	**Making certification activities part of educational programs** in higher education
P15 – [9]	**Trustworthiness or security** of combined OSS and closed source components	**Open model approach** to guarantee secure code, security analysis in cases of closed source components, partitioning and hardware virtualization as solutions
P16 – [10]	**Impacting factors for confidence** in OSS vs. closed source systems	Evidence collected in **virtual certification repository** to be used by the Certification Body for assessment
P17 – [5]	**What evidence to produce** for product-focused certification of OSS?	**Anti-patterns** collected, formalized, and ontologically related by OSS community.

4   Discussion

Our scoping review indicates a comparably low level of research activity on the specific issues related to the certification of OSS systems and components. The lack of research activity in this area could be due to the fact that OSS have only recently been considered for critical system domains and high assurance applications, i.e., during the last decade. Another possible explanation may be that researchers may view certification issues in closed source systems as substantially similar to certification issues in OSS. Our scoping review has indicated, however, that this assumption may not hold in general and that there are indeed different issues to consider when certifying OSS systems.

All reviewed studies agree that OSS certification efforts should focus on product-based assurances, as process-based assurances may be impractical in loosely controlled, "bazaar-style" development communities. This shift away from process-based certification may not be detrimental, as process-based assurances have limited power in predicting product-quality [18].

Interestingly, the open, community-style nature of typical OSS projects may, in fact, make product-focused assurances more economically feasible, by applying a crowd-sourcing paradigm to assurance and certification. This hypothesis can be seen as an implication of "Linus' Law", as stated by Raymond [20]: "Given enough eyeballs, all bugs are shallow". While significant controversy still prevails about the general validity of this law, Khoroshilov points out ways to organize the community to provide certification services [14]. More empirical and theoretical research is needed on its applicability in context of OSS certification. Important research questions include "How do certification concerns shape and impact OSS communities?" and "How to organize open source communities for effective and economic certification?".

The availability of source code for OSS components provides opportunities for scrutiny by third party certification bodies. However, the complexity, size and evolving nature of many OSS projects severely limit the practicality of such efforts, unless the software is developed "with certification in mind". Cotroneo's pre-certification kit [7], Comar et al.'s Open-DO continuous certification process [6], Fusani and Marchetti's virtual certification repository [10], Kakarontzas et al.'s OPEN-SME reuse process [11] are examples for approaches to develop "for certification". Some of these proposals can be considered complimentary, others are alternatives. Little empirical evidence is available to-date about their effectiveness in practice. As an increasing number of OSS systems are subject to certification and may consider these proposals, the community will need more empirical evidence on their effectiveness.

5   Limitations

A possible bias in results of this scoping review is in the selection of relevant papers. We mitigated this threat to validity by using clearly predefined inclusion/exclusion criteria and having a second reviewer checking the selection performed by the first author on a random sample of the query results.

Another threat to validity is in the selection of data sources. The choice to perform electronic search could potentially exclude publications that might have been relevant to include, and therefore pose a risk of external validity. However, we believe that this risk is minimal as OSS is a relatively new research topic and the fact that it belongs to the research domain of software engineering safeguards that there is not much that is not indexed electronically.

However, there are certain peculiarities when it comes to electronic search that could alter the results, although not substantially. For example, during the course of the study, SpringerLink was migrating from an older to a newer website. Since the older website offered more comprehensive and robust search options, and was still available, we decided to continue using it as our source. However, before the study was finished the publisher disabled access to the older website, and we could not use two of our keyword combinations. We feel confident that the search would not produce additional results, because we were at a point in our study where the last keyword combinations did not produce any additional results in any of the other digital libraries either. Nevertheless, we are acknowledging this as a potential limitation to our study.

A final concern is whether there is any potential threat to reliability. We expect that replications of our study would offer results similar to ours. This, of course, depends also on the comprehensiveness of the research questions used, especially the synthesis and discussion. The approach followed by other researchers in discussing and interpreting the results may bring different insights, but we believe that the underlying findings and trends identified would remain the same.

6 Conclusion

In this paper we have presented a scoping review on certification of OSS systems. By following a systematic approach in searching existing literature, we identified 125 papers. After screening for inclusion and exclusion criteria, our analysis yielded 17 primary studies (inclusion rate 13.6 %). We gave a summary for each of the primary studies, and summarized the issues of certification for OSS that have been studied in the primary studies. The issues included OSS certification compared to closed source certification, challenges due to certification economics, development processes, OSS in development of inherently complex application domains, as well as certification of OSS security.

References

1. Bunyakiati, P., Finkelstein, A.: The compliance testing of software tools with respect to the UML standards specification - the ArgoUML case study. In Workshop on Automation of Software Test **2009**, 138–143 (2009)
2. Austin, A., Smith, B., Williams, L.: Towards improved security criteria for certification of electronic health record systems. Workshop on Software Engineering in Health Care, pp. 68–73. ACM, New York, NY, USA (2010)
3. Bergquist, M., Ljungberg, J.: The power of gifts: organizing social relationships in open source communities. Inf. Syst. J. **11**(4), 305–320 (2001)
4. Bertrand, C., Fuhrman, C.P.: Towards defining software development processes in DO-178B with openup. In: Canadian Conference on Electrical and Computer Engineering, pp. 851–854 (2008)
5. Cerone, A., Settas, D.: Using antipatterns to improve the quality of FLOSS development. Electron. Commun. EASST **48**, 16 (2011)

6. Comar, C., Gasperoni, F., Ruiz, J.F.: Open-Do: an open-source initiative for the development of safety-critical software. In: 4th IET International Conference on Systems Safety, pp. 1–5 (2009)
7. Cotroneo, D., Di Leo, D., Silva, N., Barbosa, R.: The precertification kit for operating systems in safety domains. In: Workshop on Software Certification (WoSoCER), pp. 19–24 (2011)
8. Fabbrini, F., Fusani, M., Marchetti, E.: Process scenarios in open source software certification. Electron. Commun. EASST **48**, 15 (2011)
9. Feuser, J., Peleska, J.: Security in open model software with hardware virtualization: the railway control system perspective. Electron. Commun. EASST **33**, 14 (2010)
10. Fusani, M., Marchetti, E.: Damages and benefits of certification: a perspective from an independent assessment body. Electron. Commun. EASST **33**, 3 (2010)
11. Kakarontzas, G., Katsaros, P., Stamelos, I.: Component certification as a prerequisite for widespread OSS reuse. Electron. Commun. EASST **33**, 20 (2010)
12. Helms, E., Williams, L.: Evaluating access control of open source electronic health record systems. In: Proceedings. of the 3rd Workshop on Software Engineering in Health Care, pp. 63–70. ACM. New York, NY, USA (2011)
13. von Hippel, E., von Krogh, G.: open source software and the "private-collective" innovation model: issues for organization science. Organ. Sci. **14**(2), 209–223 (2003)
14. Khoroshilov, A.: Open source certification and educational process. Electron. Commun. EASST **20**, 8 (2009)
15. King, J.T., Smith, B., Williams, L.: Modifying without a trace: general audit guidelines are inadequate for open-source electronic health record audit mechanisms. In: International Health Informatics Symposium, pp. 305–314. ACM (2012)
16. Kitchenham, B.A., Pfleeger, S.L., Pickard, L.M., Jones, P.W., Hoaglin, D.C., El Emam, K., Rosen Berg, J.: Preliminary guidelines for empirical research in software engineering. IEEE Trans. Softw. Eng. **28**(8), 721–734 (2002)
17. Kitchenham, B., et al.: Systematic literature reviews in software engineering - a systematic literature review. Inf. Softw. Techn. **51**(1), 7–15 (2009)
18. Maibaum, T., Wassyng, A.: A product-focused approach to software certification. Computer **41**(2), 91–93 (2008)
19. Morasca, S., Taibi, D., Tosi, D.: Towards certifying the testing process of open-source software: new challenges or old methodologies? In: Workshop on Emerging Trends in Free/Libre/Open Source Software Research and Development, pp. 25–30. IEEE (2009)
20. Raymond, E.S.: Cathedral and the Bazaar. SnowBall Publishing, La Vergne, TN (1999)
21. Rumrill, P.D., Fitzgerald, S.M., Merchant, W.R.: Using scoping literature reviews as a means of understanding and interpreting existing literature. Work (Reading, Mass.) **35**(3), 399–404 (2010)
22. Samoladas, I., Gousios, G., Spinellis, D., Stamelos, I.: The SQO-OSS quality model: measurement based open source software evaluation. In: Russo, B., Damiani, E., Hissam, S., Lundell, B., Succi, G. (eds.) Open Source Development, Communities and Quality. IFIP AICT, vol. 275, pp. 237–248. Springer US, New York (2008)
23. Sethi, R., Azzi, D., Khusainov, R.: Interoperability and standardisation in community telecare: a review. In: IET Seminar on Assisted Living, pp. 1–6 (2011)
24. Smith, B., et al.: Challenges for protecting the privacy of health information: required certification can leave common vulnerabilities undetected. In: Security & Privacy in Medical & Homecare Systems, pp. 1–12 (2010)
25. Van der Leest, S.H.: ARINC 653 hypervisor. In: IEEE/AIAA 29th Digital Avionics Systems Conference (DASC), pp. 5.E.2–1–5.E.2–20 (2010)

26. Wassyng, A., Maibaum, T., Lawford, M.: On software certification: we need product-focused approaches. In: Choppy, C., Sokolsky, O. (eds.) Monterey Workshop 2008. LNCS, vol. 6028, pp. 250–274. Springer, Heidelberg (2010)
27. West, J., O'Mahony, S.: The role of participation architecture in growing sponsored open source communities. Ind. Innov. **15**(2), 145–168 (2008)
28. Zhao, L., Elbaum, S.: Quality assurance under the open source development model. J. Syst. Softw. **66**(1), 65–75 (2003)

Classifying Organizational Adoption of Open Source Software: A Proposal

Stephen Murphy$^{(\boxtimes)}$ and Sharon Cox

School of Computing and Digital Technology, Birmingham City University,
Birmingham, UK
{stephen.murphy, sharon.cox}@bcu.ac.uk

Abstract. Staged adoption models are a common feature of information systems (IS) adoption literature, yet these are rarely used in open source software (OSS) adoption studies. In this paper, a staged model for classifying the organizational adoption of OSS is proposed, based upon a critical review of existing staged adoption models and factors identified from OSS adoption literature. Innovations in the proposed model include: defined transition pathways between stages, additional stages and a decomposition of cessation of use into four distinct pathways.

Keywords: Open source software · Technology adoption · Staged adoption model · Innovation diffusion theory · Organizational adoption · Factor based model · Adoption pathway

1 Introduction

Software developed by communities using the open source methods espoused by Raymond [1] is increasing in popularity [2]. While exact usage figures are uncertain, some studies have put usage levels as high as 85 % [3] and in some specialist fields, close to 100 % [4]. Open Source Software (OSS) usage had previously been the preserve of programmers and software experts [5, 6], but this 'second wave' [7] of OSS adoption by businesses and non-technical users has led to greater press and academic attention [8]. However, much of this attention has focused on OSS development methods and processes [9], with studies of adoption being under-represented [10–13]. This paper aims to partly address this gap through the achievement of the following objectives:

1. highlighting that most previous OSS adoption studies are not cognizant of the staged nature of the adoption process;
2. showing that where such studies are stage aware, that the models used to classify adoption are incomplete;
3. showing that existing staged adoption models do not identify all progression pathways;
4. and proposing a model to remedy shortcomings in existing models.

© IFIP International Federation for Information Processing 2016
Published by Springer International Publishing Switzerland 2016. All Rights Reserved
K. Crowston et al. (Eds.): OSS 2016, IFIP AICT 472, pp. 123–133, 2016.
DOI: 10.1007/978-3-319-39225-7_10

2   Literature Review

2.1   Technology Adoption

Adoption is defined as "choosing something for one's use or practice" [14]. The adoption of technology is a long standing area of academic research [15], but the focus has largely been on the individual as the unit of analysis [16]. While personal technology adoption may be a near-binary state, organizational adoption is a complex process [16] and will naturally follow a more structured and tentative path. This path may be non-linear [17], as options are explored, barriers uncovered and priorities identified.

Two broad classifications of adoption theory exist: process based and factor based [18]. Numerous factor based theories have been proposed to aid in understanding the adoption of technologies, such as Technology Acceptance Model (TAM) [19], TAM2 [20], Unified Theory of Acceptance and Use of Technology (UTAUT) [21], Technology Organization and Environment (TOE) model [22] and Innovation Diffusion Theory (IDT) [16]. While there are numerous examples where these theories have been applied to studies of technology adoption (see [23] and [24] for OSS specific examples), there has been some criticism that this application has become formulaic, leading to a degree of stagnation [15]. Despite this criticism, there are few studies of OSS adoption [10–12], and this is an area where understanding remains limited [25].

While factor based theories allow the classification of drivers and barriers, as well as the ability to identify causality, they do not explain how the unit of analysis reached the observed level of adoption [18]. Such single-epoch methods have been criticized as too simplistic to capture the full complexity of adoption [26], leading to a loss of processual detail [27]. Of the above theories, only IDT, with its commensurate Innovation Decision Process (IDP) [16] fully acknowledges a process view of adoption.

Staged adoption models are one method by which an adoption process can be more richly documented. Figure 1 shows an existing staged adoption model used by Glynn et al. [28]. From this, it could be argued that an organization at any stage of this model, other than awareness or interest, could be said to be an adopter. Yet the commitment and maturity of the deployment for those in the evaluation/trial stage will differ greatly from those classified as a general deployment. Only if adoption studies classify their sample by stage can the level and commitment to that adoption be determined and stage specific barriers and drivers identified. A study that does not classify its sample risks missing stage significant factors due to heterogeneous sample composition and potentially limits comparability and generalizability.

Fig. 1. Levels of OSS adoption (redrawn from Glynn et al. [28])

Examples of the application staged adoption models to information technologies can be found dating back to the early days of mass-market computing (e.g. [29]). However, while existing studies of OSS have sought to examine drivers and barriers to OSS adoption (e.g. [23, 30, 31]), few have identified at what stage adoption is within a unit of analysis [32]. When staged adoption models are used in OSS studies, critique of the models is limited, even where shortcomings have already been identified in their native field [33]. This paucity of use and critique contrasts with practice in similar literature, such as the adoption of e-business systems. This field has benefited from numerous staged adoption models [34, 35], with this pedigree leading to critique and the development of more complex contingent [33] and latterly hybrid models [36].

2.2   A Critique of Existing OSS Classification Models

Table 1 illustrates staged models used in previous OSS adoption studies, aligned to the more generic IDP [16] and Fichman and Kemerer's models [37]. It can be seen that there is generally good agreement between these generic models, and those of Glynn et al. [28] and Fitzgerald [38] used in previous OSS studies. This similarity is perhaps not surprising, as these models have been adapted from the work of Fichman and Kemerer.

Looking at the differences, the models of Fichman and Kemerer, Glynn et al. and Fitzgerald show that the software lifecycle used by Shaikh and Cornford [39] is incomplete, with early stages relating to awareness and exploration of possible solutions omitted. Likewise, it can also be seen that the IDP lacks resolution at the implementation stage, where software is commonly deployed in several phases of 'roll out' [40].

The models of Kwan and West [41] and Miralles et al. [42] appear classificatory of an organization, rather than explanatory of the adoption process. Many stages appear to be absent compared to alternatives and as such these have been discounted as the basis for the new model and are presented only for completeness.

OSS adoption can fail [43, 44], a fact acknowledged in OSS specific models by Fitzgerald alone. None of the models used in existing OSS studies classify cessation of use, despite this being a feature of both the IDP and Fichman and Kemerer's model. This decomposition of cessation is important. Early rejection will leave little or no legacy data and an essentially unchanged business process. This contrasts with late-stage discontinuance, which will leave behind legacy data and the need to restore old systems, or seek new ones.

Despite some categorization, the IDP and Fichman and Kemerer's model are also incomplete with regard to cessation of use. Late stage discontinuance may arise as a natural evolution of the business as the process supported by the software is retired. In other cases, use of the existing software may be discontinued in favor of a new solution or upgraded to a newer version of the existing product. No model fully acknowledges these nuances and as such omits data that may be valuable to the researcher.

Many organizations are unaware of OSS, a factor cited as hindering adoption [45]. None of the models used in OSS studies have a stage acknowledging this, perhaps explained by their lineage. All have been adapted from generic technology adoption models, perhaps suggesting that such a stage was previously unnecessary due to

Table 1. Existing staged models used in OSS studies [28, 38, 39, 41, 42] aligned to the IDP [16] and Fichman and Kemerer's [37] models

Expanded Rogers' IDP	Fichman and Kemerer's Adoption Stage	Glynn et al.'s Adoption stage	Miralles et al.'s Adoption Groups	Kwan and West's Adoption Stage	Fitzgerald's Assimilation Stage	Shaikh and Cornford's Lifecycle stage	Explanation of stage
Knowledge	Awareness	Awareness	Non-adopters		Awareness/Interest		Organization is aware of innovation
Persuasion	Interest	Interest	Willing			Select	An attitude to innovation is formed by increased knowledge
Decision	Evaluation/ Trial	Evaluation/ Trial		Laboratory	Evaluation/Trial	Acquire	Engaging in activities that lead to selection
Implementation	Commitment	Commitment			Limited Deployment	Implement	Innovation put into use
	Limited Deployment	Limited Deployment	Specialized				
	General Deployment	General Deployment	High Users	Strategic Mission Critical Support	General Deployment:	Use	
Confirmation							Decision regarding innovation reviewed
Discontinuance	Discontinuance				Abandonment	Retire	Use of a previously adopted innovation ceases
Rejection	Rejection				Abandonment		An innovation is discounted as potentially adoptable
	Base from which many others are developed	No exit stages	Classifies only usage type, not adoption.	Classifies only usage type, not adoption.	Limited early stage resolution No exit classification	Limited early stage resolution No exit classification	**Comments on model**

widespread awareness of the technology in their native field. Another possible explanation is that they have been primarily used to classify existing adoption, and not map the whole adoption process *per-se*.

Many of the existing models imply a linear progression between stages, with Fichman and Kemerer being explicit about linearity in their work. However, this may not always be the case, something staged models from other disciplines [35] and the IDP do note. The path taken through the adoption process, and thus any representative staged model, may have an impact on success or the barriers encountered. For example, a deployment that omits a limited trial may encounter numerous deployment issues which could have been identified and avoided without omission of this stage. However, for certain smaller deployments, it is likely that stages may be safely omitted or combined [34] with a successful outcome maintained, or that experience of similar products allows valid short-cuts to be made [25].

This lack of focus on the adoption process has been previously highlighted as a weakness in OSS adoption studies [10] and is something that any new model should attempt to address.

3   Proposed Model

The review of literature has highlighted that existing staged adoption models are incomplete when applied to the field of OSS. The authors therefore propose a hybrid staged model [46] for classifying OSS adoption (Fig. 2) built upon the foundations of the IDP and Fichman and Kemerer's models to address the concerns highlighted in the previous section. While many of the stages of Fichman and Kemerer's model are adopted here, the commitment stage is not as the authors believe this represents a transition pathway, not a stage.

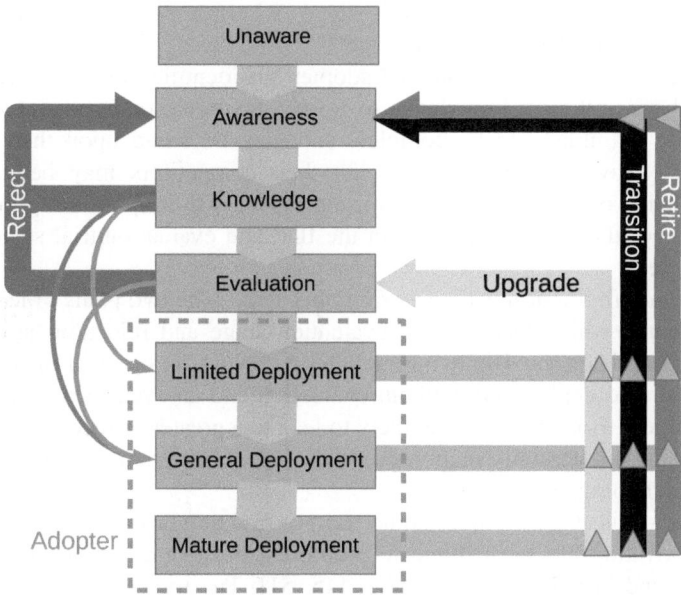

Fig. 2. Proposed OSS staged adoption model

The model has a general element of linearity, proceeding from the top, to the bottom, as indicated by the green arrows. A contingent approach was considered and rejected; the authors being unable to identify evidence to suggest OSS adoption is anything other than progressive. However, it is conceivable that some stages may be skipped [25, 34], with orange and red arrows showing pathways that allow stages to be omitted. The color coding indicates the expected increase in risk of failure based upon the deployment following that pathway, with green least risk, orange intermediate and red the highest.

Unlike the OSS specific model of Miralles et al. [42] and how Fichman and Kemerer used their model, the individual OSS package, not the organization, is used as the unit of analysis. This means an organization may occupy many stages at any one time if multiple deployments are proceeding in parallel [47].

3.1   Explanation of Stages

Unaware – this new stage indicates that the potential adopter is unaware that OSS is an option. This allows the model to fulfill the criteria defined by Morgan and Finnegan [45]. The only progression pathway is into the awareness stage as a potential user must become aware of OSS before they can progress with adoption.

Awareness – an adopter proceeds into this stage when they become aware that OSS is a potential solution to their real or perceived need. This is analogous to the knowledge stage of the IDP and the awareness stage of Fichman and Kemerer. There is only one progression pathway from this stage, where a potential solution can be explored to progress to the knowledge stage.

Knowledge – at this stage a potential adopter has identified one or more potential solutions and have sufficient knowledge to form a favorable or unfavorable opinion. This knowledge is unlikely to be complete and may be based upon their own perceptions (which may be biased) [48], what their competitors may be using [42], opinions of existing users within the organization [49], or those promoting the solution [50]. This matches the persuasion stage in the IDP and evaluation/trial stage of Fichman and Kemerer.

There are four progression pathways from this stage. The two paths of least risk are a positive outcome which leads to the evaluation stage and rejection based upon a perceived inappropriateness. The two remaining pathways, in order of increasing risk, are a jump to limited deployment without evaluation and an even riskier jump path to general deployment. Both of these are likely to lead to a greater chance of failure due to the software being a potentially inappropriate fit to the business needs or incompatible with existing technologies.

Evaluation – this stage involves some form of trial and/or evaluation. The ease of trialling an innovation has been found to promote a positive adoption outcome, both generally [16], and in OSS specific studies [45, 51]. The trial can range from installation on a single machine for formal or informal testing, to a more structured evaluation process. This is analogous to the IDP's decision stage and the evaluation/trial stage of Fichman and Kemerer. Even though the software may be being used to some extent by a member of the organization, this may not be an objective evaluation [17] and this use may only be fleeting.

Due to the limited investment of resource needed to achieve this stage rejection is still a relatively low risk option. Transition pathways from this stage include rejection, or progression to limited deployment if the evaluation proves successful. A jump path to general deployment is available, but this increases the risk of failure as many lessons about avoiding deployment issues can be learned via a limited deployment.

Limited Deployment – here a solution has been selected to carry out a business process in a limited way (e.g. the 'germ cell' deployment for the City of Munich [40]). This may be limited to one department, or a limited use throughout the organization. This is an ideal opportunity to identify deployment barriers and usage issues, while the limited scale renders them easier to mitigate or correct. This stage is identical to Fichman and Kemerer's stage of the same name and a sub-division of the IDP's deployment stage.

Transition pathways include a low risk progression path to general deployment if the limited deployment proves successful. At this stage, there is still limited commitment to the software, so exit pathways are still a relatively low risk option. Direct rejection is not a possibility as there will be a small amount of legacy data that needs to be dealt with and business processes will require amendment if use is ceased. The exit pathways are therefore retirement, upgrade or migration (which are discussed in detail later).

General Deployment – in this stage the solution is now deployed such that it impacts large numbers of users or widely impacts upon business critical processes. Despite being widespread, the deployment is still immature with problems being encountered and resolved, but these will relate to the larger scale of implementation. This matches Fichman and Kemerer's stage of the same name, and is a subdivision of the IDP's deployment stage.

Successful continued use will allow progression to mature deployment once all deployment issues have ceased. There will be an increasing amount of business data stored in the system, so exiting use is increasingly challenging, but still possible. The exit pathways are therefore retirement, upgrade and migration.

Mature Deployment – in this new stage, the solution has been in general deployment for some time and a great deal of resource has been invested over a lengthy period. It is considered 'the' way the business process is carried out by staff. Few issues will be discovered at this stage, as the organization has a legacy of support and deployment for the solution. There is likely to be a large amount of data stored in the system making direct abandonment at this stage too costly to consider. The only pathways from this stage are retirement, upgrade and migration.

3.2   Exit Pathways

As already discussed, models previously used in OSS studies do not classify the ceasing of software use [39]. In their model, Fichman and Kemerer offer some classification, but as categories [37] (it is not fully clear how these differ from a stage in their model). Here it is proposed that cessation is not thought of as a stage, but a pathway to another stage. This model proposes the following exit pathways:

Rejection (blue arrow) – where a yet to be implemented OSS solution is no longer deemed suitable during the evaluation or awareness stage it can be rejected. This is analogous to the descriptions used in the IDP and by Fichman and Kemerer. There is little cost to this pathway as it will leave no residual business data and there is no culture of acceptance within the organization to resist removal. The pathway will result in an exit to the awareness stage, as a new solution will need to be sought.

Discontinuing use after deployment is more complex and, as such, there are three pathways discussed in order of increasing risk of failure:

Retirement (black arrow) – software will be retired when the business process it supports is no longer utilized. The data from this software is therefore likewise redundant and may be archived in some form for record keeping purposes. No replacement software is needed, so the process enters the awareness stage as the organization is aware that OSS is a potential solution should a similar need arise in the future.

Upgrade (orange arrow) – if the business process is still relevant, the software may be upgraded to a newer, more functional version. This may be a trivial upgrade or a major new version, but in any event, the new version and the process needed to deploy it will need evaluating prior to widespread use. For this reason, this exit pathway terminates in the evaluation stage.

While there is some risk that the upgrade will fail, this is less likely than if an entirely new solution is implemented. Unless the upgrade involves a significant change in functionality or user interface, it is likely that this will cause minimal disruption to the organization and that there will be little chance of rejection.

Transition (red arrow) - a decision is taken to adopt a completely new solution. This is the highest risk option in terms of potential failure as the new solution may be incompatible with existing systems, practices and data. This pathway terminates at the awareness stage as the organization will be seeking a replacement but must already be aware of OSS to be on this pathway. Careful analysis during the awareness and evaluation phases will be needed to ensure it is well fitted to business processes and any legacy data. Data may need to be migrated to the new system; a time consuming, expensive and sometimes inexact process. Users are likely to require retraining and may oppose the transition, potentially leading to rejection or further transition.

4   Conclusion and Contribution

Hauge et al. [13] exhorted OSS researchers to focus upon topics relevant to organizations, with Aksulu and Wade [10] specifically highlighting the lack of understanding of the organizational adoption process. This paper has attempted tackle this gap by discussing the importance of a staged adoption process and has cited evidence to suggest models of such are poorly utilized in existing OSS adoption studies (objective 1). Without classification and awareness of adoption stages, adoption studies risk conflating dissimilar situations leading to inconsistent conclusions and limited generalizability.

While there have been several staged adoption models used is OSS studies, none have fully addressed all needs identified by previous literature and there has been little critique compared to related fields. This appears to be the first paper to evaluate existing staged adoption models used in OSS studies and propose a new OSS specific model to address apparent issues. Issues identified include: implications of linearity, missing stages, insufficient resolution at the implementation stage, a lack of detail regarding ceasing software use and a lack of focus on the adoption process (objective 2). A new model is proposed that builds on the theoretical foundation of Rogers' IDP [16] and the model of Fichman and Kemerer [37] to address these issues.

The proposed model appears to be the first to utilize a stage where the organization is unaware of OSS and to fully decompose discontinued use into four distinct pathways (rejection, upgrade, transition and retirement). In addition, three stages are used to indicate deployment based upon the maturity and spread of the software, with the aim of increasing classificatory resolution of deployment scale and the degree of acceptance. This contrasts with the one stage used by the IDP and two offered by Fichman and Kemerer. The model makes use of defined transition pathways, classified according to risk. These have the additional benefit of allowing the model to be used to track the adoption process as well as classify its current state. Both linear and non-linear paths can be followed through the model and allow adoption to be tracked on a pathway basis to allow successful and failed adoption to be potentially linked to omitted or truncated stages (objectives 3 and 4).

5 Future Work

The proposed model is a theoretical construct based upon issues identified from the literature. Future work will involve:

- Testing the model to validate stage descriptions and transition pathways. Data will be gathered from field studies to verify the presence of each stage and confirm entry and exit pathways, and criteria.
- Applying the proposed model to classify data from existing studies to potentially resolve inconsistencies related to heterogeneous sample composition. This may allow the resolution of issues where apparently similar studies have led to inconsistent results.
- An analysis of adoption paths through the model for different categories of software (e.g. infrastructure, end user software etc.) in a variety of environments (e.g. differing organizational size, sector etc.) to explore success strategies and pathways that commonly lead to failure.

References

1. Raymond, E.S.: The cathedral and the bazaar. First Monday **3** (1998)
2. Black Duck Software: The Ninth Annual Future of Open Source Survey. https://www.blackducksoftware.com/future-of-open-source
3. Gartner: User Survey Analysis: Open-Source Software, Worldwide. Gartner, Stamford (2008)
4. Top500.org: List Statistics | TOP500 Supercomputer Sites. http://www.top500.org/statistics/list/
5. Levesque, M.: Fundamental issues with open source software development. First Monday **10** (2004)
6. Raza, A., Capretz, L.F., Ahmed, F.: Users' perception of open source usability: an empirical study. Eng. Comput. **28**, 109–121 (2012)
7. Choi, N., Chengalur-Smith, I.: An exploratory study on the two new trends in open source software: end-users and service. In: Sprague Jr., R.H. (ed.) 42nd Hawaii International Conference on System Sciences. HICSS 2009, pp. 1–10. IEEE (2009)
8. Dafermos, G., van Eeten, M.J.G.: Images of innovation in discourses of free and open source software. First Monday **19** (2014)
9. Grand, S., von Krogh, G., Leonard, D., Swap, W.: Resource allocation beyond firm boundaries. Long Range Plann. **37**, 591–610 (2004)
10. Aksulu, A., Wade, M.: A comprehensive review and synthesis of open source research. J. Assoc. Inf. Syst. **11**, 576–656 (2010)
11. Mount, M.P., Fernandes, K.: Adoption of free and open source software within high-velocity firms. Behav. Inf. Technol. **32**, 231–246 (2013)
12. Ramanathan, L., Krishnan, S.: An empirical investigation into the adoption of open source software in information technology outsourcing organizations. J. Syst. Inf. Technol. **17**, 167–192 (2015)
13. Hauge, Ø., Ayala, C., Conradi, R.: Adoption of open source software in software-intensive organizations – a systematic literature review. Inf. Softw. Technol. **52**, 1133–1154 (2010)

14. OED Online: adoption, n., http://www.oed.com
15. Venkatesh, V., Davis, F., Morris, M.G.: Dead or alive? the development, trajectory and future of technology adoption research. J. Assoc. Inf. Syst. **8**, 268–286 (2007)
16. Rogers, E.M.: Diffusion of Innovations. Free Press, New York (2003)
17. Howcroft, D., Light, B.: The social shaping of packaged software selection. J. Assoc. Inf. Syst. **11**, 123–148 (2010)
18. Newman, M., Robey, D.: A social process model of user-analyst relationships. MIS Q. **16**, 249–266 (1992)
19. Davis, F.D.: A technology acceptance model for empirically testing new end-user information systems: theory and results (1986)
20. Venkatesh, V., Davis, F.D.: A theoretical extension of the technology acceptance model: four longitudinal field studies. Manag. Sci. **46**, 186–204 (2000)
21. Venkatesh, V., Morris, M.G., Davis, G.B., Davis, F.D.: User acceptance of information technology: toward a unified view. MIS Q. **27**, 425–478 (2003)
22. Tornatzky, L.G.: The Processes of Technological Innovation. Lexington Books, Lexington (1990)
23. Ellis, J., Van Belle, J.-P.: Open source software adoption by South African MSEs: barriers and enablers. In: Proceedings of the 2009 Annual Conference of the Southern African Computer Lecturers' Association, pp. 41–49. ACM, New York (2009)
24. Gurusamy, K., Campbell, J.: A case study of open source software adoption in Australian Public Sector organisations. In: Proceedings of the Pacific Asia Conference on Information Systems (PACIS) 2011. Queensland University of Technology, Brisbane (2011)
25. Poba-Nzaou, P., Raymond, L., Fabi, B.: Risk of adopting mission-critical OSS applications: an interpretive case study. Int. J. Oper. Prod. Manag. **34**, 477–512 (2014)
26. Kurnia, S., Johnston, R.B.: The need for a processual view of inter-organizational systems adoption. J. Strateg. Inf. Syst. **9**, 295–319 (2000)
27. Benbasat, I., Barki, H.: Quo vadis Tam? J. Assoc. Inf. Syst. **8**, 212–218 (2007)
28. Glynn, E., Fitzgerald, B., Exton, C.: Commercial adoption of open source software: an empirical study. In: International Symposium on Empirical Software Engineering, 2005, pp. 225–234. IEEE, Los Alamitos (2005)
29. Nolan, R.L.: Managing the computer resource: a stage hypothesis. Commun. ACM **16**, 399–405 (1973)
30. Nagy, D.: Understanding Organizational Adoption Theories Through the Adoption of a Disruptive Innovation: Five Cases of Open Source Software (2010)
31. Kuechler, V., Jensen, C., Bryant, D.: Misconceptions and barriers to adoption of FOSS in the US energy industry. In: Petrinja, E., Succi, G., El Ioini, N., Sillitti, A. (eds.) Open Source Software: Quality Verification, pp. 232–244. Springer, Berlin (2013)
32. Nelson, M., Sen, R., Subramaniam, C.: Understanding open source software: a research classification framework. Commun. Assoc. Inf. Syst. **17**, 266–287 (2006)
33. Levy, M., Powell, P.: Exploring SME internet adoption: towards a contingent model. Electron. Mark. **13**, 173–181 (2003)
34. Lefebvre, L.-A., Lefebvre, É., Elia, E., Boeck, H.: Exploring B-to-B e-commerce adoption trajectories in manufacturing SMEs. Technovation **25**, 1443–1456 (2005)
35. Subba Rao, S., Metts, G., Mora Monge, A.: Electronic commerce development in small and medium sized enterprises a stage model and its implications. Bus. Process Manag. J. **9**, 11–32 (2003)
36. Elia, E., Lefebvre, L.-A., Lefebvre, É.: Focus of B-to-B e-commerce initiatives and related benefits in manufacturing small and medium-sized enterprises. Inf. Syst. E-Bus. Manag. **5**, 1–23 (2006)

37. Fichman, R.G., Kemerer, C.F.: The assimilation of software process innovations: an organizational learning perspective. Manag. Sci. **43**, 1345–1363 (1997)
38. Fitzgerald, B.: Open source software adoption: anatomy of success and failure. In: Koch, S. (ed.) Multi-Disciplinary Advancement in Open Source Software and Processes, pp. 1–23. IGI Global, Hershey (2011)
39. Shaikh, M., Cornford, T.: Total Cost of Ownership of Open Source Software: A Report for the UK Cabinet Office Supported by Openforum Europe. UK Cabinet Office, London (2011)
40. Silic, M., Back, A.: Technological risks of open source software adoption in the organizational context – linux in Munich (LiMux) case. In: SSRN (2015)
41. Kwan, S.K., West, J.: A conceptual model for enterprise adoption of open source software. In: Bolin, S. (ed.) The Standards Edge: Open Season, pp. 51–62. Sheridan Books, Ann Arbor (2005)
42. Miralles, F., Sieber, S., Valor, J.: CIO herds and user gangs in the adoption of open source software. In: ECIS 2005 Proceedings (2005)
43. Goode, S.: Something for nothing: management rejection of open source software in Australia's top firms. Inf. Manage. **42**, 669–681 (2005)
44. Huysmans, P., Ven, K., Verelst, J.: Reasons for the non-adoption of Openoffice.org in a data-intensive public administration. First Monday **13** (2008)
45. Morgan, L., Finnegan, P.: How perceptions of open source software influence adoption: an exploratory study. In: Osterle, H., Schelp, J., Winter, R. (eds.) Proceedings of the Fifteenth European Conference on Information Systems (ECIS 2007), pp. 973–984. University of St. Gallen, St. Gallen (2007)
46. Panayiotou, N.A., Katimertzoglou, P.K.: Micro firms internet adoption patterns: the case of the Greek jewellery industry. J. Enterp. Inf. Manag. **28**, 508–530 (2015)
47. Saini, S.K., Krishnan, C.N., Rajaram, L.N.: open source adoption index: quantifying FOSS adoption by an organisation. Int. J. Open Source Softw. Process. **2**, 48–60 (2010)
48. Wilkinson, J.: Vendor rating and the evaluation of risk in new software: a view from outside. Logist. Inf. Manag. **8**, 10–12 (1995)
49. Ven, K., Verelst, J.: The organizational adoption of open source server software: a quantitative study. In: ECIS (2008)
50. Howcroft, D., Light, B.: IT consultants, salesmanship and the challenges of packaged software selection in SMEs. J. Enterp. Inf. Manag. **21**, 597–615 (2008)
51. West, J., Dedrick, J.: Scope and timing of deployment moderators of organizational adoption of the linux server platform. Int. J. IT Stand. Stand. Res. IJITSR **4**, 1–23 (2006)

In-between Open and Closed - Drawing the Fine Line in Hybrid Communities

Hanna Mäenpää[1](✉), Terhi Kilamo[2], and Tomi Männistö[1]

[1] Department of Computer Science, University of Helsinki, P.O. 68,
Gustaf Hällströmin katu 2b, 00014 University of Helsinki, Finland
{hanna.maenpaa,tomi.mannisto}@helsinki.fi
[2] Department of Pervasive Computing, Tampere University of Technology,
Korkeakoulunkatu 1, 33720 Tampere, Finland
terhi.kilamo@tut.fi

Abstract. Today, the community driven development model extends into a variety of new, often web based collaborations. Among these are hybrid open source development set ups in which various online tools are used to facilitate cooperation between virtual teams of commercial and voluntary stakeholders. As yet, how these relationships form and evolve is not understood extensively. This article presents a longitudinal case study of a smartphone startup that founded its early product development strategy on reliance on feedback from its customers through a web based question and answer forum. With this, the company managed to extend values typical for open source communities to support development of its proprietary software. Our main findings include that the challenge in similar settings lies in striking the right balance between the open and the proprietary – while overt openness may risk the competitive advantage of a company, leaving too much behind closed boundaries can create unnecessary friction in the relationship.

Keywords: Crowdsourcing · Customer community · Open source software

1 Introduction

The open innovation approach allows profit-oriented companies to outsource tasks that are essential for their production process to the general public, yielding results for significantly less expense than companies would otherwise be willing to invest [1–3]. A desired audience for these collaborations are lead users who pioneer in identifying needs for technical solutions and are willing to bear some of the costs and risks of fulfilling them [4]. Therefore, collaborating with Open Source Software (OSS) communities and adopting their ways of working have been identified as promising growth strategies for software companies [5]. These opportunities are especially highlighted at both early stages of product development [6] and when introducing new innovations to the marketplace [1,7,8].

Understanding how these relationships in between companies and their 'unpaid employees' [1] can form and be managed has not yet received much attention from the scientific community. Future research is called for to understand reasons for entering these relationships [5], as well as on principles, processes [9] and forms of control [10] that take place in their governance.

The main contribution of our paper is to report how proprietary software development can be supported by an open innovation community for customers, describing how knowledge can act as both a reward and a detriment for motivation in this setting. In the next section, a theoretical background is laid for understanding the context of our study. Section 3 introduces the research approach. A description of the case company is provided in Sect. 4, followed by results of the study in Sect. 5. The work is concluded by discussing implications in Sects. 6 and 7.

2   Background

Open Source Software communities consist of individuals, many of whom participate voluntarily and out of their own inherent interests in the development activities. Here, decision power is distributed among people who belong to the same community and individuals are empowered to make decisions based on their personal merit [9,11,12]. When commercial stakeholders enter this environment, their interests become blended with those of the voluntary contributors, creating a hybrid environment where a balance needs to be struck between the community based decision making and centralized governance that is typical for companies [11,13,14].

In these collaborations, the commercial stakeholder must often be prepared to align its own strategy to fit that of the existing community – or to establish a new one [8]. In the latter case, the amount of power vested in external collaborators can manifest in initial decisions about who gets to participate in the activities, how responsibilities are shared [15] and how rights to contribute to decisions are gained [9]. An apt division of knowledge, labor and decision power is needed to build trust and reciprocity between the stakeholders [10,11,16]. This balance can be achieved through conscious decisions on how the community is built and governed and what socio-technical infrastructure it is to be supported by [17].

When voluntary, non-affiliated individuals affect product development remarkably, an unclear legal relationship between a company and its contributors may emerge [18]. This can be managed by keeping the intellectual property rights of selected software assets in the company, creating a "gate" for the voluntary contributors [17]. This limits their possibilities to not only modify and re-use the software, but also to know about and have influence on its development decisions [17]. As the values of community driven development ideology become compromised, the motivation of contributors decrease as they feel their opinions are not being heard [9,19]. In this context, encouraging a global voice of the customers on open platforms may prove harmful as users willingly share their bad experiences in public. Therefore it is important to have a strategy for curating the community created content and for evaluating users by their trustworthiness. Equally important to identifying malicious users is rewarding users that are influential and produce interactions that are of a high quality [20]. A visible commitment from top management is often required [5,16].

Research is called for to understand the reasons why companies choose to use OSS collaborations as the core of their value creation processes (Henttonen et al. 2012), what principles and processes constitute community management in this environment (O'Mahony 2007) and how these managerial practices can evolve on a longitudinal perspective (Di Tullio et al. 2013).

3   Research Approach and Questions

We employed a mixed method case study [21,22] on a longitudinal perspective from December 2013 to November 2015, focusing on how a company created and managed an online customer community[1]. Our aim was to answer the following research questions:

RQ1: How can an open community aid the development of proprietary software?

RQ2: How can a company **initiate an open community** for collaboration in software development?

RQ3: How can a company **manage the collaboration** with its open community?

As the phenomenon in focus is inseparable from its context, a combination of different viewpoints, data sources and research methods were used to create a realistic representation [22]. These are overviewed in the following subsections.

3.1   Viewpoint of the Company

Our research started by characterizing the company and forming a general understanding of its crowdsourcing strategy. For this, freely available documents such as press releases, blog posts and social media interactions of managers were observed manually. This was continued until the end of the research period.

In January 2014, we selected two of the company's employees based on their active role in the customer community and performed an in person, semi structured interview to understand their conscious aims in building the community. Questions included: "What is your role in your company's internal software development process? How do you use the knowledge from the online community in your work?". Follow-up interviews were performed in June 2014 later in April 2015 to review how the community created knowledge was currently influencing software development decisions, how the managerial practices had evolved and what concrete new forms the collaboration had taken throughout the months.

---

[1] http://together.jolla.com.

3.2 Viewpoint of Customers

From early on, we recognized the need for including the customers' viewpoint in the study. To prepare for this, a semi structured telephone interview was performed with a voluntary community moderator (CM) in June 2014, seeking answers to questions such as: "What have been the success factors and pitfalls of building the community? Why do people choose to work for the benefit of the company without rewards? How do you see the role of the online platform in this collaboration?" Results highlighted the need for understanding motivation of individual community members and prepared us for choosing a theoretical alignment for addressing it [12]. We composed a survey with 12 Likert scale questions of motivational factors and two open ended questions about other reasons for participating. The survey was instrumented to the online community website on June 25th 2014, yielding 192 responses through the three week survey period. This study was repeated in November 2015 to review whether the motivation of the members had changed along time. The latter survey received 101 responses.

3.3 Actions of the Stakeholders

In addition to self reporting by individuals, we wanted an objective representation of actions the community members had performed during the research period. For this aim, the community created content was first sampled in February 2014 with the help of a web crawler[2]. A quantitative overview of meta keywords attached to the messages by community members was formed to distinguish the most common discussion topics. 25 examples of discussions were chosen and qualitative analysis of their textual content was performed to model their interaction sequences, two of which are illustrated in Fig. 2. In addition to the community created content, we harvested all freely available user profile records to review the growth of the registered user base.

An identical data set was yielded later in November 2015 using a Software as a-Service tool tool[3] and a retrospective of the community's development and concrete actions its members had engaged in could be formed. The number of items in each data sample are presented in Table 1. Due to the space limitation, we are able to present only a summary of this work.

Table 1. Data items in the customer community content data samples

Sample	February 2014	November 2015
Number of messages	2 473	13 332
Keywords in the content	1 151	10 577
User profile records	2 716	8 449

---

[2] Scrapy Python script.
[3] Cloudscrape.

4   Case: Jolla Together

The case company, Jolla, was established in 2011. Their first product, a smartphone, was launched by a crowdfunding campaign in May 2013 and delivered to pre-order customers in 136 countries in December 2013 [23]. The devices were equipped with Sailfish, an operating system (OS) founded on open source components such the Linux kernel[4], Mer OS middleware[5] and application layer framework Qt[6]. The company's collaboration strategies with the external OSS communities were various: work of the Linux community set the foundation of their product. They sought benefit from and contributed to the work of the Mer and Qt communities. For application development, Jolla chose to host an application store platform - trusting that an ecosystem of independent application developers would emerge among their first customers.

Jolla's largest contribution to Sailfish OS were libraries that defined fundamentals of user experience, including hand gestures, user interface themes and basic applications for calling, messaging and managing contacts. For them, a proprietary licensing strategy was chosen, securing the company's competitive advantage of building an user experience "unlike" those of its competitors. Figure 1 presents the Sailfish OS software architecture, related licensing models and the collaboration strategies.

Sailfish OS was introduced as a minimally viable prototype to the customers and the smartphone was to be used as a toolkit for lead user innovation in early product development. For harvesting feedback, an online forum, together.jolla.com, was opened. Later in the text, we call this forum *the online (customer) community* or *Together* for short. Users of the forum we refer to as *online community members* or *customers*. The following sections present our findings on how this relationship was initiated and what practices were used in guiding the customer community to support the company's internal proprietary software development process. Implications for similar settings are discussed later in Sect. 6.

5   Results

While Sects. 5.1 and 5.2 address RQ2. Sections 5.3 and 5.4 seek to provide answers for RQ3. Based on these, RQ1 is later discussed in Sect. 6.

5.1   Initiating the Customer Community

Jolla used minimal marketing efforts in initiating the customer community: new smartphone owners had received an invitation in their delivery box and management had sent Twitter messages [24] welcoming people to join. The online community platform[7] allowed asking questions, answering and commenting on them,

---

[4] https://www.kernel.org/.
[5] http://merproject.org.
[6] http://qt.io.
[7] http://www.askbot.com.

attaching keywords and voting publicly on any piece of the content created. *"The first evening we had hundreds of people logged in and contributing"*, explained the quality manager in January 2014. Jolla's value proposition was "We want to create an innovation platform for ideas, opportunities and openness." To highlight this, customers were engaged with aspects that were not commonly discussed in public such as packaging and manuals[8], brand values[9], delivery strategies[10] and future visions of the hardware[11]. Ideas were vividly shared, refined and ranked by voting. Section (A) of Fig. 2 displays a typical idea harvesting interaction pattern. As the Askbot platform supported gathering personal "karma" community members were allowed to self-organize: moderators were elected via a process of self-representation and voting and best practices for content organization were agreed upon. In addition to the moderator status, employees of the company were marked with a logo alongside their member profile. Jolla's software quality manager (QM) established a visible and interactive role among the community members. *"He did great work in focusing the discussion and solving conflicts constructively. [sic] He wanted to have both customers and employees have an equal voice in both asking and answering questions"*, a community moderator explained in April 2014.

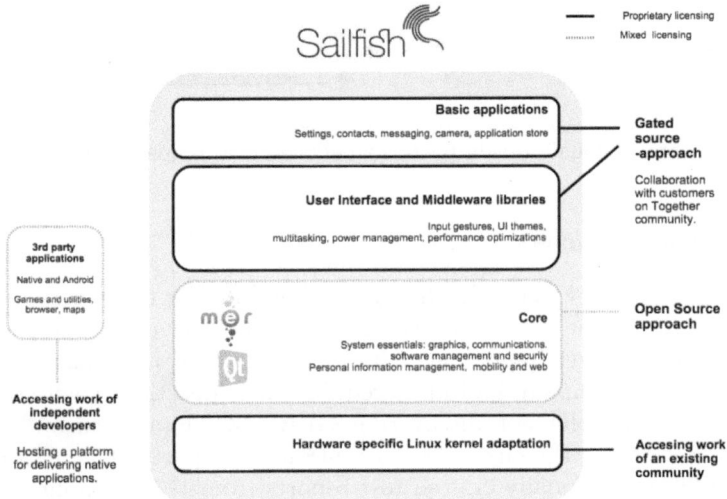

Fig. 1. Licensing architecture of Sailfish OS and the company's strategies for collaborating with external communities. Adapted from https://sailfishos.org/about/

---

[8] "What's missing from the user guide?".
[9] "What does Jolla mean to you?".
[10] "What hardware/devices would you like to see Sailfish OS on?".
[11] "Poll: The Other Half of Your Dreams".

(A) Harvesting ideas from customers

(B) Reporting and pre-processing a defect

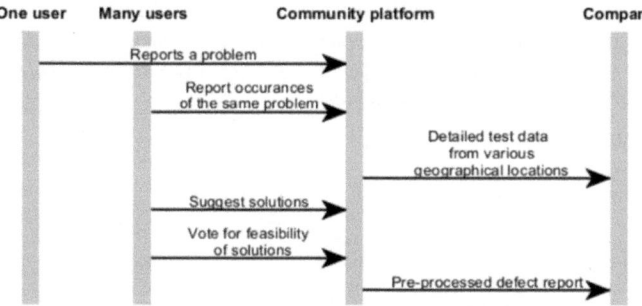

Fig. 2. Typical collaboration patterns between the company and customers

5.2 Creating a Focus

The online community acted as the first touchpoint for customers and defects quickly emerged as the most discussed topic. A majority of questions concerned elementary interactions: importing contacts, typing text, using email and browsing the web. The company had prepared for this - questions such as "Did you have trouble with Jolla not discovering GPRS/3G data settings?" had been submitted to wait for the customers' attention. This particular question briefly resulted in 29 professionally crafted test reports from 17 geographical locations around the world.

Most defects were submitted by the customers themselves and were followed by comments with rich detail of the testing process. As a defect had been described satisfyingly, community members created hypotheses about its origins and presented suggestions for solving it. Voting complemented these interactions by providing indicators on the urgency of the problem, feasibility of the solutions and quality of related comments. Figure 2(B) presents a common defect reporting interaction. After six months, feedback from the customer community had become the main source of knowledge for the company's software product development decisions.

5.3   Sustaining Motivation of Contributors

As already in February 2014 the company's integration and release mechanism allowed a stable software update to be delivered monthly, discussing a bug and then seeing it fixed was gratifying for all involved. Members had become aware of the value of their contributions, demanded more say on prioritization[12] and information about the progress of the development[13]. *"Customers are demanding in this regard. Sometimes we give a time window for releases but it is not enough. When the window is starting to get smaller, users ask: Hey Where is the update, What's happening? I want it now!"* QM explained. Here, the software program manager (PM) came to be in a key role to control visibility to the progress. Status codes began to be marked by modifying headlines of the original defect report messages (Fig. 3).

As pointed out by the forum moderator, the Askbot platform "had not served its purpose well". Rapid pace of interactions encumbered organization of the content and voting based community evaluation emphasized opinions of the most active and loudest members. *"Even if crucial, a feature that is important to a niche user segment does not reach enough attention to be noticed by the company"* he explained. At the same time, the extensive input from the customer community seemed to be overwhelming for the company. *"In some cases it might not be feasible to implement even those (features) that the great majority advocates for"* the quality manager explained. However cumbersome managing the in- and outflow of knowledge was, the company still ruled out giving visibility to their internal bug reporting and workflow coordination tools.

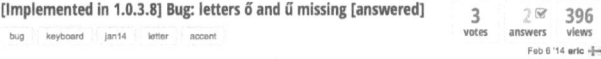

Fig. 3. Notification of progress in a message headline on together.jolla.com

For the proprietary licensing of the user experience components, community members perceived the subject of their contributions as a black box. While no external rewards or guarantees on uptake of their innovations were made by the company, the motivation of the participants became of interest. Our first survey was performed in June 2014 for 193 customer community members. Results revealed that a total of 89 % were owners of the Jolla smartphone and 32 % indicated an affiliation with OSS development. A prime motivator was to make a better product for themselves (92 % agreed) and to receive (90 %) and to give (77 %) help in using the smartphone. While creating new ideas inspired the customers (77 %), a majority of the respondents wanted to help the company directly to succeed (90 %).

---

[12] "Jolla should target business users".
[13] Which features do you crave and would like to know its roadmap status on?.

The second survey of 101 persons in November 2015 confirmed that the motivational factors had not changed in almost two years. The most active online community members had remained smartphone owners (83 %) and the proportion of open source developers in the population was roughly one third. Contributors were still inspired by the product, the company's way of working and altruism. A noteworthy change was that neither recognition among peers (8 % positive, 26 % negative) nor showcasing expertise to the company (7 % positive, 26 % negative) were dominant among the community members. Willingness to help the company to succeed had decreased only somewhat (Strongly agree -19 %, agree somewhat -12 %). Still, as the company faced the need for steamlining its operations in November 2015, the loyalty of the customers manifested as initiatives for crowdfunding campaigns[14] to help the company.

When asked about the members' "other" and "ideological" reasons for participating, a clear majority reported being motivated by characteristics of the OSS ideology: freedom, openness and empowerment of individuals to control their own information and assets. As one respondent summarized: *"I love the idea to exit from iOS, Windows and especially Android world: with Sailfish we're talking about real open source, freedom and the close contact between us users and the Company giving us the possibility to do something new, unlike and interesting."*.

5.4   Evolution of Practices

As the number of Sailfish OS devices grew, pre-release testing had gained emphasis and the company strengthened its internal process with a small, closed group of community members who were given release candidates *before* they were delivered to the customers. *"This helps us to confirm the quality of our releases before they are released to the rest of our customers."* explained the software program

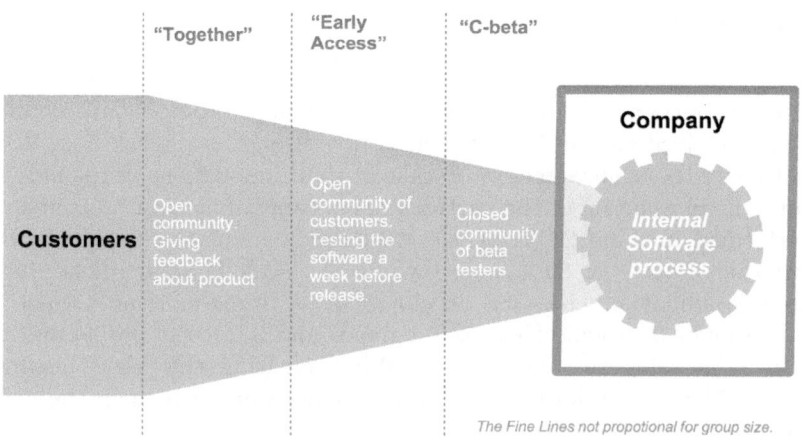

Fig. 4. Roles of customers in supporting the company's internal software process

---

[14] https://together.jolla.com/question/122312/emergency-crowdfunding/.

manager in March 2015. Later, the company had started an "early access" test community by providing any Sailfish OS user with an unreleased version of the OS after the C-Beta group had sufficiently tested it. *"If no critical issues are found from in field, we release the update to the rest our end users."* After the improvements, feedback from the web based question and answer forum started to have less impact on the company's short term planning compared to its early stages. *"Decisions mostly rely on technical know-how and debts in software to stir the development in the right direction"* explained the software program manager in March 2015, continuing: *"Feedback and reports from Together still guide us to identify the most painful issues for our end users."* Fig. 4 displays the relationship of the described sub communities to the whole customer population.

6   Discussion

First, limitations of the study are described. Sections 6.2 and 6.3 provide answers to research questions RQ2 and RQ3, laying the foundation of understanding how the open community model can aid the development of proprietary software (RQ1) in similar settings. This question is discussed in Sect. 6.4 with implications.

6.1   Limitations

Several factors of both the phenomenon and our study design limit generalisation of the results. Our surveys, in spite of the high number of participants, represent at best only a fraction of the Together community's active members who on their part represent a limited subset of Jolla's customers (see Fig. 4). Our sampling strategy is thus inclined to present characteristics of not a random set but a purposefully selected sample [22] of those customers who are the most actively involved in the community. We claim that these people have been some of the most influential in the relationship and argue that the set represents that of early adopters (i.e. lead users) of the Sailfish OS technology. The history of the company as a continuum of Nokia's work may partly explain the community's loyalty and proneness to support values of OSS development. Therefore, the results can not be generalized to any product development context as is. However, we claim the results to be directional to situations where both the product in question relies on OSS software and at the same time a large personal investment on a hardware product has already been made.

6.2   Initiating the Collaboration

Offering the smartphone as a pre-order campaign helped the company to test the viability of the product concept and size of its market. Customers made an initial financial commitment to the company and were set to expect an unpolished product. This, combined with an invitation to help build the product together with the company and low barrier of communication with employees created a promising start for the collaboration.

The OSS related history of the product resonated strongly with a small, yet very active group of lead users. However, using an independent, web based community platform that anybody could easily register to invited non-technical users to participate in the collaboration. While the platform supported merit based self-representation and autonomous decision making, users were given tools to organize and manage their own contributions. Even though the customer community was open for anybody to join, a between-the-lines prerequisite was the customership: discussions dealt almost solely with either using or not being able to use the product. This created an aim for contributors: to solve problems and help others in doing so. Personal achievement and helping others were altruistically celebrated. As the community managed its own contributions the company was relieved from curating the content. Voicing constructive criticism was allowed, increasing the quality of contributions while multiple viewpoints could be represented. Benefits for the crowdsourcing practise were indisputable. As at that time the company operated in only two cities in Finland, the extent of the testing activities could not have been achieved without the help of its customers.

6.3   Managing the Collaboration

The company had chosen a gated source approach for the UX components of Sailfish OS, yet its strategy was to acquire feedback for developing them from customers from the customer community. This allowed hiding specifics of the software process from external contributors. Surprisingly, for the first years, no visible incentives were required to sustain the collaboration.

A large reward for contributors was the frequent and timely delivery of OS upgrades and thus, knowing when and what was to be shipped acted as a powerful incentive. While the company promised its customers openness and transparency, the "gate" created pressures for disclosing information. Maneuvering the situation required careful consideration on what, where, and to whom knowledge should be let out. Neither decision power, full transparency of the development process were ever offered as incentives - the company chose to offer more information about its internal development process through personal interactions with only those customers who were willing to contribute more to their development process.

6.4   Applying the Community Driven Model in Similar Settings

Our main research question (RQ1) calls for understanding how an open community of contributors can support development of proprietary software. We described a specialized setting where a company founded its product on open source collaborations, searched a crowd for funding its development and harnessed the first customers for contributions that helped the company take its first steps for the first two years of its existence.

From this, we learned that in order to gain benefit for the proprietary development, the values of the company have to match those of the community. A sincere relationship between the stakeholders needs to be created and more interactive this relationship is, the richer results are to be expected. However, all interactions require time and effort from the company and to balance this, a sufficient degree of autonomy for the community in managing its own actions and contributions is required. From the online tools this requires support for merit-based self-representation, consensus decision making and general enough functionality that allows diverse types of interactions to emerge.

As a community matures, value of its work becomes established. Therefore, the need and means for rewarding voluntary contributors should be reconsidered from time to time. While several motivations are at play, reciprocity in the community membership experience is important, as well as sustaining the focus of the community's work on its original purpose. In our case, weaving all this together required the hosting company to have a strict policy of what knowledge to disclose, what issues to take a stand on and what not.

7   Conclusions

The interplay of community driven values and commercial interests flourish in hybrid OSS communities. To explore this phenomenon, we used interviews and surveys supported with publicly available data to follow the inception and management of an open, online customer community. Our main findings include that the challenge in similar settings lies in striking the right balance between the open and the proprietary – while overt openness may risk the competitive advantage of a company, leaving too much behind closed boundaries can create unnecessary friction in the relationship. Where the fine lines are drawn depends on how much knowledge, decision power and autonomy are vested in the community.

Acknowledgments. The authors wish to thank Digile's Need4Speed program (http://www.n4s.fi/) funded by the Finnish Funding Agency for Innovation (Tekes (http://www.tekes.fi/en/tekes/)) for its support for this research. We are also grateful to Sezin Yaman, Max Pagels, Sini Ruohomaa, Soumya Billal and Eric Le Roux.

References

1. Kleemann, F., Vo, G., Rieder, K.: Un(der)paid innovators: the commercial utilization of consumer work through crowdsourcing. Sci. Technol. Innov. Stud. 4(1), 5–26 (2008)
2. Pénin, J., Burger-Helmchen, T.: Crowdsourcing of inventive activities: definition and limits. Int. J. Innov. Sustain. Dev. 5(2–3), 246–263 (2011)
3. Estellés-Arolas, E., González-Ladrón-de, F.: Guevara: towards an integrated crowdsourcing definition. J. Inf. Sci. 38(2), 189–200 (2012)
4. von Hippel, E.: Lead users: a source of novel product concepts. Manage. Sci. 32(7), 791–805 (1986)

5. Henttonen, K., Pussinen, P., Koivumäki, T.: Managerial perspective on open source collaboration and networked innovation. J. Technol. Manage. Innov. **7**(3), 135–147 (2012)

6. Kim, J., Wilemon, D.: Focusing the fuzzy frontend in new product development. R&D Manage. **32**(4), 269–279 (2002)

7. Duarte, V., Sarkar, S.: Separating the wheat from the chaff: a taxonomy of open innovation. Eur. J. Innov. Manage. **14**(4), 435–459 (2011)

8. Schenk, E., Guittard, C.: Towards a characterization of crowdsourcing practices. J. Innov. Econ. **7**(1), 93–107 (2011)

9. O'Mahony, S.: The governance of open source initiatives: what does it mean to be community managed? Engl. J. Manage. Gov. **11**(2), 139–150 (2007)

10. Di Tullio, D., Staples, D.S.: The governance and control of open source software projects. J. Manage. Inf. Syst. **30**(3), 49–80 (2013)

11. Sharma, S., Sugumaran, V., Rajagopalan, B.: A framework for creating hybrid-open source software communities. Inf. Syst. J. **12**(1), 7–25 (2002)

12. Antikainen, M., Mäkipää, M., Ahonen, M.: Motivating and supporting collaboration in open innovation. Eur. J. Innov. Manage. **13**(1), 100–119 (2010)

13. Benkler, Y.: Coase's penguin, or linux and the nature of the firm. Yale Law J. **112**, 369–446 (2002)

14. Fitzgerald, B.: The transformation of open source software. MIS Q. **30**, 587–598 (2006)

15. Midha, V., Bhattacherjee, A.: Governance practices and software maintenance: a study of open source projects. Decis. Support Syst. **54**(1), 23–32 (2012)

16. Dahlander, L., Magnusson, M.: How do firms make use of open source communities? Long Range Plann. **41**(6), 629–649 (2008)

17. Shah, S.K.: Motivation, governance, and the viability of hybrid forms in open source software development. Manage. Sci. **52**(7), 1000–1014 (2006)

18. Wolfson, S.M., Lease, M.: Look before you leap: legal pitfalls of crowdsourcing. Proc. Am. Soc. Inf. Sci. Technol. **48**(1), 1–10 (2011)

19. Shah, S.K.: Understanding the nature of participation and coordination in open and gated source software development communities. In: Proceedings of the Academy of Management, vol. 2004, no. 1. Academy of Management, pp. B1–B5 (2004)

20. Doan, A., Ramakrishnan, R., Halevy, A.Y.: Crowdsourcing systems on the world-wide web. Commun. ACM **54**(4), 86–96 (2011)

21. Runeson, P., Höst, M.: Guidelines for conducting and reporting case study research in software engineering. Empirical Softw. Eng. **14**(2), 131–164 (2009)

22. Yin, R.K.: Case Study Research: Design and Methods. Sage publications, Thousand Oaks (2013)

23. Press release of the first smartphone pre-order campaign's progress, August 2013. https://cdn.jolla.com/wp-content/uploads/bsk-pdf-manager/5_JOLLA_PRESS_RELEASE_21.8.2013.PDF

24. Welcome message from the company to join the together.jolla.com online customer community, December 2013. https://twitter.com/JollaHQ/status/415868959519698944

Herding Cats: A Case Study of Release Management in an Open Collaboration Ecosystem

Germán Poo-Caamaño[1]([✉]), Leif Singer[1], Eric Knauss[2],
and Daniel M. German[1]

[1] University of Victoria, Victoria, BC, Canada
{gpoo,lsinger,dmg}@uvic.ca
[2] Chalmers | University of Gothenburg, Gothenburg, Sweden
eric.knauss@cse.gu.se

Abstract. Release management in large-scale software development projects requires significant communication and coordination. It is particularly challenging in Free and Open Source Software (FOSS) ecosystems, in which hundreds of loosely connected developers and their projects need to be coordinated to release software to a schedule. To better understand this process and its challenges, we analyzed over two and half years of communication in the *GNOME* ecosystem and studied developers' interactions. We cataloged communication channels, categorized high level communication and coordination activities in one of them, and triangulated our results by interviewing developers. We found that a release schedule, influence instead of direct control, and diversity are factors that impact positively the release process in the GNOME ecosystem. Our results can help organizations build better large-scale teams and show that research focused on individual projects might miss important parts of the picture.

1 Introduction

Releasing a single software product is already challenging, but consider the challenges of releasing a complex product that consists of a multitude of independent software products. Each of these individual software products is developed autonomously, with distributed teams of developers, different motivations, many of them working as volunteers. And yet, most of the time, the complex product with all its individual pieces is released on time and in high quality. The developers of each of these pieces must communicate and coordinate effectively to achieve the goal of release a cohesive product.

A FOSS ecosystem is a set of independent, interrelated FOSS applications that operate together to deliver a common user experience. Examples of these ecosystems include Linux distributions (such as Debian), KDE and GNOME (GUI set of applications for the desktop), or the R ecosystem (R language, libraries and tools).

© IFIP International Federation for Information Processing 2016
Published by Springer International Publishing Switzerland 2016. All Rights Reserved
K. Crowston et al. (Eds.): OSS 2016, IFIP AICT 472, pp. 147–162, 2016.
DOI: 10.1007/978-3-319-39225-7_12

In a FOSS ecosystem, a release is composed by many different independent applications. The release management of the ecosystem can be significantly more difficult than any of its applications alone. Release managers need to coordinate the goals and schedules of multiple teams to deliver, from the point of view of the user, one single release. However, little is known about how ecosystems conduct release management.

The goal of this paper is to understand communication and coordination for the purpose of release management in a software ecosystem. In particular, we studied how the GNOME project does release management. GNOME is a FOSS project whose main goal is to create a platform to build applications for the desktop for Linux and Unix-like systems. We chose GNOME because it is a large and mature software ecosystem [18], it has been studied before [7,11,14,16, 17,24,28], its official release is a single product comprised of many independent and distributed projects, and **more important, it has a successful and stable release schedule:** a new GNOME release is issued every 6 months. We studied the high level communication of the release management process across 5 releases. To understand how developers in a FOSS ecosystem communicate and coordinate to build and release a common product based on different projects, we answer the following research questions:

1. What are the communication channels used for release management?
2. How do developers communicate and coordinate for release management?
3. What are the release management tasks in a FOSS ecosystem?
4. What are the challenges that release managers face in a FOSS ecosystem?

2   Background and Related Work

A software ecosystem is a set of software projects that evolve together, share infrastructure, and are themselves part of a larger software project [15,17]. Regardless of its size, an ecosystem can be studied in-the-large or in-the-small [18]. That is, the interactions with external actors, or the inner ones, respectively. Our research is focused in the inner parts of a large software project, that is, an ecosystem "in-the-small".

In FOSS, software ecosystems are composed of multiple individual projects, although they might be invisible for a user of such software. For example, a typical GUI desktop system is composed of a file manager, text editor, email client, web browser, window manager, and the underlying libraries to build applications. All of them work as a single integrated system, even if each is developed independently. Each might have its own release cycle, yet it needs to coordinate with the other parts of the large scale software ecosystem to properly function as a whole.

Previous research on communication and coordination in software ecosystems has focused in a temporal analysis of information flows [13], and then obtained a structural map about flows between actors [12]. However, the requirements and challenges that release managers face in software ecosystems have not been explored.

Previous research on software ecosystems has focused on analyzing the software development process [9], the intersection of roles among developers and their activities [18], the organizational structure and how it evolves over time [10], studying the workload across projects and across contributors [27], and exploring correlations between discussions in mailing lists and activity in software contributions [8].

Previous research on release management in FOSS has focused on single projects, with emphasis on time-based schedules, challenges that FOSS projects face and practices they use to cope with them [19].

This paper aims to further the communication and coordination understanding in software ecosystems with respect to release management. We studied the enabling factors to deliver a product in a FOSS ecosystem with many individual projects. To this end, we considered the organizational structure, its communication channels, and the interaction between developers of different projects towards a common goal.

3   Study Design

To answer the research questions, we used a mixed methods approach [4] that employs data collection and analysis with both quantitative and qualitative data analysis [3, 23, 29]. The study was composed of four steps: (1) we identified the main communication channel used for high level coordination between projects and teams within the ecosystem (2) we collected and cleaned the data from that channel (3) we analyzed the data collected and extracted discussion themes, and (4) we conducted interviews to triangulate our findings and obtain additional insights from developers.

Communication Channel Selection. To identify the communication channels used for release management, we explored the GNOME organization by gathering and consolidating information found on its website. Two main communication channels are recommended: mailing lists and IRC. We focused in mailing lists, as they are archived and publicly available. We did not find evidence that communication over IRC was archived by GNOME, which makes its historical analysis harder, if not impossible.

Data Collection and Cleaning. We identified 285 mailing lists archived in the GNOME ecosystem. We searched for mailing lists used for cross-project communication and release management. We found that the Release Team recommends to its new team members to follow two mailing lists (*desktop-devel-list* and *release-team*); such recommendation is to help new Release Team members to grasp background information about the development process within the ecosystem [26].

We identified the Desktop Development mailing list[1] as the main channel for information related to release management: it is where the discussion of the desktop and platform development takes place. To study the communication

---

[1] https://mail.gnome.org/mailman/listinfo/desktop-devel-list.

across several releases, we retrieved data for 32 months spanning from January 2009 to August 2011. We used MLStats [22] to split into threads the mailing list archive data sets. We found this period interesting because it comprises 5 release cycles, including the transition between two major releases—from the series 2.x to 3.x. In total, we analyzed 6947 messages (an average of 214 messages per month). These were grouped into 945 discussions with 1 to 50 participants each, and a median of 2 participants per discussion.

To consolidate multiple email addresses associated with a single individual, we created clusters of similar identities and then manually processed them [1]. To match identities, we also collected names and email addresses from other data sources, such as commit logs and projects' metadata.

Analysis. We followed a grounded theory [2,3] approach to analyze the discussions in the *desktop-devel-list* mailing list. In grounded theory, researchers label or code openly the data to uncover themes and extract concepts. Through manual analysis we segmented the email subjects into categories and labeled them with a term, extracting themes from the discussion threads.

To code the messages we read the email subjects and associated a code to each thread. The code then represented the message's theme. Whenever the subject was unclear, we read the discussion thread in detail, and searched in other data sources (e.g. wiki, websites, related bugs and source code commits referenced in the discussion) for additional clues about the topic discussed. Thus, we also considered the role in the ecosystem of the person initiating a discussion, the roles of the other participants in the discussion, the number of messages in such discussion, the number of participants in a discussion, and the time in the release cycle were the discussion occurred—from early planning to finally release a stable version. We used those details as follows:

Role (initiator)	To know an individual's status in a project within the ecosystem, and the potential motivations to bring a topic to discuss. We assumed that the intention of a message may vary depending of the sender (*user, regular developer, project maintainer*, or *team member*)
Role (participants)	To know specialities and type of discussion they became involved with. We could distinguish among people who replied to regular developers or newcomers in the mailing list, and whether developers would participate in familiar subjects or in broader discussions
Number of messages	To order the discussions. Discussions with only one message (no reply) were left to the end
Number of participants	To order the discussions. Discussions with several participants were investigated with more detail
Release cycle time	To contextualize the discussions studied and determine discussion patterns that depended on the stage in the release cycle

We clustered codes into categories of communication and coordination. Later, we validated these categories through interviews with the corresponding developers.

Interviews and Triangulation. The purpose of interviewing developers were twofold: first, to triangulate our findings, and second, to enrich our finding with additional insights of the development practices and release management process. We conducted semi-structured interviews with GNOME developers who had actively participated in the discussions we studied. We recruited 10 (out of the top 35 candidates) developers during GNOME's main conference, the *GUADEC*.

The interviews consisted of three parts: (1) inquiry about roles in the project and communication channels our interviewees used (2) to comment on our findings; to probe the extend to which our findings matched their perception of their and others communication and collaboration activities (3) to comment specific interactions with other developers and the circumstances they would feel inclined to discuss with them.

4   Findings

In this section we present our findings structured by the respective research questions they answer. As we divided research question Q_1 into several questions, we answer each of the sub-questions separately. To illustrate our findings, we provide quotations from interviews and provide some developers' point of view. Among similar opinions, we chose to quote only the one we considered the most representative for each case.

4.1   What Are the Communication Channels Used for Release Management?

The Release Team recommend participating in three mailing lists (*release-team*, *desktop-devel-list*, and *devel-announce-list*) and one IRC channel (*#release-team*). The Release Team gives special importance to *desktop-devel-list*, even though its description— *"GNOME Desktop Development List"*—seems unrelated to release management. *desktop-devel-list* is the mailing list where developers from different projects converge to discuss about GNOME. As indicated by a former Release Team member:

> *"[The Release Team] may include any input [—data source or communication channel—] when they decide."*

Hence, the Release Team chooses to monitor diverse communication channels to have multiple sources of information that could be relevant to a release.

Mailing lists. In GNOME, there are internal and global mailing lists. The former are used by teams for their own purposes, the latter are used to discuss topics that concern the whole ecosystem. The Release Team uses an internal mailing list (*release-team*) to discuss and decide issues directly related to release management, and a global one (*desktop-devel-list*) for the whole ecosystem.

> " If you [need] high level coordination that affect the entire project that tends to be on the mailing lists."

Membership to the internal list is limited to the Release Team members, although it can receive emails from any address and the archives are publicly available.

IRC. An interactive chat system. Similar to mailing lists, there are internal and global chat channels. The Release Team holds meetings once or twice per release cycle using an internal channel (*#release-team*), which is also used for discussions within the team and for developers to get quick answers on release management. For awareness of the ecosystem, the Release Team monitors *#gnome-hackers*.

> "If people are already involved in working on something, IRC works very nicely for coordination."

Bugzilla. A Web-based bug tracking system. In GNOME, developers track and discuss bug reports or feature requests that. The Release Team uses Bugzilla to keep track of features and critical bugs for future releases. The bug tracker is also used in conjunction with mailing lists and IRC to obtain awareness of issues that must be solved or require further discussion.

> "[Using Bugzilla] is easier to keep track of the progress over a longer time because an IRC conversation is very transient."

Wiki. It is defined as *"GNOME's development and community organization space"*. Here the Release Team maintains information of the release process, provides instructions for developers to make releases, and details of the current release schedule, such as important dates.

> "In each cycle, we draft [the schedule] on the wiki, ask on the development list for feedback, after a while, we make a final [version] and we announce [it] ... we expect the core modules in GNOME and its maintainers to stick to it."

Blogs. To increase awareness, the developer blogs are aggregated in a common location called *Planet* (*"a window into the world, work and lives of GNOME hackers and contributors"* [25]. The audience expected is wider than the subscribers to a mailing list or regular participants on an IRC channel. Some Release Team members use them to communicate release-related decisions and to inform others about the release status. Developers also express their points of view regarding the project.

> "On blog posts it is easier to keep the tone of the conversation healthy, because people-wise the blogs are very attached to their public image, it is more [visible] than a comment inside the blog of another person. So, when the conversation happens between blogs, within the context of Planet GNOME, it is more productive, or more detailed."

Conferences. GNOME holds an annual conference where the Release Team presents the state of the project. In a panel, the team discusses GNOME's future with developers. For the Release Team it is an opportunity to have a face-to-face meeting.

> *"GUADEC, and other conferences and hackfests, are very valuable for having face to face contact with people ... you have a lot more bandwidth."*

Hackfests. Hackfests are focused face-to-face meetings of developers to work on a specific project, feature, or release. Depending on the topic, some Release Team members are invited to participate to bring their perspective. These meetings are organized by developers, however the foundation can fund developers to attend.

> *In GNOME, the Release Team uses mailing lists and IRC as the main communication channels for coordination; for long term discussions, and for quicker decisions that involve less than four people, respectively. Regardless, the Release Team might use multiple channels as input to gauge their decisions, including face-to-face meetings.*

4.2 How Do Developers Communicate and Coordinate for Release Management?

We found that developers use different communication channels, some of them specific to a particular topic or project and others for wider discussion. In the latter, discussions can be either about process management, technical issues, or both.

From our analysis of the *desktop-devel-list* mailing list, nine discussion categories emerged. Five of them are directly related to release management activities:

Request for comments. Long-term proposals that affect the entire ecosystem and require a high level of coordination. They may involve discussing the vision of the project for the next releases and beyond or major changes whose execution could take one or more releases. These discussions start at the beginning of each release cycle, and revisited during the release cycle. The Release Team gauges the overall sentiments. Examples: *"empathy integration with the desktop"*, *"Consolidating Core Desktop libraries"*, *"RFC: gtk-doc and gobject introspection"*.

> *"Part of the purpose of doing these discussions [is] to figure out what people concerns are, and make sure they can be addressed."*

Proposals and discussions. Short-term proposals focused on the current release cycle and tied to a particular project, but with potential indirect impact on other projects or teams. For example, a project wanting to use a library that is external to GNOME must submit a proposal. Other projects interested in the library might support the idea or raise concerns if they are already using an alternative library. The Release Team may raise concerns regarding the long-term sustainability of the external library—such as development activity, availability, or the library's track record regarding security fixes. Examples: *"systemd as external dependency"*, *"Module Proposal: GNOME Shell"*, *"New proposed GnomeGoal: Add code coverage support"*.

Announcement. Notifications for developers about the status of a component or the whole project. The purpose is to raise awareness among developers and keep them engaged. Announcements include the releases of new versions, a new branch, new external dependencies, and status reports of the project goals. Examples: *"GNOME 3.0 Release Candidate (2.91.92) Released!"*, *"GNOME 3.0 Blocker Report"*.

Schedule reminders. Specific type of *announcement* used by the Release Team to send periodic reminders of the release cycle's stage. The Release Team reminds developers to release a new version, start the period of feature proposals, and so on. Its nature and recurrence make it worth a category by itself. Examples: *"Release Notes time!"*, *"GNOME 2.29.90 beta tarballs due"*, *"Last call for comments on module proposals"*.

Request for approval. Request to break the *freeze* period at the end of the release cycle, once the Release Team controls the changes (See Sect. 4.3). The discussion is open to everyone, but the decision is taken by the Release Team, the Documentation Team, or the Translation Team. These requests require a timely decision as they occur close to the release date. All decisions require at least two votes from the Release Team. Changes in translatable strings will also require the approval of the Documentation and Translation Teams. Changes in the user interface will also require the approval of the Documentation Team. Examples: *"Hard code freeze break request for gvfs"*, *"[Freeze break request] gtksourceview crash"*, *"String change in gnome-session"*.

Table 1 presents the amount of discussions and messages during the period studied. Both help to balance their importance. Although there are less *Request for comments* and *Proposal and discussions* than *Announcements*, the proportion of messages of each of them reflects that those are the core of the discussions in the mailing list.

We noticed that discussions started by well-known developers attract other well-known developers, more than discussions started by other people. Our interviewees reported that they would be more inclined to participate in a discussion started by known developers, as they already know their expertise.

The remaining four categories are less relevant to release management activities: *Events coordination* (special type of announcement related to the organization of conferences, sprints, or hackfests), *expertise seeking* (questions on seeking others working on or in charge of a specific part in GNOME), *knowledge seeking* (questions from developers on specific organizational issues), and *Out of scope* (any other message).

Table 1. Summary of discussions and messages per category.

Category	Discussions		Messages		Messages per discussion
	#	%	#	%	Median
Request for comments	181	19.15	2,505	36.06	6
Proposals and discussions	219	23.17	2,074	29.85	4
Announcement	238	25.19	740	10.65	1
Schedule reminders	45	4.76	236	3.40	2
Request for approval	22	2.33	83	1.19	3
Events coordination	27	2.86	44	0.63	1
Expertise seeking	25	2.65	184	2.65	3
Knowledge seeking	151	15.98	764	11.00	3
Out of scope	37	3.92	317	4.56	2
Total	945	100.00	6,947	100.00	

> *The release schedule of GNOME guides the type and timing of coordination activities discussed in the main communication channel. The scope of decisions more from project-wide to focalized the more the project approaches the release.*

4.3 What Are the Release Management Tasks in a FOSS Ecosystem?

As we described earlier, the objectives of the Release Team are (1) defining the requirements of GNOME releases, (2) coordinating and communicating with projects and teams; and (3) shipping a release within defined quality and time specifications. With respect to the communication categories, the first objective maps to *Request for comments* and *Proposals and discussions*; the second maps to *Proposals and discussions, Schedule reminders,* and *Request for approval*; and the third objective maps to *Announcement, Schedule reminders,* and *Request for approval*.

To facilitate coordination, the Release Team prepares the release schedule and announces it. Based on the schedule, developers propose new features early in the release cycle. The Release Team coordinates the community, helps reaching consensus, and discusses and decides the adoption of proposals. Different stages in the schedule require different coordination and communication activities.

The importance of the Release Team for the success of the project can be seen in the stabilization phase. The Release Team takes control of the changes planned to be included in the release. As the release date approaches, the project maintainers require approval to make changes in their projects. The Release Team also coordinates the release notes, working with developers and teams— such as the marketing team—to write cohesive release notes for GNOME.

To make a release, the Release Team builds every component and validates that the software runs as expected. If a build fails, the Release Team will get in touch with the developers of the failing component to fix the build. Release Team members acknowledged that this is one of the most time-consuming tasks. By continuously building and testing a planned release, the Release Team monitors the quality of the product during the whole release cycle. They determine critical bugs and follow-up with developers to fix them. They also coordinate with distributors of GNOME regarding potential issues.

> *The Release Team defines what a GNOME release is, sets the schedule, coordinates with projects and cross-cutting teams to reach the goal on time, integrates and validates the product as a whole, and releases GNOME.*

4.4   What Are the Challenges that Release Managers Face in a FOSS Ecosystem?

From our analysis and interviews, we identified the four major challenges that release managers face in the GNOME ecosystem, they: (1) need to coordinate projects and teams of volunteers without direct power over them (2) keep the build process manageable (3) monitor for unplanned changes, and (4) test the GNOME release.

Coordinate Projects and Teams of Volunteers Without Direct Power over Them. GNOME contributors participate as volunteers, even though some of them are paid by external companies for their involvement. Projects are *"owned"* by the contributors who actively work on them, and these people make decisions regarding their projects.

> *"Maintainers have the last word most of the time. If the conflict is about a maintainer not agreeing with your vision ..., with specific technical decision, then it is [the maintainer's call]."*

The Release Team does not have any official power over developers, it relies on building consensus based on technical merit. One challenge the Release Team faces is to convince developers of its judgment and knowledge in the release process.

> *"It is difficult to coordinate well; there are so many people, so many teams. You need to be sure that everybody is aware on what is going on, that everybody is really involved when you need input. It is hard to coordinate people, it is really hard ... we try to do the best we can, but still is not perfect."*

The Release Team builds awareness of the whole release process by increasing the community participation. The time-based schedule facilitates this task by providing the same information to everyone beforehand [20], providing developers a sense of ownership of specific tasks and to become more involved in the process. This emphasizes the importance of social skills and power of persuasion of the Release Team members.

Keep the Build Process Manageable. GNOME is composed of multiple piece of software, each one with its own set of dependencies. When the dependencies grow, building the whole GNOME becomes cumbersome as it takes longer, and with more points of build failures. As a consequence, less volunteers build and test the whole GNOME before the release; which also increases the workload of the Release Team.

The Release Team addresses the scalability issue by keeping the *building stack* as small as possible, however, it is challenging to keep the stack small. We learned this observation directly from the interviews, as a Release Team member stated:

> *"In GNOME 3, we tried to make the stack smaller, [by reducing] the set of modules. For a short while we managed to get it below 200 [dependencies]. But then, new dependencies trap you back and now we have like 220 or so."*

One way to make the *building stack* smaller is by avoid managing external dependencies whenever is possible. Thus, the Release Team defines two kind of dependencies: system dependencies and regular dependencies. The system dependencies are the preferred external dependencies as they are mature enough that are available in the most common distributions. The regular dependencies are any other and must be built by GNOME, they can be software within GNOME or an external dependency.

Monitor for Unplanned Changes. Changes in the Application Programming Interfaces (API) and Application Binary Interfaces (ABI) of libraries pose a challenge to release managers. The libraries that GNOME provides try to guarantee stability in both API and ABI; thus, any application that uses a public API of a stable series will continue working with future releases without recompilation. Because the GNOME stack has several libraries, each one maintained by different people, it is challenging to track unintentional breakages before a release. Some API/ABI changes might work well in some build configurations, but break in others; or may be specific for a platform or architecture. To illustrate this observation, a Release Team member indicated:

> *"A change ... that works fine in my local system, maybe breaks some application somewhere else in the stack, or maybe it breaks only on a 32-bits system that I don't test locally because my laptop is 64-bits. Or in some parts of our stack ... we have to be worried about Windows or FreeBSD."*

Each project can decide on its own whether to add a new public API. However, the Release Team monitors the API and ABI stability, and makes sure the API documentation is up-to-date. To this end, the Release Team needs to detect API changes and make sure they follow the programming guidelines.

Test the GNOME Release. The number of projects to coordinate, as well as dependencies on external projects, make cumbersome testing the latest development version of GNOME. These quality assurance activities are performed

by a small group of developers, mainly the Release Team as who is in charge
of continuous integration. In the words of a Release Team member, continuous
integration is a necessity:

> "[full automated continuous integration] would allow us [to be] more aggressive: if
> something causes a problem, we can just back it out. Nowadays we commit some-
> thing [that] works in our systems, and people keep working on top. [Months] later,
> we find out ... problems somewhere else, but nobody noticed them because nobody
> managed to build the whole tree and actually test it."

OSTree [28] is a project that aims to address this issue by continuously
building GNOME and providing a testable system ready to be downloaded and
run. The Release Team uses it to build and test GNOME.

---

*The challenges of the Release Team in GNOME are associated with the size
and complexity of managing multiple independent projects, and developed by
volunteers in a distributed setting.*

---

5   Discussion

Any software system needs to plan and manage its releases. In large ecosystems of interrelated independent project this task is much more complex than
in a single system. **The Release Team plays a coordination role without
participating directly in any project in particular.** The release management activities are not recorded in commits of any project, but in discussions
in various channels, including email, IRC, and even face-to-face. For researchers
studying coordination, this role can be overlooked.

We found that Release Team members underestimate their role because of
lack of official power over developers. However, the evidence shows that the
Release Team decisions are respected even when some disagree. Even if developers do not align with the decisions of the Release Team, they accept them and
act upon them.

Overall, we extracted some lessons learned which we explain below.

**A successful Release Team requires both, good technical and social
skills.** Technical skills are needed to build consensus on technical merits and
convince the developers of their judgment; they need social skills to convince
developers to perform the necessary actions to deliver the software on time.

Need a common place for coordination. Single software projects have their
own communication infrastructure (such as the one provided by services like
GitHub or BitBucket). However, to coordinate multiple projects is necessary
to have infrastructure that sits on top of the infrastructure of each of these
projects. This will allow the Release Team to more easily track the progress
of all the projects, and communication to flow from the Release Team to the
projects and vice-versa.

A Release Team needs to be diverse. Its members are recruited from many different teams and with many different skill sets. This will help having first-hand knowledge of the different projects and teams, and to be able to reach everybody in the ecosystem. This diversity is also likely to provide different points of views. They also need to be (or at least have been) members of the teams that they expect to guide. By being "one of them", both sides will be able feel more affinity to the challenges and problems of the other side, specially when the Release Team makes decisions that contravene the wishes of a given team. In a way, the Release Team are not only release managers, but they are also representatives of the teams. Their are expected to make the best decisions that benefit both the ecosystem and the individual teams as a whole.

Need of multiple communication channels. The Release Team needs to communicate in a variety of ways. They use electronic channels that vary from asynchronous (such as email and blogs) to more direct, interactive ones (such as IRC). They value face-to-face communication; for this purpose they organize gatherings (such as conferences and hackfests) where the Release Team can host sessions to address specific issues, or communicate one-on-one with some contributors.

A formal release process with a well defined schedule helps the Release Team in the coordination process. Once the coordination process is internalized by the community, the Release Team can focus its efforts on other challenges. In addition, the time-based schedule release provides the Release Team a powerful tool: even though the Release Team might not know beforehand the features to be included in any release ahead, it is certain—for the Release Team and the community—when the features will be discussed, decided and released. The time-based release schedule sets the expectations for developers and stakeholders, enabling them to plan ahead with confidence [20].

6   Threats to Validity

We studied one of the two main communication channels in GNOME. As we focused on communication on one mailing list, we might have missed some interactions occurring on other channels. There could also be GNOME developers who do not participate in mailing lists at all and instead rely on other communication channels. However, previous research suggests that most discussions occur in mailing lists [1,6,7,21]. We also triangulated our results by interviewing key developers. It is thus unlikely that our analysis missed important coordination types, patterns, strategies, or challenges.

The most important threat to construct validity is the manual categorization of email subject fields, which might introduce subjective bias in the results. We followed a grounded theory [2,3] approach for coding, which consists in to abstract common patterns in the communication process. We extracted the topics to build the categories based on our interpretation of the subject field of each email thread. To address any possible misinterpretation of the actual discussion, before coding we familiarized with the email threads, and later we triangulated our results by interviewing developers.

The results of a single case study cannot be generalizable. However, a single study case can lead to a generalization through analytical generalization, which is performed by comparing the characteristics of a case to a possible target [5]. The case study presented can facilitate the analytical generalization and comparison with other cases.

7   Conclusions and Outlook

We explored the GNOME ecosystem to gain a deeper understanding of its dynamics. We determined the main communication channel used to coordinate the ecosystem, extracted meaningful discussion topics, determined the relevant actors, whose later confirmed and enriched our findings.

The Release Team as a key player in the communication and coordination among developers in GNOME. The communication coverage that the Release Team has in the GNOME community is far-reaching. This phenomenon has so far been undocumented. Our interviewees were surprised by this finding, yet they all agreed that it made sense.

In GNOME, the Release Team members come from a variety of teams or projects, as some of their members acknowledged in the interviews. Some of them are from the system administrators team, bug squadron, accessibility team, or maintainers of individual projects. This variety allows the Release Team to monitor and address almost all communications. Our interaction analysis could be beneficial for the Release Team, either to detect communication anomalies in time or to discard irrelevant issues faster.

The Release Team leads the coordination efforts in GNOME, it is the glue that keeps multiple projects and teams working together towards a goal. It is a crucial team for the success of GNOME, even if some of its members write little or no code at all.

The operational details of release management among ecosystems might vary. The lessons learned in this case study can be compared against other ecosystems through analytical generalization in future research.

References

1. Bird, C., Gourley, A., Devanbu, P., Gertz, M., Swaminathan, A.: Mining email social networks. In: International Workshop on Mining Software Repositories, Shanghai, China, pp. 137–143 (2006)
2. Corbin, J.M., Strauss, A.: Grounded theory research: Procedures, canons, and evaluative criteria. Qualitative Sociology **13**(1), 3–21 (1990)
3. Creswell, J.W.: Research Design: Qualitative, Quantitative, and Mixed Methods Approaches, vol. 2. Sage Publications, Thousand Oaks (2009)
4. Easterbrook, S., Singer, J., Storey, M.-A., Damian, D.: Selecting empirical methods for software engineering research. In: Shull, F., Singer, J., Sjøberg, D.I.K. (eds.) Guide to Advanced Empirical Software Engineering, pp. 285–311. Springer, London (2008)

5. Flyvbjerg, B.: Five misunderstandings about case-study research. Qual. Inq. **12**(2), 219–245 (2006)
6. Fogel, K.: Producing Open Source Software: How to Run a Successful Free Software Project. O'Reilly Media Inc., Sebastopol (2005)
7. German, D.M.: The GNOME project: a case study of open source, global software development. Softw. Process Improv. Pract. **8**(4), 201–215 (2003)
8. German, D.M., Adams, B., Hassan, A.E.: The evolution of the R software ecosystem. In: 17th European Conference on Software Maintenance and Reengineering, Williamsburg, USA, pp. 243–252. IEEE (2013)
9. Goeminne, M., Mens, T.: Towards the analysis of evolution OSS ecosystems. In: The 8th BElgian-NEtherlands Software EVOLution Seminar, pp. 30–35 (2009)
10. Goeminne, M., Mens, T.: Analyzing ecosystems for open source software developer communities. In: Goeminne, M., Mens, T. (eds.) Software Ecosystems, pp. 247–275. Edward Elgar Publishing, Cheltenham (2013)
11. Jergensen, C., Sarma, A., Wagstrom, P.: The onion patch: migration in open source ecosystems. In: 19th ACM SIGSOFT Symposium and the 13th European Conference on Foundations of Software Engineering, FSE 2011, Szeged, Hungary, pp. 70–80 (2011)
12. Knauss, E., Damian, D., Knauss, A., Borici, A.: Openness and requirements: opportunities and tradeoffs in software ecosystems. In: 2014 IEEE 22nd International Requirements Engineering Conference (RE), August 2014, pp. 213–222. IEEE (2014)
13. Knauss, E., Damian, D., Poo-Caamaño, G., Cleland-Huang, J.: Detecting and classifying patterns of requirements clarifications. In: 2012 20th IEEE International Requirements Engineering Conference (RE), Chicago, IL, USA, September 2012, pp. 251–260. IEEE (2012)
14. Koch, S., Schneider, G.: Effort, co-operation and co-ordination in an open source software project: GNOME. Inf. Syst. J. **12**, 27–42 (2002)
15. Lungu, M.: Towards reverse engineering software ecosystems. In: 2008 IEEE International Conference on Software Maintenance, September 2008, pp. 428–431. IEEE (2008)
16. Lungu, M., Lanza, M., Gîrba, T., Robbes, R.: The small project observatory: visualizing software ecosystems. Sci. Comput. Program. **75**(4), 264–275 (2010)
17. Lungu, M., Malnati, J., Lanza, M.: Visualizing gnome with the small project observatory. In: 6th IEEE International Working Conference on Mining Software Repositories, Vancouver, Canada, pp. 103–106 (2009)
18. Mens, T., Goeminne, M.: Analysing the evolution of social aspects of open source software ecosystems. In: 3rd International Workshop on Software Ecosystems (ISWSECO 2011), Brussels, Belgium, pp. 1–14 (2011)
19. Michlmayr, M.: Quality improvement in volunteer free and open source software projects exploring the impact of release management. Ph.D. thesis, University of Cambridge (2007)
20. Michlmayr, M., Hunt, F., Probert, D.: Release management in free software projects: practices and problems. In: Feller, J., Fitzgerald, B., Scacchi, W., Sillitti, A. (eds.) Open Source Development, Adoption and Innovation. IFIP, vol. 234, pp. 295–300. Springer, Heidelberg (2007)
21. Mockus, A., Fielding, R.T., Herbsleb, J.D.: Two case studies of open source software development: Apache and Mozilla. ACM Trans. Softw. Eng. Methodol. **11**(3), 309–346 (2002)

22. Robles, G., González-Barahona, J.M., Izquierdo-Cortazar, D., Herraiz, I.: Tools for the study of the usual data sources found in libre software projects. Int. J. Open Source Softw. Process. **1**(1), 24–45 (2009)

23. Runeson, P., Host, M., Rainer, A., Regnell, B.: Case Study Research in Software Engineering: Guidelines and Examples. Wiley Blackwell, Hoboken (2012)

24. Sarma, A., Maccherone, L., Wagstrom, P., Herbsleb, J.D.: Tesseract: Interactive visual exploration of socio-technical relationships in software development. In: 2009 IEEE 31st International Conference on Software Engineering, Vancouver, BC, Canada, pp. 23–33. IEEE (2009)

25. The GNOME Project. Planet GNOME Guidelines (2011). https://wiki.gnome.org/PlanetGNOME

26. The GNOME Release Team. Guide for New Release Team Members (2011). https://wiki.gnome.org/ReleasePlanning/NewReleaseTeamMembers

27. Vasilescu, B., Serebrenik, A., Goeminne, M., Mens, T.: On the variation and specialisation of workload - a case study of the GNOME ecosystem community. J. Empir. Softw. Eng. **19**, 4 (2013)

28. Walters, C., Poo-Caamaño, G., German, D.M.: The future of continuous integration in GNOME. In: 1st International Workshop on Release Engineering (RELENG), pp. 33–36 (2013)

29. Yin, R.K.: Case Study Research: Design and Methods (Applied Social Research Methods), 4th edn. Sage Publications, Thousand Oaks (2008)

Women in Free/Libre/Open Source Software: The Situation in the 2010s

Gregorio Robles[1]($\boxtimes$), Laura Arjona Reina[2], Jesús M. González-Barahona[1], and Santiago Dueñas Domínguez[3]

[1] GSyC/LibreSoft, Universidad Rey Juan Carlos, Madrid, Spain
{grex,jgb}@gsyc.urjc.es
[2] Universidad Politécnica de Madrid, Madrid, Spain
laura.arjona@upm.es
[3] Bitergia, Madrid, Spain
sduenas@bitergia.com

Abstract. Women are underrepresented in the IT sector. But the situation in FLOSS (free, libre, open source software) development is really extreme in this respect: past publications and studies show a female participation of around 2 % to 5 % and have shed some light into this problem. In this paper, we give an update the state of knowledge to the current situation of gender in FLOSS, by analyzing the results of surveying more than 2,000 contributors to FLOSS projects in 2013, of which more than 200 were women. Our findings confirm that women enter the FLOSS community later than men, do primarily other tasks than coding, participate less if they have children, and have slightly different reasons to enter (and to stay in) the development communities they join. However, we also find evidence that women are joining FLOSS projects in higher numbers in recent years, and that the share of women devoting few hours per week to FLOSS and full-time dedication is higher than for men. All in all, comparing our results with the ones from the 2000s, the context of participation of women in FLOSS has not changed much.

Keywords: Gender · FLOSS · Free software · Open source · Survey

1 Introduction, Motivation and Goals

The percentage of female participation in FLOSS projects is by all means very low (from 2 % to 5 % according to several surveys, such as FLOSS 2002 [7]). Although the IT industry already shows a disparity in gender, the amount of women is estimated to be between 25 % and 30 % [8], in FLOSS projects this disparity is even larger. Some projects, such as GNOME, have been actively promoting participation of female collaborators by means of scholarships exclusively for women. In many projects, as for instance Debian, there are specific mailing lists to welcome new female contributors and discuss how to increase participation of women. However, even if this fact has been known for over a decade now, the situation changes at a slow rate.

K. Crowston et al. (Eds.): OSS 2016, IFIP AICT 472, pp. 163–173, 2016.
DOI: 10.1007/978-3-319-39225-7_13

The goal of this paper is to provide some insight on the current partici-pation of women in FLOSS development communities, testing and extending findings from previous studies on female participation in FLOSS. For that, we have used data obtained by means of an open web survey, answered by FLOSS contributors. We have analyzed answers by men and women to different ques-tions, mainly regarding their involvement with FLOSS, their educational level and background, and their personal status.

The structure of this paper is as follows: next, related research, in particular studies on the involvement of women in FLOSS, is presented. Section 3 contains the research questions. Then, we will introduce the methodology. Section 5 offers the results obtained for the research questions. Finally, some conclusions are drawn.

2   Related Research

An ample research literature exists on gender issues in IT. In the context perti-nent to this paper, many efforts have been devoted to better understand why the number of women in science, technology, engineering and mathematics (STEM) is so low [8]. It is interesting to note that this gender gap has not only been reported at the professional level, but as well on related activities such as access-ing the Internet [2]. In this regard, scholars have studied whether the problem of such a low share of women lies in a "leaky pipeline" or in a "gender filter" [4], even to the point of asking students directly about this issue [11], and have theorized about it [15].

Among STEM, computer science and programming are areas where male predominance is among the largest [10], something which is not easy to explain. Some recent studies postulate that a wider perspective of the problem is needed, keeping into account "metaphors of programming, inclusion and exclusion, the notion of beautiful code, understandings of masculinity and programming" to "obtain a more complex analysis than a dualistic focus on differences between men and women" [3].

Some studies focus on the area of FLOSS, where the amount of women is dra-matically low [5]. For example, Adam has written about gender and the hacker phenomenon [1], or Vasilescu et al. have studied StackOverflow, the largest Q&A site for programming and technical questions nowadays, to measure quantita-tively online participation and representation of gender [16].

Other studies have studied female joining and participation patterns in FLOSS (and if they differ from the ones of males). So, Qui et al. have stud-ied how women join and socialize in the KDE-women group [13], while Kuechler et al. found a disproportionate participation rate in several FLOSS projects under study [9].

Probably, the most significant effort on the gender issue on FLOSS is the inte-grated report of findings authored by Nafus, Leach and Krieger in the framework of the European funded FLOSSPOLS research project [12]. As one of the key findings, FLOSSPOLS states that "[w]omen are actively (if unconsciously) excluded rather than passively disinterested" and offers some interesting insight on how this is related to the hacker ethic. The research presents some evidence that women start later using computers and having computers on their own, and explains some of its findings by stating that women engage mainly in activities different than coding or that women have a burden as they normally still assume a disproportionate amount of domestic responsibilities. To some extent, this research wants to update the findings from the FLOSSPOLS project, with data from almost a decade later – the FLOSSPols data is from 2005, while the one used in this research is from late 2013.

3   Research Questions

This paper addresses specifically the following questions:

1. Do men and women incorporate themselves to the FLOSS movement at the same age? Is the number of women entering FLOSS growing in the last years?
2. Do men and women perform the same type of contributions in FLOSS projects? Do they lead (coordinate) the same number of projects?
3. Is the proportion of men and women with children and collaborating in FLOSS projects similar?
4. Are reasons to start and to stay in FLOSS development similar for men and women?
5. Do men and women devote the same amount of time to FLOSS projects?

With these questions, we aim to address not only the reasons, as perceived by the studied individuals, but also the actual situations that could help to learn about the context for those reasons.

Finally, we would like to compare our results with the ones known from the FLOSSPOLS project, to see if any changes can be seen in the "gender issue" in FLOSS after one decade.

4   Methodology

The data used for this research has been obtained by means of a survey. This survey, called FLOSS 2013, tried to follow the same philosophy as the one of the original, and well-known FLOSS 2002 survey [7]. Thus, it is an open web-based survey, where participation is self-selected. The strategy to attract survey respondents has been to announce the survey in those channels where FLOSS developers communicate, specifically community news sites (such as Slashdot) and mailing lists. In addition to communication flows already used in FLOSS 2002, we spread the news of the survey through Twitter and other (free) social networks.

We made an important effort to preserve the privacy of the survey respondents. Thus, the survey could be answered anonymously, as IP addresses of respondents were not tracked and cookies were not used. However, participants were asked to provide their e-mail address –or some part of it– to validate that they really were FLOSS contributors. Respondents were also informed that their answers would be made publicly available in an anonymized way. Hence, if the e-mail address had been introduced, this would be handled as private information that would not be made public or shared with other research groups.

We intended to be as close as possible to the original FLOSS 2002 questionnaire in order to allow comparisons. However, some questions were added, others removed and some modified, after over a dozen meetings involving the authors where the questions were individually addressed for their meaning and goals. Mainly the changes were because of the following reasons: (1) the experience from the original FLOSS 2002 survey had shown that the question was not clear enough; (2) we modified the question adopting it to the current situation; (3) we wanted to obtain information about a new phenomenon/situation that was not relevant ten years ago; and (4) we removed the question because we thought it was of no interest for the survey or that this information can be gathered by other means, such as by mining software repositories (versioning systems, issue tracking systems, mailing lists, Q&A-sites, etc.).

An example of a question added to address the current situation (type 2 and 3) is the one related to the type of contribution to FLOSS. The original FLOSS 2002 survey focused exclusively on software developers, but the FLOSS phenomenon, even if the final product is a software, includes a number of other participants that do not code, such as translators, artists, community managers, promoters, etc. As a consequence, we target with FLOSS 2013 not only FLOSS developers, but all type of contributors. To implement this, a first question was added asking about the type of contribution to FLOSS projects by the respondent. This was a branching question, as subsequent developer-related questions were only shown to developers. All questions in the survey were optional except this first one.

The survey consisted of a total number of 58 questions[1]. The survey opened November 12th 2013 and closed December 6th 2013. The survey responses are publicly available on the survey website in several formats and is described in [14].

A limitation of the methodology is that our results are not representative of the percentage of women in FLOSS projects in general. This is because of the self-selected participation in the survey. However, the results of our survey allow to draw a picture of the context in which participation in FLOSS occurs, trying to identify differences. Actually, the survey has been especially promoted in female-specific mailing lists and communication channels to have sufficient respondents to be representative of this context.

---

[1] The complete questionnaire, including answers, can be obtained from http://floss2013.libresoft.es/.

5   Results

Table 1 provides the number of respondents to the FLOSS 2013 survey by gender. As respondents could leave any question unanswered, from the total number of 2,183 respondents, we only have information on the gender of 2,002 of them. 226 of them are women.

Table 1. Gender self-definition: number of respondents.

Gender	Respondents	Percentage
Male	1,776	81.36 %
Female	226	10.35 %
Other	33	1.51 %
NA's	148	6.78 %
Total	2,183	100.00 %

The question was addressing gender self-definitions (*"Which of the following describes how you think of yourself?"*) so a third option "In another way" with a textbox was included. Since the total number of respondents who selected this option is small (less than 50), we have chosen only men and women as groups of study. As there are almost 10 times more men than women who answered the survey, our results are given in relative terms.

5.1   Age and Date of Entry

Figure 1 shows how old respondents were when they entered the FLOSS movement – the figure on the left is the one for men, women are depicted on the right. We can infer visually that men start participating at an earlier age than women. So, while men and women peak both at 21 years, the tail for men is much more abrupt than for women; the values for men in the early 30s are a third of the ones of 10 years younger, while for women the values in the early 30s are over 70 % the ones in the 20s.

Table 2. Distribution of age when starting to participate in FLOSS projects.

	Min.	1st Qu.	Median	Mean	3rd Qu.	Max.
Men	10.00	19.00	23.00	24.49	28.00	55.00
Women	13.00	22.00	26.00	28.01	33.00	55.00

Table 2 provides a basic statistical analysis for this question[2]. As it can be seen, the age of incorporation for women is always higher than for men,

---

[2] 10 and 55 is given as the minimum/maximum age, because the survey allowed only responses such as "10 years or less" or "55 years or more".

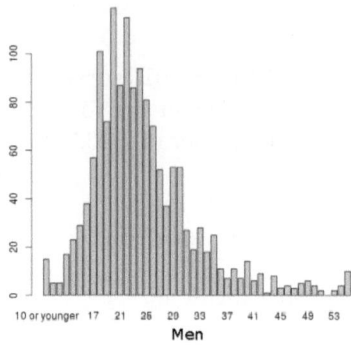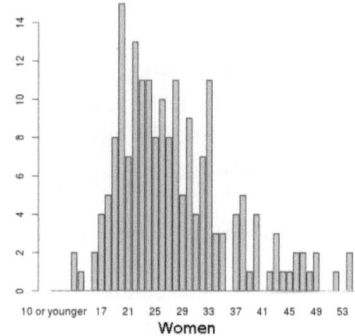

Fig. 1. Age of first contribution to FLOSS (men left, women right). The horizontal axis is in years, while the vertical axis gives the number of respondents of that age.

Table 3. Year of entry in FLOSS

	Men	%	Women	%
Before 1990	58	3.69	0	0,00
1990–1999	315	20.03	21	10.24
2000–2009	905	57.53	105	51.22
2010–2013	295	18.75	79	38.54
Total	1573	100.00	205	100.00

in general from three to five years. So, while half of the male contributors enter during their university years or before, for female this happens when many are already professionally active.

Table 3 shows that women entered the FLOSS movement more recently: 38.54 % of women have started in the last four years (compared to only 18.75 % of men) prior to the survey.

5.2 Type of Contributions and Number of Projects Involved

The FLOSS 2013 survey, in contrast to the original FLOSS survey from 2002, was open not only for FLOSS developers, but also to any other person who performed other type of contributions to FLOSS projects. Therefore a question was included, where respondents could specify if they were mainly coders, performed other activities (such as documentation, translations, tests, artwork...) or both.

Table 4 and Fig. 2 show that men are mostly devoted to coding and that the amount of male contributors who perform other tasks lies slightly above 20 %. However, the distribution of contributions for women is different. In this case, other type of contributions is the main task performed (with almost 45 %), while coding comes next (31 %).

Table 4. Type of contributions to FLOSS projects.

Type	Men	Women
Code, programming	903	71
Other	440	101
Both	433	54

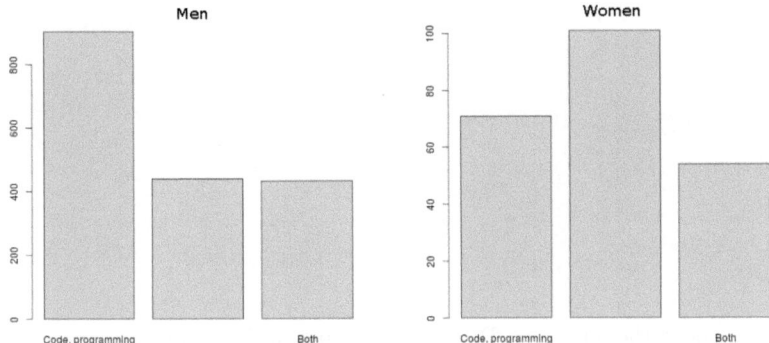

Fig. 2. Type of contributions to FLOSS projects (men left, women right). The vertical axis is given in number of respondents for the three choices: "code programming", "other type of contributions" and "both".

The survey asked in how many projects respondents were involved in as project leader, coordinator or administrator. Table 5 shows that 51.49 % of women were involved in these kinds of tasks (compared to 65.89 % of men). However, probably due to women entering FLOSS more recently, only (approx) 5 % of women coordinate more than 3 projects (compared to 18.47 % of men).

Table 5. Number of projects as leader, coordinator, or administrator.

	Men	Women
None	34.11 %	48.51 %
1	24.20 %	21.78 %
2	14.41 %	18.32 %
3	8.82 %	5.94 %
4 or more	18.47 %	5.45 %

5.3   Children

Figure 3 provides information on how many FLOSS contributors have children, sorted by gender. Results are presented in a bar plot, in such a way that the height of the "No" answer is the same, thus allowing to compare the proportions.

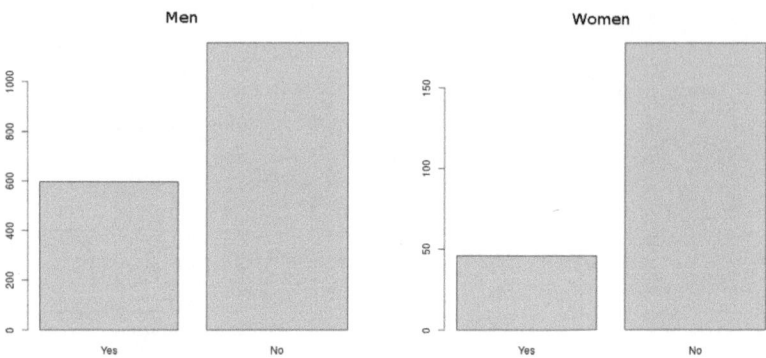

Fig. 3. Answers to the question "Do you have children?" (men left, women right). The vertical axis is given in number of respondents; it should be noted that the scale used in both graphs is not the same as it has been adjusted so that the number of "No"s are represented at the same height.

The graph shows that a minority of contributors to FLOSS have children, but that the number of men with children (34 %) is proportionally twice as high as the number of women with children (19 %).

5.4   Reasons to Start (and to Continue) Contributing to FLOSS

Table 6 shows the top seven reasons (with 20 % or more respondents selecting them) to start in FLOSS for men, while Table 7 shows the reasons for women[3].

The top reason for starting to contribute to FLOSS for both groups is to learn and develop new skills. Women give more importance to participate in new forms of cooperation, and men to improve FLOSS products of other developers. Improving job opportunities looks more important for women, but this could be because women are entering the FLOSS scene more recently, when the open source market has become more mature.

To find out if the reasons to stay contributing were the same or not, we have selected women and men that started later than 2011 in FLOSS, and checked the respondents of the multiple-optional question *"And today? For what reason(s) do you go on with contributing to FLOSS?"*. Learning and sharing knowledge and skills are still at the top both for men (58.98 % and 57.28 %)

---

[3] The multiple-optional question was: "Remembering the time you started contributing to FLOSS, what was the reason for this?".

Table 6. Top 7 reasons to start in FLOSS (men)

Reasons to start	% Men
To learn and develop new skills	62.39
To share my knowledge and skills	38.01
To improve FLOSS products of other developers	35.87
To participate in the FLOSS scene	29.56
Because I think that software should not be a proprietary product	25.79
To participate in new forms of cooperation	25.23
To improve my job opportunities	19.65

Table 7. Top 7 reasons to start in FLOSS (women)

Reasons to start	% Women
To learn and develop new skills	67.70
To participate in new forms of cooperation	38.94
To share my knowledge and skills	37.17
To improve my job opportunities	34.07
To participate in the FLOSS scene	33.63
Because I think that software should not be a proprietary product	28.32
To improve FLOSS products of other developers	21.24

and women (64.78 % and 62.26 %), and participating in new forms of cooperation is still more important for women (31.45 %) than for men (25.10 %), while men still focus on improving FLOSS products of others (39.18 %, against 28.30 % of women). However, improving the job opportunities is a similar concern for both genders (25.85 % of men, 25.79 % of women selected that option).

5.5 Involvement in FLOSS

While FLOSS was merely a volunteer activity in the mid-90s, in the last decade it has seen a high professionalization [6] and more contributors work full or part-time on FLOSS projects. Figure 4 presents the amount of time that respondents commit to FLOSS by gender. Although the distribution seems very similar at first, it is noteworthy that the share of women devoting less than 5 hours/week (53.69 %) is higher than for men (49.71 %), and that the amount of women working 40 or more hours per week (14.77 % of women, 12.01 % of men). So, when contributing to FLOSS projects women are over-represented among the less active participants or among the *professional* full-time FLOSS contributors, in the latter case probably working for an industrial software company.

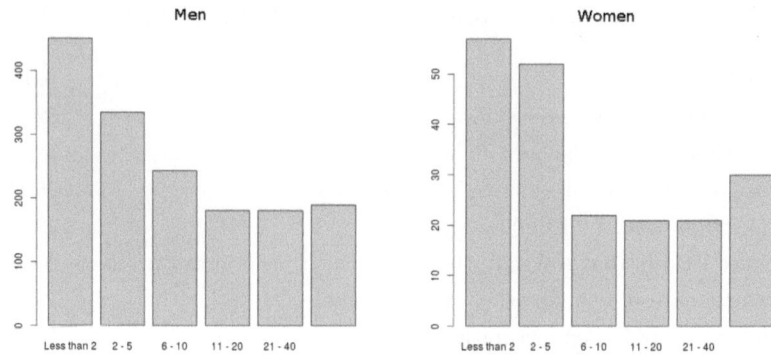

Fig. 4. Number of hours per week devoted to contributing to FLOSS projects (men left, women right). The vertical axis is given in number of respondents. Graphs have different scales.

6   Conclusions

In this paper we targeted a number of research questions presented in Sect. 3. Our results show that:

1. Women start to participate in FLOSS projects at a later age than men, and have begun to enter FLOSS projects in growing numbers in recent years.
2. Women perform majoritarily other types of contributions than coding, while men mostly contribute with code. More than half of the women are involved in leading, administering or coordinating FLOSS projects. The share of women leading projects is lower than for men.
3. The proportion of men with children contributing to FLOSS projects is almost twice the proportion of women.
4. Reasons to start and to stay in FLOSS development are similar for men and women, but men tend to focus on the product, and women in the forms of cooperation.
5. The share of women who devote less than 5 h and more than 40 h per week is higher than for men.

Our results confirm (and extend) the main ones from the FLOSSPOLS study, even if almost 10 years have passed between both. So, although it is possible that the percentage of women in FLOSS may have slightly increased during these years[4] –probably due to the involvement of the software industry–, many contextual patterns have remained the same. We can therefore talk about a *lost decade* in the general inclusion of women in FLOSS.

As future work, we plan to extend this study with the other questions included in the survey that might give more insight into the gender issue.

---

[4] A study of GitHub developers from 2015 found that only around 6 % were women, see http://www.toptal.com/open-source/is-open-source-open-to-women.

References

1. Adam, A.E.: Hacking into hacking: gender and the hacker phenomenon. ACM SIGCAS Comput. Soc. **33**(4), 3 (2003)
2. Bimber, B.: Measuring the gender gap on the internet. Soc. Sci. Q. **81**(3), 868–876 (2000)
3. Boivie, I.: Women, men and programming: knowledge, metaphors and masculinity. In: Gender Issues in Learning and Working with Information Technology: Social Constructs and Cultural Contexts, pp. 1–24 (2010)
4. Blickenstaff, J.C.: Women and science careers: leaky pipeline or gender filter? Gend. Educ. **17**(4), 369–386 (2005)
5. David, P.A., Shapiro, J.S.: Community-based production of open-source software: what do we know about the developers who participate? Inf. Econ. Policy **20**(4), 364–398 (2008)
6. Fitzgerald, B.: The transformation of open source software. Mis Q. **30**, 587–598 (2006)
7. Ghosh, R.A., Glott, R., Krieger, B., Robles, G.: Free, libre, open source software: survey and study (2002)
8. Hill, C., Corbett, C., Rose, A.S.: Why So Few? Women in Science, Technology, Engineering, and Mathematics. ERIC (2010)
9. Kuechler, V., Gilbertson, C., Jensen, C.: Gender differences in early free and open source software joining process. In: Hammouda, I., Lundell, B., Mikkonen, T., Scacchi, W. (eds.) Open Source Systems: Long-Term Sustainability. IFIP AICT, vol. 378, pp. 78–93. Springer, Heidelberg (2012)
10. Margolis, J., Fisher, A.: Unlocking the Clubhouse: Women in Computing. MIT Press, Cambridge (2003)
11. Miliszewska, I., Barker, G., Henderson, F., Sztendur, E.: The issue of gender equity in computer science-what students say. J. Inf. Technol. Educ. Res. **5**(1), 107–120 (2006)
12. Nafus, D., Leach, J., Krieger, B.: Gender: Integrated report of findings. FLOSSPOLS, Deliverable D 16 (2006)
13. Qiu, Y., Stewart, K.J., Bartol, K.M.: Joining and socialization in open source women's groups: an exploratory study of *KDE-Women*. In: Ågerfalk, P., Boldyreff, C., González-Barahona, J.M., Madey, G.R., Noll, J. (eds.) OSS 2010. IFIP AICT, vol. 319, pp. 239–251. Springer, Heidelberg (2010)
14. Robles, G., Reina, L.A., Serebrenik, A., Vasilescu, B., González-Barahona, J.M.: Floss 2013: a survey dataset about free software contributors: challenges for curating, sharing, and combining. In: MSR, pp. 396–399 (2014)
15. Trauth, E.M., Quesenberry, J.L., Morgan, A.J.: Understanding the under representation of women in it: toward a theory of individual differences. In: Proceedings of 2004 SIGMIS Conference on Computer Personnel Research: Careers, Culture, and Ethics in a Networked Environment, pp. 114–119. ACM (2004)
16. Vasilescu, B., Capiluppi, A., Serebrenik, A.: Gender, representation and online participation: a quantitative study of stackoverflow. In: 2012 International Conference on Social Informatics (SocialInformatics), pp. 332–338. IEEE (2012)

Short Papers and Tool Demonstration

An Open Continuous Deployment Infrastructure for a Self-driving Vehicle Ecosystem

Christian Berger[(✉)]

Department of Computer Science and Engineering,
University of Gothenburg, Gothenburg, Sweden
`christian.berger@gu.se`

Abstract. Self-driving vehicles are an ongoing research and engineering topic even though first automotive OEMs started to deploy such features to their premium vehicles. Chalmers University of Technology and University of Gothenburg are operating and maintaining a vehicle laboratory comprising 1/10 scaled cars, a Volvo XC90, and a Volvo FH truck to conduct studies with automated driving. This laboratory is used both from researchers from different disciplines and in education. The experimental software for all these platforms is powered by the same software environment for different hardware architectures. Therefore, maintaining and deploying new features and bugfixes to the users of this laboratory in a fast way needs to be organized in a reproducible yet easily maintainable manner. This paper outlines our open approach to encapsulate our build, test, and deployment process using VirtualBox, Docker, and Jenkins.

1 Introduction

Today's engineers are challenged by the development and maintenance of increasingly complex autonomous driving systems. To conduct research within this domain, our laboratory setup comprises a virtual test environment to experiment with algorithms for such vehicles, a fleet of standardized 1/10 scale miniature cars, and a workshop housing a Volvo XC90 and a Volvo FH truck. Our algorithms on these different platforms are powered by our open-source middleware OpenDaVINCI[1] and the vehicle software environment OpenDLV[2].

Having a unified and open-source software environment for all these different platforms, where we have full flexibility and design freedom, allows us to conduct our research and education in the way that is supporting the goals of the laboratory with the different vehicles in the best way. However, preserving the full flexibility in design and implementation requires also to maintain a certain level of deployment infrastructure to support the different research and educational projects with "ready-to-use" packages that work on the different development platforms.

---

[1] http://code.opendavinci.org.
[2] https://github.com/chalmers-revere/opendlv.

© IFIP International Federation for Information Processing 2016
Published by Springer International Publishing Switzerland 2016. All Rights Reserved
K. Crowston et al. (Eds.): OSS 2016, IFIP AICT 472, pp. 177–183, 2016.
DOI: 10.1007/978-3-319-39225-7_14

To underline the challenge, an embedded systems course taken by around 75–80 students every year is using our scaled cars with ARM-based hardware environments for educational purposes. Therefore, maintaining pre-compiled packages while having a low response time to react on feature and change requests as well as on unveiled issues while testing the resulting packages on the different architectures is resource-intense.

In this paper, we outline the technical setup that realizes our goal to reduce the manual maintenance and deployment work by highly automating software building, testing, packaging, and deployment using VirtualBox, Docker, and Jenkins; as such, the software architecture and algorithms for the self-driving vehicles are not in the paper's focus (cf. [Ber14] for further background). Having our infrastructure in place, we achieve (a) reproducible build and packaging environments, (b) can directly test pre-compiled binary packages by setting up Docker containers imitating a client environment using "throw-away" containers [Ber15], and (c) have the possibility to rollback and restore a previous release if something went unexpectedly wrong.

The rest of the paper is structured as follows: Sect. 2 summarizes related work and Sect. 3 describes the technical setup for the encapsulated build environment. Section 4 concludes the paper and discusses future topics to be addressed.

2   Related Work

Build farms for open-source software to support a professional deployment of software packages are available with different foci: The GCC compile farm [WWWb] provides different hardware and software platforms (Linux and BSD); however, the offered operating systems are not up to date as required for our laboratory. The Debian Linux distribution is providing a build service [WWWa] targeting package maintainers and release managers. Such deb-packages can also be automatically built by using Launchpad [WWWc] aiming at Ubuntu-based distributions; however, rpm-packages would not be supported (even though the tool `alien` could transform a deb-package into an rpm one and vice versa). In contrast, OpenSuSE's build farm [WWWd] is offering a build environment for different packages, even though it is primarily used for rpm-based platforms.

As our goal is to achieve a high-degree of automation and documentation of the entire deployment process without administering different build farms, we decided to setup and maintain our own environment. The closest concept to our demands would be Docker's own build procedure [Fra15] that we partially explored in our previous work [Ber15]. As we have to maintain the technical infrastructure for a Docker-based continuous deployment anyways, this paper is complementing our previous work addressing the packaging for different Linux distributions using automated and encapsulated builders and distribution testers.

We have released all essential scripts as open-source: https://goo.gl/XhEq15.

3   Encapsulated Build Environment

The open-source software environment OpenDaVINCI used for the vehicle laboratory is the result from the research and experience of developing several self-driving vehicular systems during the last years: Started at the 2007 DARPA Urban Challenge [RBL+09], over a self-driving experimental SUV car [Ber10], up to a research and educational 1/10 scale vehicle platform [Ber14] (Fig. 1).

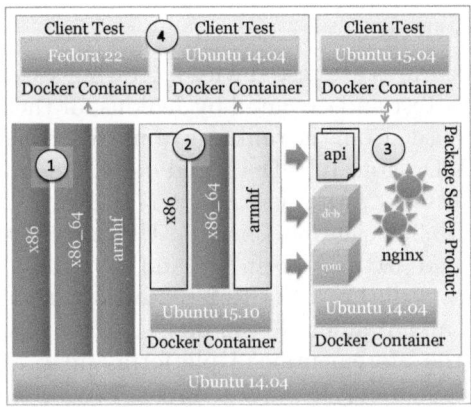

Fig. 1. Encapsulated build environment: (1) building binaries on native platform, (2) building binaries within Docker, (3) package server as Docker image, and (4) regression tests with typical client setups.

3.1   OpenDaVINCI Software Environment

The open-source software environment OpenDaVINCI is a lean and portable C++ middleware to realize distributed software components exchanging messages. The core functional properties comprise encapsulation of typical programming idioms used with distributed, data-exchanging software components like concurrency, UDP-, TCP-, and serial-communication, abstraction of shared memory and time, and publish/subscribe and round-robin coordinated data exchange.

These low-level functional features are extended by a domain-specific library providing additional functions typically required by automotive software systems to realize self-driving functionality: Methods to describe a logical road network, a visualization environment (bird's eye perspective as well as 3D rendering), and components to embody simulations (vehicle kinematics, sensor simulations for a virtual camera, infrared, and ultrasonic sensors).[3]

The different components are compiled into individual static and dynamic libraries as well as stand-alone applications. The libraries enable the transparent reuse in headless simulations as part of unit-tests[4], while the stand-alone

---

[3] https://goo.gl/7SGR7G.
[4] https://goo.gl/tKCEp1.

applications can be distributed to different machines and supervised by a central component `odsupercomponent` to monitor their life-cycle, to provide either uncoordinated publish/subscribe communication, or to enforce deterministic communication and scheduling following the round-robin pattern.

Our Jenkins build system is using CMake and GCC 4.8 or higher on the Linux and BSD platforms, Clang on Mac OS X, and Visual Studio 2013 on Windows.

3.2 Regression Testing

The aforementioned features are tested with a growing set of more than 570 unit tests realized with CxxTest and executed by Jenkins for the following 64 bit platform configurations chosen from the rankings from DistroWatch.com: ArchLinux, CentOS7, Debian 8.2, DragonFlyBSD 4.2 and 4.4, ElementaryFreya, Fedora 21-23, FreeBSD 10.2, MacOS X, Mageia 5, Mint 17.3, NetBSD 7.0, OpenBSD 5.8, openSuSE 13.1 and 13.2, Scientific Linux 7, Ubuntu 14.04.3 LTS, 15.04, and 15.10, Windows 8.1 and 10, and Zorin 9.1 and 10. The following 32 bit environments are tested as well: FreeBSD 10.2 (32 bit), Mint 17.1 (32 bit), Ubuntu 14.04.3 LTS (32 bit), and Windows 7 (32 bit).

Jenkins is using the aforementioned platforms on a Mac OS environment with VirtualBox while running itself in a VirtualBox virtual machine itself for simplified maintainability allowing a regular backup to rollback in the case of issues when updating the individual platforms. All platforms are accessed via SSH to unify the scripting of the build process and to report back the results from the build and the CxxTest test suites.

The regression testing is following a 12 h schedule per day; as the typical development environment is Ubuntu 14.04.3 LTS, this platform is additionally triggered by any new commit to the master branch on GitHub. Thus, developers have to wait a maximum of around twelve hours to know whether their changes run safely on all supported platforms.

3.3 Encapsulated Continuous Deployment

The project's central GitHub page provides access to the latest features and reports also the results from the Jenkins regression tests. Thus, members of the research laboratory as well as students using the source distribution can simply pull therefrom – either the current development head or a stable release.

As the complete compilation on a single core machine takes around 15 min, we also offer pre-compiled binary packages[5] for Ubuntu 14.04.4 LTS and 15.04 (i386, armhf, and amd64), Ubuntu 15.10 (amd64), and Debian 8.2 (i386, armhf, and amd64) as deb, and for CentOS 7, Fedora 21 and 22, and openSuSE 13.1 and 13.2 (i686, amd64, and armhf) as rpm.

Our deployment process is incorporating regression testing as well: All created binary packages are tested on a fresh system environment before the new release is being publicly accessible to the world.

---

[5] http://goo.gl/BTEHEs.

Regression Deployment. Any new release is deliberately initiated but Jenkins is triggering a "dry-run deployment" on any newly pushed change to our master branch to report whether a release would succeed or fail. This "dry-run deployment" is using the same build and test environment as the script for the real deployment process executed on Ubuntu 14.04 LTS (64 bit).

As a first step, the local working copy is updated to the respective revision. Next, the source tree is built for x86-64 systems using GCC 4.8.4. Afterwards, the 32 bit variant is compiled using the same compiler adjusted therefor. Finally, the source tree is built for ARM systems using the arm-linux-gnueabihf tool chain 4.8.2 for hard-float environments as our miniature vehicle fleet is using the Odroid XU3 platform. Once a respective build has completed, the resulting binaries and libraries are bundled into deb and rpm packages.

As the resulting binaries would not be directly usable on Ubuntu 15.10, the actual build process would need to be executed on a different software setup. For this purpose, we have encapsulated the actual build into a Docker image.[6]

The Dockerfile for this image bases on the Ubuntu 15.10 distribution and contains the required build environment and the required library dependencies for OpenDaVINCI. The final step for the Docker container is the execution of the actual build. The build itself is simply running the same steps as described for manually compiling OpenDaVINCI from sources on Ubuntu 15.10.[7] As the source folder is that part of the Docker image, which is changing the most, it is simply mapped into the running Docker container. The resulting build is executed as follows: `docker run --rm=true -v $HOME/OpenDaVINCI:/opt/OpenDaVINCI seresearch/wily:latest`.

The advantage of this approach is the textual description and full automization of the actual build process. Thereby, further build environments can be added and maintained easily. The regression testing builds as described in Sect. 3.2 including running all test suites in the VirtualBox environments take approximately 15–20 min per platform; the encapsulated Docker build takes around 17 min to complete.

Testing Pre-compiled Packages. After all packages have been successfully built, the webserver environment for delivering these packages is encapsulated in a Docker image as well. Thereby, not only the complete runtime configuration for the production server providing the packages is described and documented but it also allows for a safe rollback to previous versions if an issue occurs. Furthermore, migrating the production server to a different hardware server or even a Cloud-infrastructure is possible.

Before the newly produced production server will be enabled for world-wide access, it will be started as "production-server-under-test" for internal access on a specific port only. Thus, the produced binary packages can be tested in a user-like configuration environment to ensure that the user-workflow is running as expected.

---

[6] https://goo.gl/ueqTpH.

[7] http://goo.gl/yR1JDe.

Therefore, a fresh client setup for the specific Linux distribution will be created with Docker adding the "production-server-under-test" as package source. Then, the pre-compiled binaries will be installed and a small test program will be compiled and executed[8]; afterwards, the images therefor will be discarded afterwards [Ber15].

The freshly produced pre-compiled binaries are tested on the following client configurations: CentOS7 (rpm), Debian 8.2 (deb), Fedora 21 & 22 (rpm), openSuSE 13.2 (rpm), and Ubuntu 14.04 & 15.04 (deb). Thereby, the typical Linux distributions that are used by the users of the vehicle laboratory are covered. After all these tests have been successfully passed, the currently running production server is deactivated and the freshly created Docker image containing the new pre-compiled binaries will be activated.

3.4 Completing Continuous Deployment

Besides the actual pre-compiled binaries that are served by the production's server web environment, the project's website is added as well as the software's API documentation.[9] Finally, the software's tutorials are automatically generated on any new commit to our GitHub repository from the ReadTheDocs.org service.[10] In total, a complete deployment running all the different Docker-encapsulated builders and tests takes around 90 min.

4   Conclusion and Future Work

Our university's laboratory equipment comprises a fleet on miniature vehicles, a Volvo XC90 SUV, and a Volvo FH truck. To facilitate algorithm reuse and exchange as well as preserving full flexibility and design freedom in our source code, we are providing and maintaining the open-source software environment OpenDaVINCI powering these vehicles. To simplify the use of this software in research projects but especially for large-scale student project courses, we also provide pre-compiled binaries and tutorials.

In this paper, we have outlined our technical infrastructure enabling continuous deployment while preserving even regression testing of the deployment itself by encapsulating the build, test, and deployment processes into different Docker images. While initial effort needed to be spent to setup such an environment, the monthly maintenance effort like regular system updates is very low by having a high degree of automation using a precise documentation of the realized processes in the supporting scripts and build files. As part of this paper, we release the scripts for our continuous deployment infrastructure as open-source.

Future work will address the parallelization of the different builders to further reduce the deployment time. Additionally, further platforms and builders are planned to be added to extend the repository of offered pre-compiled binaries.

---

[8] https://goo.gl/1Wq9hf.
[9] http://api.opendavinci.org.
[10] http://docs.opendavinci.org.

Acknowledgments. The Chalmers REVERE laboratory is supported by Chalmers University of Technology, AB Volvo, Volvo Cars, and Västra Götalandsregionen.

References

[Ber10] Berger, C.: Automating Acceptance Tests for Sensor- and Actuator-based Systems on the Example of Autonomous Vehicles. Shaker Verlag, Aachener Informatik-Berichte, Software Engineering Band 6, Aachen, Germany (2010)

[Ber14] Berger, C.: From a competition for self-driving miniature cars to a standardized experimental platform: concept, models, architecture, and evaluation. J. Softw. Eng. Robot. **5**(1), 63–79 (2014)

[Ber15] Berger, C.: Testing continuous deployment with lightweight multi-platform throw-away containers. In: Großpietsch, K.-E., Kloeckner, K. (eds.) Proceedings of the 41th EUROMICRO Conference on Software Engineering and Advanced Applications (SEAA), Funchal, Madeira, Portugal, August 2015

[Fra15] Frazelle, J.: New Apt and Yum Repositories, July 2015. https://blog.docker.com/2015/07/new-apt-and-yum-repos/. Accessed 15 Jan 2016

[RBL+09] Rauskolb, F.W., et al.: Caroline: an autonomously driving vehicle for urban environments. In: Buehler, M., Iagnemma, K., Singh, S. (eds.) The DARPA Urban Challenge. STAR, vol. 56, pp. 441–508. Springer, Heidelberg (2009)

[WWWa] Debian Build Service. https://buildd.debian.org. Accessed 15 Jan 2016

[WWWb] GCC Compile Farm. https://gcc.gnu.org/wiki/CompileFarm. Accessed 15 Jan 2016

[WWWc] Launchpad. https://launchpad.net. Accessed 15 Jan 2016

[WWWd] OpenSuSE Build Service. http://build.opensuse.org. Accessed 15 Jan 2016

Towards Open Source/Data in the Context of Higher Education: Pragmatic Case Studies Deployed in Romania

Alexandru Coman[✉], Alexandru Cîtea[✉], and Sabin C. Buraga[✉]

Faculty of Computer Science,
"Alexandru Ioan Cuza" University of Iaşi, Iaşi, Romania
{iosif.citea,busaco}@info.uaic.ro
http://profs.info.uaic.ro/~busaco/

Abstract. The open source ideology is unfortunately not so popular in Romania. This subject represents, to this day, an untackled problem especially in various local educational areas. The paper describes an interesting initiative taken this year by the Faculty of Computer Science, University of Iaşi, Romania to change the collective opinion by progressively pushing the new generations of students through a binding process with the ideas involved in the open source philosophy. Three ongoing initiatives addressing this problem are detailed, including the results we have obtained so far through them, and also the steps that are planned to be taken soon on the matter.

1 Introduction

Based on multiple discussions with students in various events around the country, we observed that a high percentage of those with whom we talked have a few bad preconceptions when it comes to the open source ideology, from the fact that someone will use/steal your work to the idea that open source software is of poor quality. We set out to change that perspective and build a better community around the concept of open source software, ideally promoting collaboration and teamwork among fellow and future engineers [3].

The paper presents several details about three ongoing initiatives – sharing via GitHub of the most interesting student projects (*Awesome FII Projects*), a two-day national conference on various open source technologies (*Open Source Camp*), and an academia-industry joint training event (*CloudbaseLABS*) – in order to help current and new generations of students get initiated and accustomed to the open source philosophy, methodologies, techniques, and tools in the context of actual Romanian higher education system – in particular, the Faculty of Computer Science from Iaşi, Romania. Several insights about these ongoing activities are provided, followed by conclusions and further work.

© IFIP International Federation for Information Processing 2016
Published by Springer International Publishing Switzerland 2016. All Rights Reserved
K. Crowston et al. (Eds.): OSS 2016, IFIP AICT 472, pp. 184–191, 2016.
DOI: 10.1007/978-3-319-39225-7_15

2   Advantages of a Fully Open Faculty

Each year, the students tackle a series of challenges meant to prepare them for real-life scenarios in the industry and sharpen their skills. Some of these challenges imply working in teams and using a wide range of industry technologies (e.g., various programming paradigms, languages, methodologies, software tools). Most of their work usually gets lost and is not saved and archived to be available online, and for that reason multiple generations of students receive similar tasks, those tasks not keeping up with developments in the industry. Also, each generation of students starts from scratch and usually has little ways of interacting with more experienced, older students. According to the Open Education Consortium[1], "education is sharing knowledge, insights and information with others, upon which new knowledge, skills, ideas and understanding can be built."

From our point of view, there are multiple advantages to a open-source-oriented faculty. Besides knowledge not getting lost, multiple generations can contribute to the same project over time. Additionally, there will be a high concentration of educational materials and resources that students can access to be able to get up to speed faster. Furthermore, due to the work older generations put in place, the bar is raised each year as a side effect. Another key feature of such a faculty is the fact that it offers its students a higher grade of visibility, resulting in more opportunities to get integrated in the job market.

In addition, we consider that our proposal approaches could be a suitable solution for learning beyond the classroom [11], by adopting both formal and informal instruction virtual spaces – in this case, focusing on open source code/data public repositories stored by GitHub.

3   Our Current Situation

At the moment, several disciplines taught at the Faculty of Computer Science Iasi (FII) already encourage students to build software projects under various open source licences, for various disciplines: *Operating Systems*, *Computer Networks*, *Web Technologies*, *Software Engineering*, etc. As an example, at the *Web Application Development* course, students receive specifications for projects (such as *Ark*, *FaW*, and *SAPA*)[2] that are based on reusing open data, including governmental data, to be able to build public REST APIs that offer valuable machine-processable information.

Several timid initiatives to publicly offer content from the faculty have appeared due to enthusiastic professors, but unfortunately only reserved to specific disciplines and not driven by a unitary educational policy at the faculty, institutional or governmental level. These initiatives tackle student projects, that

---

[1] Open Education Consortium: http://www.oeconsortium.org/.

[2] List of projects developed in 2015/2016 by the postgraduate students enrolled at Web Application Development discipline: http://profs.info.uaic.ro/~busaco/teach/courses/wade/projects/.

could eventually be of interest to the industry, or content to be able to educate students in the means of open source possibilities.

Multiple types of materials have emerged from these initiatives, from presentations, tutorials, workshops and seminars (available in Romanian or English) to a wide variety of events organised at FII such as RoPython, Open Source Iaşi 2014, Design Jam (2011, 2012, 2014, in collaboration with Mozilla Foundation), Web Technologies local workshops (2001–2007, 2010–2014). Other national important initiatives are the series of "Informatica la Castel" Summer School on Linux and Open Learning Environments (since 2004), ROSEdu (Romanian Open Source Education) community projects, InfoEducation (a national contest on software, Web, and robotics – established in 1993). Various details regarding the history and experiences of using open virtual environments in Romania are presented in [7,8].

4 First Steps: Initiatives in Progress

With the help provided by the FII academic staff, we started three projects to help new generations of students get initiated and accustomed to the open source philosophy, methodologies, and techniques. Their purpose is to not only build up interest in the Open Source subject, but also initiate and support the transition to a fully Open Source Faculty by offering the students a spectrum of opportunities to interact with the concept.

Each of the proposals has a specific objective, some of them ongoing and some already offering us a set of results to analyse.

4.1 Awesome FII Projects

Our first task was to solve the problem of lost knowledge (and wheel reinvention) over multiple generations. In that sense, we started a project entitled *Awesome FII Projects*[3]. This project represents our initiative to build a virtually-stored open knowledge library for future students to browse through and keep as a reference to their work. With its purpose in mind, we built an organisation on the GitHub online platform [5] associated with the FII in order to keep track and store the top ranking projects, homeworks, assignment papers, technical/scientific articles, or useful posts.

Currently, three pilot courses students take in their first year of pursuing a Bachelor's Degree and the first year of pursuing a Master's Degree. Those courses are *Introduction to Programming*, *Object-Oriented Programming*, and *Web Application Development*. Also, students are encouraged to use a version control system. We are planning to extend this initiative to other disciplines of interest: *Web Technologies* and *Human-Computer Interaction*.

To be able to automate the process of adding the projects to the repository, we developed a REST API built upon the one exposed by GitHub which will

---

[3] Public repository of the most interesting projects developed by the FII students: https://github.com/info-uaic/awesome-fii-projects.

help us manage the students and the projects they are building each year. When a new team of students is formed, a new repository is automatically created. After the evaluation period has ended, based on the obtained grade and a set of default thresholds (e.g., grade bigger than 7, "readme" and "changelog" files present, code available under the terms of a specific open source license), matched projects are moved into the Hall Of Fame.

In the case of already published projects, a crawler was built – based on the GitHub API and GitHub Search Engine[4]. This tool is able to search for projects having specific keywords directly related to FII disciplines (usually, these terms are predefined by the professors). As an example, if we search for "web fii", we can find 9 repositories and approximately 40 000 occurrences in the source-code. Every found repository is then going through a validation process in which the authors of the project are verified against a list of the enrolled students. If the authors of the repository match students from our faculty and those students form a known team, we can proceed in processing that repository.

Discussing results, due to the current student evaluation schedule, for *Awesome FII Projects* only one course (*Introduction to Programming*) has finalised out of the three pilot courses. This introductory discipline covered the basics of programming (arrays, functions, recursive functions, basic algorithms) over the span of 14 weeks of teaching. Each first year student (from the 14 groups, each containing on average 28 persons) had to develop – as a last laboratory evaluation step – a simple application chosen from a list of proposed projects by using the procedural paradigm (i.e. C language). At the end of the evaluation period, we selected the top ranking projects in terms of complexity and quality and added them to the *Awesome FII Projects* list. From 392 built and successfully assessed projects, we chose about 2 % and added them to the faculty's GitHub public repository[5]. We observed that each repository has an average of 6 commits and an average of 2391 lines of code.

In the near future, about 35 projects of the *Web Application Development* discipline will be assessed – using a combination of criteria adapted from [1, 4, 6] – and the best of them will be chosen to be included into the specific *Awesome FII Projects* collection. The project (developed by a team of 2–4 students) consists of an application built by using the existing social and semantic Web technologies. There are no restrictions regarding the implementation solution, but the open source approaches are highly encouraged. All data managed by the developed Web application must be modelled by using the RDF (Resource Description Framework) specifications [1, 6]. The project should be developed and deployed according to the actual practices in software/Web engineering by using a cloud-based approach for the code management.

Having established such a software project collection, we will able to assess the usability, usage spread, code quality and evolution of the most popular sub-repositories, following the ideas and proposals enumerated by [9, 10].

---

[4] GitHub Developer: https://developer.github.com/.

[5] *Introduction to Programming* selected projects: https://github.com/info-uaic/.

4.2   Open Source Camp

The second project is called *Open Source Camp*[6] and is meant to be a three-in-one event consisting of a conference, a hackathon, plus several workshops, during two days (7–8 May 2016). The purpose is to gather various professionals from the industry and, with their help, build an event for all skill levels and perspectives (open source or not) and gather as much interest in the community.

Open Source Camp is based upon the idea launched in 2014 and called "Open Source Iaşi", a 10-hour local event gathering about 100 participants. This year, we are taking our event to a national level and hopefully gathering more than 300 students and developers, currently managed to invite a large part of the local and national communities dedicated to the open source movement: RoPython, ROSEdu, Rogentos, Open Knowledge Romania, and others to be investigated and contacted. We are further preparing the event and gathering support to promote the open source values and best practices.

4.3   CloudbaseLABS

The third already started project is *CloudbaseLABS*[7], initiated in collaboration with Cloudbase Solutions, a private IT company having an office in our city. With its help, we envisioned a two week training event for groups of eight students that will cover multiple technologies and pragmatic knowledge used in the industry – e.g., system and network administration, virtualisation, OpenStack[8] architecture, Python programming.

We created a campaign in order to evaluate the number of students interested in open source. Out of 1873 contacted students, only 146 students actually opened our message – from those, 105 accessed our online provided resources (about 5 %). After organising a social event and another campaign, we managed to climb to 7 % of the students. Thus, there is much work to be done concerning the promotion of what the FLOSS movement is and its benefits for education. Finally, 24 students were selected to be part of the training program. Due to the large number of applications, this event was hosted in two rounds at FII.

During the training program, the main methodologies of development in open source projects were promoted. The participants had at their disposal a code repository[9] with a series of challenges which they were asked to solve. For each proposed solution, the participants received feedback from the organisers and the other students and were encouraged to improve their code.

As expected, their work progressed very well after a few days of constant feedback and supervising. The participants offered daily anonymous feedback to signal any problems and also to suggest what other things may be of interest to them. Accordingly, the training program was adapted to suit their needs and unanswered questions. Analysing the data from the provided source-code,

---

[6] Open Souce Camp: https://oscamp.eu/.
[7] CloudbaseLABS: http://labs.cloudbase.it/.
[8] OpenStack official Website: https://www.openstack.org/.
[9] CloudbaseLABS challenges: https://github.com/alexandrucoman/labs.

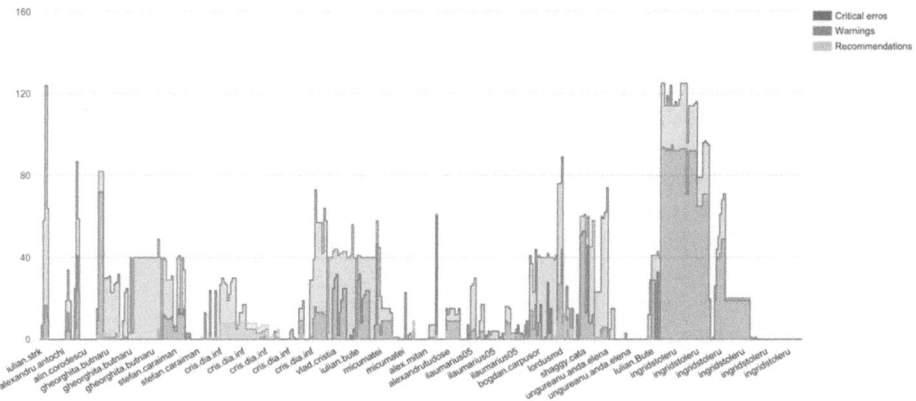

Fig. 1. Visualising data regarding source-code quality of student projects

a positive tendency is observed, from commits with large amount of issues to more refined code with a lower number of problems – see Fig. 1.

5 Conclusion and Future Work

The three described initiatives join together in the same idea: to offer students the opportunity to learn about and interact with the open source ideology. Even if several disciplines encourage students to use open source software and to provide their code and data under the terms of open licenses, there is a large amount of potential. We have managed to awaken the curiosity and enthusiasm of a small group of people, which we hope will help us further to promote the FLOSS values and build an educated generation of students further, including the academic motivation and self-regulation while learning online by inspecting, understanding, and contributing to the existing knowledge [2].

We plan to integrate a semantic Web-based system that outputs statistics and metadata from all of the FII projects in the RDF format, following the *Linked Open Data* initiative [6]. Using this system, we will be able to provide multiple types of information regarding each repository – e.g., the evolution of our students at a technical level, security problems in several types of applications, the most common mistakes found in code writing, and many others.

Appendix

Reference presentations publicly available for students as open educational resources under the terms of "Creative Commons (CC) Attribution-NonCommercial-ShareAlike License" [10]:

---

[10] http://creativecommons.org/licenses/by-nc-sa/4.0/.

- S. Buraga, Code in the Clouds (2015, in Romanian):
  http://www.slideshare.net/busaco/cu-codul-n-nori
- S. Buraga, Web Developer?! (2015, in Romanian):
  http://www.slideshare.net/busaco/dezvoltator-web-varianta-2015
- S. Buraga, Towards 5-star Data in the E-university (2014):
  http://www.slideshare.net/busaco/towards-5star-data
- S. Buraga, REST and some Python (2014):
  http://www.slideshare.net/busaco/rest-and-some-python
- S. Buraga, Web Game Development (2013):
  http://www.slideshare.net/busaco/web-game-development
- S. Buraga, Architecture of the Web Browser (2012):
  http://www.slideshare.net/busaco/web-browser-architecture
- S. Buraga, Semantic Social Web (2009):
  http://www.slideshare.net/busaco/semantic-social-web
- S. Buraga, Why Web 3.0? (2008):
  http://www.slideshare.net/busaco/why-web-30-presentation
- A. Cîtea, Security Problems in Software Applications (2015, in Romanian):
  http://tinyurl.com/h5mesda
- A. Cîtea, Software Panic?! (2015, in Romanian):
  http://slides.com/alexcitea/panel-securitate-9#/
- A. Coman, A Briefer History of bcbio-nextgen(-vm) (2015):
  https://slides.com/alexcoman/bcbio-nextgen
- A. Coman, Cherrypy Framework (2014, in Romanian):
  http://slides.com/alexcoman/framework-ul-cherrypy
- A. Coman, Cross Site Request Forgery (2014, in Romanian):
  http://slides.com/alexcoman/cross-site-request-forgery
- A. Coman, Python Coding Standards (2014, in Romanian):
  http://slides.com/alexcoman/standarde-de-scriere-in-python
- A. Coman, Deploy OpenStack Kilo with DevStack (2015, in Romanian):
  http://tinyurl.com/deploy-openstack
- A. Coman, Create a cluster on Windows Azure (2015, in Romanian):
  http://tinyurl.com/cluster-on-azure
- A. Coman, VirtualBox driver for OpenStack (2015, in Romanian):
  https://cloudbase.it/virtualbox-openstack-driver/
- A. Coman, PythonLAB (2015, in Romanian):
  https://github.com/c-square/python-lab

References

1. Allemang, D., Hendler, J.: Semantic Web for the Working Ontologist, 2nd edn. Morgan Kaufmann, Burlington Massachusetts (2011)
2. Artino, A., Stephens, J.: Academic motivation and self-regulation: a comparative analysis of undergraduate and graduate students learning online. Int. High. Educ. **12**(3–4), 146–151 (2009)
3. Atenas, J., Havemann, L. (eds.): Open Data as Open Educational Resources: Case Studies of Emerging Practice. Open Knowledge, Open Education Working Group, London (2015)

4. Casteleyn, S., Daniel, F., Dolog, P., Matera, M.: Engineering Web Applications. Springer, Heidelberg (2009)
5. Chacon, S., Straub, B.: Pro Git. Apress, New York (2014)
6. Heath, T., Bizer, C.: Linked Data: Evolving the Web into a Global Data Space. Theory and Technology. Synthesis Lectures on the Semantic Web: Morgan & Claypool, San Rafael, California (2011)
7. Jalobeanu, M.: From web-based teaching to virtual learning environment and towards social media used in education. In: International Conference on Social Media in Academia: Research and Teaching (SMART 2013), Bacau (2013)
8. Jalobeanu, M.: A 43 years history, passing from the gutenberg project initiative to the open educational resources movement. In: 10th International Scientific Conference "eLearning and Software for Education", Bucharest (2014)
9. Syeed, M.M.M., Hammouda, I.: Who contributes to what? exploring hidden relationships between FLOSS projects. In: Corral, L., Sillitti, A., Succi, G., Vlasenko, J., Wasserman, A.I. (eds.) OSS 2014. IFIP AICT, vol. 427, pp. 21–30. Springer, Heidelberg (2014)
10. Rajanen, M., Iivari, N.: Examining usability work and culture in OSS. In: Damiani, E., Frati, F., Riehle, D., Wasserman, A.I. (eds.) Open Source Systems: Adoption and Impact. IFIP Advances in Information and Communication Technology, vol. 451, pp. 58–67. Springer, Heidelberg (2015)
11. Scott, K., Sorokti, K., Merrell, J.: Learning "beyond the classroom" within an enterprise social network system. Int. High. Educ. **29**, 75–90 (2016)

BugTracking: A Tool to Assist in the Identification of Bug Reports

Gema Rodríguez-Pérez(✉), Jesús M. Gonzalez-Barahona, Gregorio Robles, Dorealda Dalipaj, and Nelson Sekitoleko

GSyC/LibreSoft, University King Juan Carlos, Fuenlabrada (Madrid), Spain
{gerope,ddalipaj,snelson}@libresoft.com, {jgb,grex}@gsyc.com
http://libresoft.es
http://gsyc.es

Abstract. Issue tracking systems are used, in most software projects, but in particular in almost all free open source software, to record many different kinds of issues: bug reports, feature requests, maintenance tickets and even design discussions. Identifying which of those issues are bug reports is not a trivial task. When researchers want to conduct studies on the bug reports, managed by a software development project, first of all they need to perform this identification.

The job for researchers here is very different from the bug triaging that researchers do. In the latter case, people with a considerable experience in the project make a decision based on the information available at that time (maybe just a short comment by some user), asking, if needed, for more details. In the former case, researchers usually have not that experience in the project, but they have at their use all the information produced, until the moment the issue was closed. This may include not only all comments and actions on the issue tracking system, but for example, discussions about a fix in the code review system, or the final fixing patch in the source code management system. Having all that information conveyed to the researchers, in an easy, flexible and quick way, accelerates and makes their decision process much more reliable. It simplifies large scale manual analysis of issues (in hundreds or thousands), helping researchers to ensure that they are really working with what they intend to work: bug reports.

This paper presents a tool designed to solve exactly the problem of providing the researchers with all the relevant information needed to decide whether an issue corresponds to a bug report or not. The tool uses information extracted automatically from the projects repositories. It offers a web-based interface which allows collaboration, traceability and transparency of the identification of bug reports. All this makes the process easier, faster, and more reliable.

Keywords: Issue tracking system · Code review system · Bug triage · Tool

© IFIP International Federation for Information Processing 2016
Published by Springer International Publishing Switzerland 2016. All Rights Reserved
K. Crowston et al. (Eds.): OSS 2016, IFIP AICT 472, pp. 192–198, 2016.
DOI: 10.1007/978-3-319-39225-7_16

1   Introduction

While a software system is being developed, software engineers use version control repositories to produce and manage their code. Researchers and testers report issues, which are then stored in other repositories, known as issue-tracking systems, where many kinds of issues can be found.

Issue-tracking systems facilitate the process of solving these bugs, but their shortcoming is the difficulty in distinguishing which of the reports are bug reports or not. These systems provide an interface to manage reports of maintenance activities where researchers can report issues describing bug reports, features or code optimizations. During the bug triage process it is difficult to distinguish bug reports from other issues; a study describes that two of five issues are misclassified [2]. This misclassification causes bias predicting bugs where non-bug reports are taken into account.

To distinguish the bug reports we could have used automatic classification systems, as described in [1], but the vocabulary used in the description of the issues could change from project to project, as well as the policy depending on the project. Consequently, data validation is recommended as mentioned in [2].

Linking a bug report in a issue-tracking system and the corresponding fix-commit may not be a trivial task. Traditionally, the methods used in link recovery [4,5] are based on text patterns or the mining of key phrases. Unfortunately, these methods include many false negatives causing bias in data [6,7]. Therefore other methods, such as the Mlink approach, have been developed to link bug report with fixes using features in the changed source files corresponding to commit logs in addition to the traditional textual features [3]. But in all of these methods, it is supposed that the issues are bug reports.

In this paper, we present a tool that displays, to the benefit of the researchers, a collection of all the necessary information needed to decide if an issue is a bug report or not. The tool, through the collection of exhaustive data on bug reports and the corresponding fix-commit, along with researchers extensive knowledge of the system, will help the last in their decision making, leading them into choosing only bug reports. This way they will not recur in any bias induced by non bug reports. To the best of our knowledge, this is the first tool that provides support to the identification of bugs and classification of bug reports. The need of the contribution of this tool arises from the increasing interest that both the academy and industry world is showing in the bug classification as a primary factor in modern software development.

2   The Tool

The tool is a web application, therefore it runs in a browser. It displays the main data for distinguishing bug reports from others issues. The researchers will be responsible for classifying the issues from Launchpad as bug reports or not, and can thereby explain their decision for each issue. The issues are what we will refer as tickets during the paper.

2.1 Architecture

The tool integrates information from Launchpad as issue-tracking system and
Gerrit as code review system. The Fig. 1 presents the architecture of the tool.
The tool was developed using JavaScript, Node, JQuery and HTML5 technologies. The queries to the API of Gerrit and Launchpad are executed on server
side. The responses are displayed on the client side. The end user can view the
information displayed and interact with the server through events. Both sides
exchange information using JSON files along with using their own REST API.
Furthermore, we use a third-party application between GitHub and the browser
in order to integrate some functionalities from GitHub.

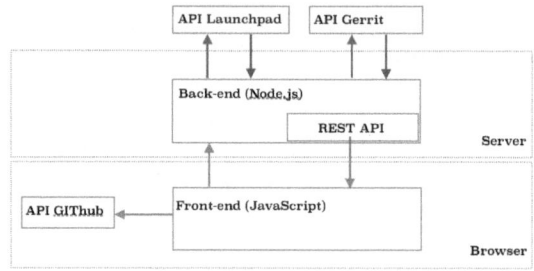

Fig. 1. Architecture of the tool.

2.2 Main Features

Figure 2 illustrates a screen short of the main tab of the tool. In particular, the
tool displays the ID of the tickets which are extracted randomly from each issue-
tracking repository of OpenStack. Other related information is displayed. Based
on all these data, the researcher can decide whether the issue is a bug report or
not. We focused on displaying the main parameters that help in the classification
of reports, such as title and description of the report, as well as the description
of the fix commit. For example for ticket ID 1531734 the tool displays the information related with the ticket in Launchpad and its corresponding review in
Gerrit.

There is other additional information that the tool does not displays. If the
researchers find it necessary, they can access the Launchapd and Gerrit web
pages, respectively of the ticket and review, through the links provided by the
tool. Thereby they can access extra information such as the comments written by
code review researchers that correspond to that particular ticket. This provides
a mean for tracking the history of the ticket from the moment it was opened
until it was closed.

The tool further facilitates researchers to record and express their opinion
about the ticket after reading all the information that is automatically displayed.
They have to classify the ticket as *Bug report* or *Not Bug report*. Due to unso-
phisticated description used in the ticket, the researchers could doubt the classification. For this reason we add an extra option in the classification, *Undecided*.

Furthermore, the researchers have a text area to write keywords found in the title, in the description of the ticket and commit message, that support their classification. Finally, they can leave their comment on why they classified a report as Bug, Not Bug or Undecided. Such information, in the future, will help us building an automatic bug classification system.

Another feature of the tool is that it allows to carry out a blind analysis of the tickets. Since all the data analysis inserted about a ticket is saved in a file on ones GitHub account, such analysis can be done by two or more researchers in parallel. By saving the data in GitHub, we could also measure the time that each researcher need for an analysis, which tickets were more difficult to analyze and other metrics that can help us understanding the current problem of issue misclassification.

The web page provides different functionalities depending on the tab the researcher is browsing. We explain these functionalities in the following:

1. Tab Repository: In this tab you can choose which repository you want to analyze. Currently the tool supports the four principal repositories of OpenStack: Cinder, Nova, Neutron and Horizon.

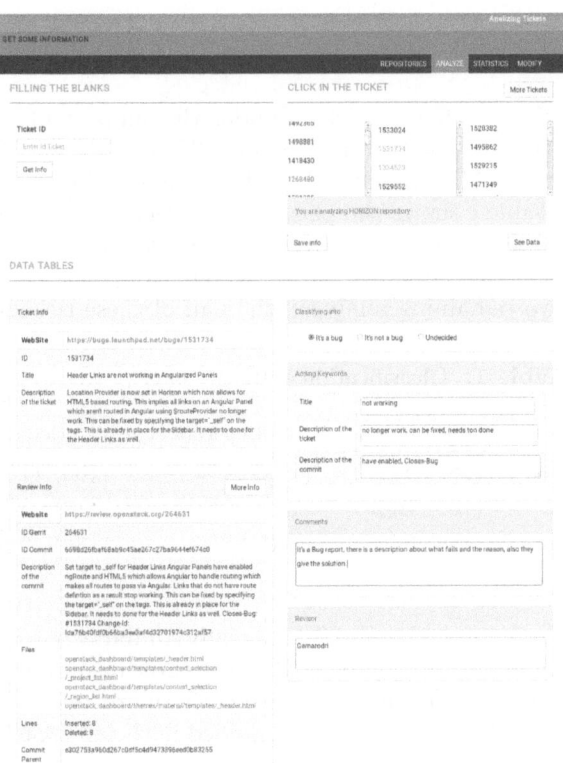

Fig. 2. Screenshot of analyze tab

2. Tab Analyze: It is the Tab illustrated in Fig. 2. It is where all the data from a specific ticket are displayed. The user can either select a random identifier or insert one of his choice. According to the data retrieved from Launchpad and Gerrit, the researcher can classify the ticket.
3. Tab Statistics: This tab extracts the data already analyzed by a researcher involved in the analysis from their user account in GitHub. It analyzes these data and displays a distribution of the classifications in a table;
4. Tab Modify: In case the researcher thinks to have inserted a mistake during the analysis, in this tab he/she can edit any of the data saved in his/her GitHub repository.

At the current state we present the initial version of the tool which is available at;[1], as well as a demonstration video[2]. It is licensed under GPL 0 (General Public License) and you can find the code at a GitHub page[3]. Anyone can use the tool, regardless of having GitHub account or not. However, it should be noted, for the researcher to save, modify data and see statistics of analysed tickets automatically, he/she should create a GitHub repository with the same name as the OpenStack project to be analysed, for example if the OpenStack project name is Nova, than the GitHub repository name should be Nova.

3   Results

We have analyzed 459 different tickets under the support of the initial version of the tool. 125 tickets where from Cinder, 125 from Nova, 125 from Horizon and 84 from Neutron. All the tickets have been analyzed by two out of the three researchers. The Table 1 shows the percentage of tickets classified as bug reports for the different researchers. These results don't report for some combinations of researchers because of in some projects, only a researcher analyzed all the tickets and the two remaining analyzed the half of these tickets each one.

Table 1. Classification statistics of each researcher

	Bug report	Not bug report	Undecided	Total
Researcher 1	(184) 55 %	(115) 34 %	(35) 11 %	334
Researcher 2	(188) 76 %	(54) 22 %	(7) 3 %	249
Researcher 3	(188) 56 %	(116) 35 %	(30) 9 %	334

The percentages between R1 and R3 are really similar, whereas the R2 has identified more Bug Reports in his analysis. But, the three results support the misclassification present in bug tracking systems. Furthermore, according to [2]'s work, approximately two of five issues are misclassified in the analysis of R1 and R3.

---

[1] bugtracking.libresoft.es.
[2] https://www.youtube.com/watch?v=q0-TIvL4mqc\&feature=youtu.be.
[3] https://github.com/Gemarodri/BugTracking.

Table 2. Concordance between each researcher in each repository

	Nova	Cinder	Horizon	Neutron	Total
R1 and R2	(44/63) 70 %	(40/52) 77 %	(37/62) 60 %	-	68 %
R1 and R3	-	(46/63) 73 %	(48/63) 76 %	(26/42) 62 %	71 %
R2 and R3	(41/62) 66 %	(10/10) 100 %	-	-	71 %

Focusing in the concordance between researchers analyzing the same ticket, 417 tickets present a double bind review process, obtaining that each ticket was analyzed by two researchers. Table 2 shows the percentage of concordance between researchers in each repository after the analysis of the tickets.

Table 2 shows that the concordance of the researchers is high, but, also demonstrate the difficulty to classify tickets as bug report or as not bug report, because each researcher can have different opinions about a specific ticket. The concordance could be higher if they were expert in the project.

All data from the analysis are available in the GitHub repositories of the researchers[4], the repositories having the same name of the projects analyzed in OpenStack.

3.1 Future Work

Since we are conducting empirical studies based on OpenStack projects, the current tool is limited to OpenStack as a pilot project. In the future, our aim is to extend the tool at extracting tickets from others bug tracking systems, such as Bugzilla or GitHub where the server will operate against them to analyze the most OSS project. Additionally, we aim to study the misclassification in this OSS projects. We would like to add more features to the tool. One of them would be to display information such as the lines of code changed in the files affected from the fix-commit, along with the code in the bug seeding moment. Furthermore, we would like to implement an automatic classifier for the tickets, based on the semantic of the description of the ticket and the fix-commit. The result will indicate a percentage of confidence about whether a ticket is a bug report or not. However, the researcher will always make the final decision. The automatic classification will enable researchers to focus only on problematic issues, which can be easily misclassified.

We also aim to investigate what will be the results if the data sources used by the tool to automatically extract tickets are used in isolation to manually classify bugs or other possible bug classifying tools. This will help us validate our results and the tool to further improve.

---

[4] https://github.com/Gemarodri,ddalipaj,nellysek.

References

1. Antoniol, G., Ayari, K., Di Penta, M., Khomh, F., Guéhéneuc, Y.G.: Is it a bug or an enhancement?: a text-based approach to classify change requests. In: Proceedings of the 2008 Conference of the Center for Advanced Studies on Collaborative Research: Meeting of Minds, p. 23. ACM, October 2008
2. Herzig, K., Just, S., Zeller, A.: It's not a bug, it's a feature: how misclassification impacts bug prediction. In: Proceedings of the 2013 International Conference on Software Engineering, pp. 392–401. IEEE Press, May 2013
3. Nguyen, A.T., Nguyen, T.T., Nguyen, H.A., Nguyen, T.N.: Multi-layered approach for recovering links between bug reports and fixes. In: Proceedings of the ACM SIG-SOFT 20th International Symposium on the Foundations of Software Engineering, p. 63. ACM, November 2012
4. Zimmermann, T., Premraj, R., Zeller, A.: Predicting defects for eclipse. In: International Workshop on Predictor Models in Software Engineering, ICSE Workshops 2007, p. 9. IEEE, May 2007
5. Zimmermann, T., Weigerber, P.: Preprocessing CVS data for fine-grained analysis. In: Proceedings of the First International Workshop on Mining Software Repositories, pp. 2–6, May 2004
6. Bird, C., Bachmann, A., Aune, E., Duffy, J., Bernstein, A., Filkov, V., Devanbu, P.: Fair, balanced?: bias in bug-fix datasets. In: Proceedings of the the the 7th Joint Meeting of the European Software Engineering Conference and the ACM SIGSOFT Symposium on the Foundations of Software Engineering, pp. 121–130. ACM, August 2009
7. Nguyen, T.H., Adams, B., Hassan, A.E.: A case study of bias in bug-fix datasets. In: 2010 17th Working Conference on Reverse Engineering (WCRE), pp. 259–268. IEEE, October 2010

Panel and Workshops

The Future of Open Source Research:
A Panel Discussion

Kevin Crowston[1], Joseph Feller[2], Carl-Eric Mols[3],
and Anthony I. (Tony) Wasserman (Chair)[4]

[1] School of Information Studies, Syracuse University, Syracuse, USA
crowston@syr.edu
[2] Cork University Business School, University College Cork, Cork, Ireland
jfeller@ucc.ie
[3] Software Intelligence, Software Development Lund,
Sony Mobile Communications, Lund, Sweden
Carl-Eric.Mols@sonymobile.com
[4] Integrated Innovation Institute, Carnegie Mellon University - Silicon Valley,
Mountain View, USA
tonyw@sv.cmu.edu

1   Description

Over the past decade, FLOSS has become mainstream. It's the technological foundation for a huge percentage of software, including products and services from both
startups and established companies, as well as the dominant approach for software
development and deployment tools. More recently, FLOSS has become the preferred
solution for a growing number of governments and non-profit organizations around the
world. What was once a niche research area has similarly become mainstream;
FLOSS-related research publications are now found across a variety of social, economic, and software-related publications and conferences. Likewise, open source
software is increasingly discussed in connection with open innovation, open government, open data, and related areas.

This growing popularity poses an interesting challenge for FLOSS research. While
there remains a core set of topics specifically related to FLOSS, e.g., software licensing,
many other topics, such as collaborative distributed development, have much broader
applicability. Some researchers who previously submitted their work to FLOSS-related
conferences and publications are now seeing many other opportunities to present their
work, describing the open source aspects of their research in a broader, domain-focused
context.

In this panel, we hope to address not only the most likely future directions for
FLOSS research, but also how FLOSS is related to other research fields and the broader
context of modern society. The panelists bring a wide variety of academic and
industrial experience with FLOSS and related subject areas.

K. Crowston et al. (Eds.): OSS 2016, IFIP AICT 472, pp. 201–203, 2016.
DOI: 10.1007/978-3-319-39225-7

2   Individual Position Statements

Kevin Crowston

My suggestions for the next phase of FLOSS research starts with observation that FLOSS is a topic, not a field, meaning that while we are looking at the same phenomenon, we do so adopting diverse approaches. So, why might sticking together make sense? A shared conference provides an opportunity to learn about work that you would miss in a disciplinary conference. But such visibility is only valuable if we can find commonalities that bring us together, e.g. sharing common inputs (e.g., datasets), common methods or complementary outputs across disciplines.

However, achieving interdisciplinarity requires a shared sense of priorities about the work to be done. A good common project would be to put our knowledge to work, that is, to tell interested parties how to have successful FLOSS projects (which would also serve as a test of our knowledge). A particular need is in the setting of scientific software. Funding agencies want to see the software they pay for reused and maintained, and openness fits the needs of science for reproducibility and auditability. What advice might we give about how to structure development to achieve quality code and to create a sustainable community around a piece of scientific software?

Joseph Feller

I will discuss the current and potential relationships between FLOSS research and emerging research areas, reflecting upon the activities of the AIS Special Interest Group on Open Research and Practice (SIGOPEN), and of other research communities.

In particular, I will discuss

- the proliferation of open phenomena (e.g. open innovation, open design, crowdsourcing, crowdfunding, volunteer computing, collective intelligence, etc.) and the challenges this proliferation creates for the research community,
- the important intellectual contribution that FLOSS research can make to these emerging fields of inquiry, and vice-versa,
- the implications of FLOSS and related research findings for the creation of a more open practice of scholarly inquiry and dissemination (e.g. open data, open access publishing, etc.), and
- the opportunity and need for greater integration, knowledge sharing, and intellectual cross-pollination between the global open research communities.

Carl-Eric Mols

My proposal for the future of Open Source research focuses on scaling up the software business aspects, in particular scaling up the Open Source maturity of organizations that develop software. While Open Source is widely used in the ICT industry, it is often in a passive, consuming way. It's uncommon to find companies that have extensive Open Source contributions and community participation as their core product/service development strategy, and even more rare to find companies that fully adapt their business models when their offering is increasingly based on Open Source.

With emerging software phenomena such as IoT, Industry 4.0, and Automotive Software, Open Source will massively impact the "traditional", non-ICT industry in many ways, not least in the way software development will need to be organized, and the way business will need to be conducted in order to avoid being eradicated by the Open Source giants. What wisdom on scaling software business can academia bring to the Open Source-challenged industry?

Anthony I. (Tony) Wasserman

I will discuss some implications of FLOSS becoming mainstream, many of which are already apparent. From a research perspective, research results that were previously published in open source research conferences and publications are now appearing in software engineering, economics, and political science conferences and publications. Open source-related research has diffused across various broader interest categories, making it more difficult to keep up with relevant research.

From a broader societal perspective, great improvements in the quantity and quality of FLOSS software has led to its adoption in a broad range of settings. As software has more and more societal impact, there is likely to be greater public demand for transparency and openness, especially for life-critical systems, such as those found in medical devices and autonomous vehicles. People will justifiably want to see the source code of heart pacemakers and vehicle control systems, which are now guarded as intellectual property by their makers; similarly people will expect governments to make extensive use of FLOSS and to make any software developed under government contracts to be released under an OSI-approved FLOSS license. These changes will, in turn, open up new areas for FLOSS-related research.

FLOSS Education and Computational Thinking Workshop @ OSS 2016

Jesús Moreno-León[1]([✉]), Terhi Kilamo[2], and Gregorio Robles[3]

[1] Programamos.es, Seville, Spain
jesus.moreno@programamos.es
[2] Tampere University of Technology, Tampere, Finland
terhi.kilamo@tut.fi
[3] Universidad Rey Juan Carlos, Madrid, Spain
grex@gsyc.urjc.es

Introduction

The presence of FLOSS in education has not stopped growing in the last years. The trend has been clear both in K-12 and higher education. While using FLOSS can support teaching computer science and other disciplines, its benefits lie in teaching FLOSS itself as part of the curriculum.

An example that can illustrate this situation is the teaching of computational thinking skills through computer programming, which is one of the latest trends in education - for instance, Finland has just added coding and computational thinking as part of the national core curriculum for primary education. This field has been globally addressed almost exclusively with FLOSS technologies, both by using FLOSS platforms and programming languages, such as Scratch or Alice, but also by including in the curriculum the social aspects of software development that characterize FLOSS movements, like sharing and contributing to the community.

The purpose of this workshop is to bring together free software experts and educators to discuss challenges that we face in the educational world at present and that we will face in the future and how they can be undertaken from a FLOSS perspective.

Topics of Interest

The topics of interest of this workshop include but are not limited to:

- Teaching experiences with FLOSS/free content
- FLOSS in higher education
- FLOSS in K-12
- FLOSS practices in education
- FLOSS in the curriculum
- Computational thinking teaching and FLOSS

Published by Springer International Publishing Switzerland 2016. All Rights Reserved
K. Crowston et al. (Eds.): OSS 2016, IFIP AICT 472, pp. 204–205, 2016.
DOI: 10.1007/978-3-319-39225-7

Specific Research Questions

Specific questions that are of special interest to this workshop are:

- Which FLOSS approaches have proven beneficial to education?
- What experiences do you have in collaboration with FLOSS communities in education contexts?
- How do you produce and share your educational materials?
- What assessment and certification models did you apply? Why have those models been chosen?
- What models for sustainability and revenue generation worked successfully?
- What efforts are undertaken to come towards a compatible or standardised curriculum?
- What indicators are measured to show strengths and weaknesses of the initiative?
- How is copyright and licensing managed in your institution/initiative? What (potential) impact does this policy have on sustainability?
- How can curricula be designed to foster the spirit of sharing?
- What FLOSS technologies do you use to teach computational thinking?
- How do you promote FLOSS social aspects in your lessons?

Programme Committee

- Yasemin Allsop, University of Roehampton (United Kingdom)
- Alessandro Bogliolo, University of Urbino (Italy)
- Jordi Freixenet, University of Girona (Spain)
- Petri Ihantola, Tampere University of Technology (Finland)
- Oystein Imsen, Lær Kidsa Koding (Norway)
- Terhi Kilamo, Tampere University of Technology (Finland)
- Simon Marsden, University of Portsmouth (United Kingdom)
- Joek van Montfort, Scratchweb Foundation (Netherlands)
- Jesús Moreno, Programamos.es (Spain)
- Eduard Muntaner, Inventors for Change (Spain)
- Peter Parnes, Luleå University of Technology (Sweden)
- Gregorio Robles, Universidad Rey Juan Carlos (Spain)

Sponsorship

This workshop is sponsored in part by the Region of Madrid under project "eMadrid - Investigación y Desarrollo de tecnologías para el e-learning en la Comunidad de Madrid" (S2013/ICE-2715).

Workshop on Contributions to Open Source Software by Public Institutions

Matthias Stuermer

Research Center for Digital Sustainability, Institute of Information Systems
at University of Bern, Engehaldenstrasse 8, 3012 Bern, Switzerland
matthias.stuermer@iwi.unibe.ch
http://www.digitalenachhaltigkeit.unibe.ch

Background, Goals, and Target Audience

Governments, universities, and other public institutions not only use open source software (OSS) but also contribute to existing OSS projects or even initiate new OSS communities. Public administrations such as City of Munich are actively involved in the development of LibreOffice (City of Munich 2012; Sneddon 2015); others like the Swiss Federal Office of Topography (swisstopo) supported the OpenLayers 3 implementation substantially via an international crowdfunding campaign (Moullet 2014). Starting a new OSS project may simply mean publishing source code on public repositories as the UK government is doing on GitHub[1] using the *GitHub and Government* service.[2] Or it may also include establishing governance rules as the Swiss Federal Court did when releasing its internal court decision administration system thus initiating the OSS project OpenJustitia (Brunner 2013).

Contributing to OSS has benefits such as lower development cost or increased transparency. Reducing IT spending is the major motivator for Swiss cantons collaboratively developing CAMAC, an open source construction permit system (Moser 2015). Transparency of the software is the reason why the Canton of Geneva plans to open-source its e-voting platform (Geneva State Chancellery 2010; Atmani 2015). Obviously committing source code and managing OSS projects does involve various challenges such as governance of user communities, establishing institutional structures, funding of ongoing development, effective release management or collaboration of public institutions with firms and volunteers.

The goal of this workshop is to share experiences and discuss solutions on how to increase contributions of public institutions to OSS and improve collaboration among all stakeholders. This workshop is targeted to practitioners with or without experience in managing OSS communities as well as academics researching governance and development processes within OSS projects.

---

[1] https://github.com/alphagov.
[2] https://government.github.com.

K. Crowston et al. (Eds.): OSS 2016, IFIP AICT 472, pp. 206–207, 2016.
DOI: 10.1007/978-3-319-39225-7